Russia and the Balkan Alliance of 1912

by the same author:
CONSERVATIVE NATIONALISM
IN
NINETEENTH-CENTURY RUSSIA

Russia and the
Balkan Alliance
of 1912

EDWARD C. THADEN

THE PENNSYLVANIA STATE UNIVERSITY PRESS
University Park, Pennsylvania

Library of Congress Catalog Card Number: 64-8086
Copyright © 1965 by The Pennsylvania State University
All rights reserved
Printed in the United States of America by
The Colonial Press Inc., Clinton, Mass.
Designed by Maxine Schein

To the Memory of Vico

CONTENTS

PREFACE

In 1912 the Balkan states finally resolved their differences and united against Turkey. At the time, well-informed Europeans realized that Russia had played an important role in the formation of the Balkan Alliance. Yet the surmises of contemporary journalists and even the conclusions of able Soviet, West European, and American historians of the 1920's and 1930's lacked proper perspective. With no adequate collection of Russian documents, especially for 1911–12, historians have frequently ignored pressures on policy makers in St. Petersburg, have often accepted uncritically the subjective judgments of contemporary non-Russian diplomats and journalists, or have used sweeping assertions based on patriotism or Marxist ideology to bridge wide gaps in their knowledge.

    Like that of other great powers, Russian foreign policy during the years immediately preceding World War I was designed to safeguard Russian strategic and political interests without risking war. Hartwig, the Russian Minister in Belgrade, and Izvol'skii, foreign minister and later ambassador to Paris, undoubtedly intrigued; and many other Russians coveted new rights for their country in the Straits and believed in its "historic mission." But after 1905 responsible officials in St. Petersburg were too well aware of Russia's political, economic, and military weakness to permit adventures in the Balkans.

During this period other powers or the Balkan states themselves, not Russia, usually took the diplomatic initiative. But Russian policy, although defensive, was certainly not passive. Faced in 1908 with Austria-Hungary's Sanjak railway project and annexation of Bosnia-Herzegovina, Izvol'skii came to believe that his own reputation and Russian prestige could only be preserved by corresponding economic and strategic advantages for Russia. In 1909 and 1910 the tsarist government encouraged the Balkan states and Turkey to proceed with their plans for a Balkan rapprochement or alliance—and in 1911 raised the Straits question when Turkish plans for naval expansion in the Black Sea, Italy's invasion of Tripoli, and French gains in Morocco and railway projects in Anatolia threatened Russia's relative power position. Finally, during 1911 and 1912 when Bulgaria and Serbia commenced serious consideration of an alliance, St. Petersburg became deeply involved in the negotiations.

Neither Izvol'skii nor Sazonov, who succeeded him as foreign minister, admitted that Russia's weakness obliged her to renounce the role of a great power. This weakness, in their opinion, was temporary. Soon, after internal pacification and consolidation, St. Petersburg could pursue its objective more energetically. Meanwhile, although Izvol'skii forgot this in 1908, it was imperative to avoid risks and adventures. Yet Russia's prestige as a great power had to be maintained, other powers had to be prevented from unilaterally altering the status quo in areas of traditional tsarist influence, and the Balkan states could not be permitted to settle independently questions concerning the future and security of the Empire.

In 1933 Otto Bickel published the standard monograph on Russia and the Balkan Alliance. Using recent British, French, and Austrian documents, he portrayed tsarist Balkan policy in more detail than had such writers as William L. Langer and Hans Kiendl.[1] But without adequate Russian sources, Bickel had to rely heavily upon the conjectures of pre-1914 diplomats, especially German. Thus he exaggerated the influence of Izvol'skii and Hartwig.[2] Bickel also believed that the Entente wanted a Balkan alliance to help encircle Germany, that Russia wanted it to block Austria-Hungary and to wring from Turkey special privileges in the Straits, and that the "driving" forces of Russian Near Eastern policy were a sense of "historic mission," the search for an outlet to the sea, and dreams of eventual possession of Constantinople.[3] Bickel's failure to correct, or at least critically modify, such popular and oversimplified interpretations was unfortunate. His study, the most detailed scholarly analysis of Russian Balkan policy between 1908 and 1912, has tended to convert these interpretations into "historical truth."

The major fresh source for this re-examination is volumes XVIII–XX of the second series of *Mezhdunarodnye otnosheniia v epokhu imperializma* published by the Komissiia po Izdaniiu Dokumentov between 1938 and 1940. These volumes cover all important questions of Russian diplomacy in Asia and Europe for the period May 14, 1911 to October 17, 1912. The coverage of Balkan events is especially complete. For the first time, hundreds of previously unpublished documents enable one to study in detail tsarist policy during the year and a half immediately preceding the First Balkan War.[4] But new international crises have made the Balkan wars seem faraway and remote, and historians have virtually ignored these materials. Soviet and German scholars have occasionally consulted the documents, but not to analyze the precise motives of St. Petersburg's diplomacy in the Balkans. In English, Philip E. Mosely's excellent but brief review article of 1940[5] remains the most noteworthy attempt to interpret Russia's Balkan policy on the basis of these sources.

In addition to *Mezhdunarodnye otnosheniia*, I have carefully re-examined the collections used by Langer, Bickel, and

others. Materials reflecting public opinion and internal conditions in Russia have also been consulted. Here the Duma debates,
memoirs, and newspapers have been especially useful. The passage of thirty years since Bickel and recent secondary Soviet
studies of Russian and European diplomacy on the eve of World
War I [6] also help place the Balkan events of the beginning of
this century in a different perspective.

One cannot always agree with Soviet historians, but they
are often most suggestive and, of particular importance, present
the results of research in Soviet archives—to which non-Com-
munist foreign historians have not yet been granted free access.
Meanwhile, I hope this study will encourage Soviet historians to
investigate more thoroughly Russian diplomacy on the eve of
the Balkan wars.

In addition, I am grateful to Professor J. Halpérin of the
University of Zürich, who first suggested further investigation of
this problem, and to Professor Pierre Renouvin of the Sorbonne,
under whose guidance I began my work on Russian Balkan diplomacy. In 1956 and 1958 two articles published in the *Journal
of Central European Affairs* summarized the results of this investigation. S. Harrison Thomson, editor of that journal, kindly
granted permission to include materials from these articles in the
first two chapters of this study. John A. DeNovo of the University
of Wisconsin and my colleague Ari Hoogenboom read a substantial part of a rough draft of the final manuscript. Their thought-
ful comments greatly helped me in making final revisions. And
thanks are due to James E. McSherry of The Pennsylvania State
University Press for his editorial skill.

I wish to acknowledge indebtedness to the staffs of the New
York Public Library, the Library of Congress, and the Penn State
Pattee Library. Ernst C. Helmreich of Bowdoin College generously allowed the use of his copy (apparently the only one in the
United States) of the *Doklad na parlamentarnata izpitatelna
komisiia*, published in 1918–19 by the Bulgarian Narodno Sŭbranie. And the Administrative Committee on Research, the

Preface

Liberal Arts College, and the Russian Area Committee of The Pennsylvania State University provided financial assistance during the preparation of this book.

E. C. T.

January 1965

INTRODUCTION

Although Turkey was a traditional enemy, on a number of occasions Russia's interests demanded an entente with the Porte. Treaties of alliance were signed in 1799 and 1805, at the time of the Directory and Napoleon, and the Treaty of Unkiar Iskelessi in 1833. In 1911 Russia even offered to guarantee the territorial integrity of the Ottoman Empire if the Straits were opened.[1] In the eighteenth century, however, tsarist diplomats sought to cooperate with Austria and partition the Turkish Empire. And they often reverted to this policy in the nineteenth and early twentieth centuries.

Between 1878 and 1908, despite sharp clashes in 1878 and 1885–87, Russian agreements with Austria-Hungary either delimited spheres of influence or maintained the Balkan status quo. Russia respected Austrian influence in Serbia and Bosnia and received implicit recognition of her own hegemony in Bulgaria. But heavy-handed agents soon alienated Bulgarian political leaders; by 1887 Russian influence, resulting from the Russo-Turkish War of 1877–78, had completely evaporated.[2] Thereafter Russian diplomacy focused on the Far East. Although events of the mid-1890's and around the turn of the century, the Armenian massacres and troubles in Crete, Greece, and Macedonia, revived some interest in the Balkans, Russian diplomats merely concluded that a more satisfactory understanding with Austria-Hungary was necessary. Thus both countries agreed in 1897 and 1903 to maintain the status quo.[3]

Commitments in the Far East precluded an active policy in the Balkans prior to the Russo-Japanese War. And after that war economic interests directed the attention of Russian leaders not to the Balkans but to the Straits, which acquired new significance in the twentieth century because of the development of heavy industry in the Ukraine and the increasing volume of trade passing from the Black Sea into the Mediterranean.[4] The Treaty of London of 1871 abrogated the clauses of the Treaty of Paris forbidding Russian and Turkish fortifications and navies on the Black Sea, but maintained the principle of closing the Straits to foreign warships established by earlier treaties. Thus during the Russo-Japanese War, Britain and Turkey would not allow exit of the Russian Black Sea fleet to reinforce naval forces in the Far East.

Although the Russian Foreign Ministry decided in 1905 that opening the Straits would not be advantageous, serious discussion of this possibility implied a shift of emphasis in foreign policy from the Far East to the Near East.[5] The task of reorienting Russian policy fell to Alexander Petrovich Izvol'skii, who succeeded V. N. Lamsdorf as foreign minister in May 1906.

Izvol'skii, an unusually able and ambitious man, was determined to minimize the effect of the Far Eastern defeat on Russia's role as a European great power. But the conduct of foreign policy could scarcely remain unaffected by economic dislocation, revolutionary unrest, and military disintegration; Izvol'skii's colleagues in the council of ministers firmly opposed any diplomatic adventures that might involve Russia in another war for which she was totally unprepared.[6] The new foreign minister therefore had to proceed cautiously with his plans to liquidate differences with Japan and concentrate on the defense of Russian interests in the Balkans and the Near East.

By 1907 Izvol'skii seems to have decided to combine the

Straits and other Near Eastern questions with an Anglo-Russian entente. The establishment of better relations with France's friend, Great Britain, was logical because of Russia's existing alliance with France and increased financial dependence on that country after the Russo-Japanese War. And Britain, threatened by growing German naval and economic power, wanted to improve diplomatic relations with Russia. Tentative conversations occurred as early as 1903 and continued sporadically during 1904 and 1905. Izvol'skii resumed these conversations in 1906 when Sir Arthur Nicolson, the new British Ambassador and an enthusiastic supporter of Anglo-Russian friendship, arrived in St. Petersburg. The success of the two countries in ironing out their differences in Iran and elsewhere in 1906 and 1907 culminated in the famous Anglo-Russian convention of August 31, 1907. The British even promised to consider Russian proposals concerning the Straits, though they carefully avoided making any definite commitments. Izvol'skii, optimistic about the future, seems to have assumed that Britain would support revision of the 1871 Treaty of London. By late 1908 he knew that Britain would not grant Russia special privileges in the Straits region, but his optimism about British goodwill helps to explain why he coupled revision of the Treaty of London with the Bosnia-Herzegovinian question earlier in the year.[7]

In a speech to the Duma on April 17, 1908, Izvol'skii spoke eloquently about Russia's responsibilities to her co-religionists and blood brothers to the south. But these fraternal ties with the Balkan Slavs did not exclude further cooperation with Austria-Hungary. Although defending friendly relations with the Habsburg Empire, Izvol'skii kept silent about his own ideas of gaining concessions in the Straits in exchange for recognition of Austria-Hungary's annexation of Bosnia-Herzegovina. Instead, he repeated to the Duma (its members had already read it in newspapers) his support of a Danube-Adriatic railway to counter the Sanjak railway project Austro-Hungarian Foreign Minister Alois Lexa von Aehrenthal had made public in January 1908.[8]

Since a Sanjak railway to Saloniki would have consolidated Vienna's economic power in the western Balkans and conceivably endangered Izvol'skii's own position as foreign minister, he demanded advantages for Serbia and Russia comparable to those sought by Aehrenthal.[9] A Danube-Adriatic railway had been seriously considered in the 1870's, and Izvol'skii's own assistant in the foreign office, N. V. Charykov, had worked for its realization in 1901 when minister to Serbia. But Izvol'skii had not encouraged the Serbs when they raised the question of an Adriatic railway in 1906 and 1907.[10] At that time he was more interested in Austrian support for revision of the Treaty of London than in helping "brother" Serbs hard pressed by Austrian economic pressure. In 1908 he advocated the Danube-Adriatic line apparently as a temporary expedient to pacify Russian public opinion and to worry Aehrenthal about the future of the Austro-Russian entente. Any doubts the Austrians might have had concerning Izvol'skii's intentions were removed on July 2, 1908, when a memorandum from St. Petersburg offered to discuss Russian recognition of the annexation of Bosnia-Herzegovina and the Sanjak in return for Vienna's support of Russia's interests in the Straits.[11]

Duma leaders, unaware of Izvol'skii's real intentions, generally reacted favorably to his speech of April 17, 1908. The liberal parties (the Kadets on the left and the Octobrists in the center) and the moderate right approved of his enthusiasm for the Slavic peoples but criticized continued cooperation with Austria-Hungary and Germany. The extreme right favored continuation of this cooperation but divided over support for the Balkan Slavs. The Social Democratic extreme left charged the foreign office with an irresponsible spirit of adventurism and support of reaction throughout Europe and of the subjugation of the Slavs in the Balkans.[12]

Only the tsar and Assistant Foreign Minister Charykov knew of the secret negotiations Izvol'skii had initiated with Aehrenthal at Buchlau in September. After the Austrian annexation of Bosnia-

Herzegovina in October, which enraged most Russians, Izvol'skii used the tsar's exclusive control of foreign policy to avoid discussion in the council of ministers.[13] Leaders of public opinion had no way of learning exactly what had taken place at Buchlau but had strong suspicions of the truth. Liberals and conservatives (as distinguished from the extreme right) had long been anti-German and anti-Austrian as well as champions of the Balkan Slavs. As early as the summer of 1907 they had advocated a Balkan alliance to halt Austro-German expansion; returning to this theme at the time of the Bosnian crisis, they criticized Izvol'skii for losing sight of the main task of Russian Balkan diplomacy.[14] As *Novoe Vremia* remarked on October 9, 1908, Russia could receive no better compensation than the "final unification of all the southern Slavs." This, *Novoe Vremia* asserted, was more important than any possible gains in the Dardanelles.[15] Izvol'skii's tactics also infuriated Premier P. A. Stolypin. Once he learned through Charykov the substance of the Buchlau conversations, he firmly opposed the foreign minister's plans.[16]

In the fall of 1908 Izvol'skii's critics in the government and press pushed for a Balkan confederation. Turkey was logically included because Turkish rights and interests were even more directly affected than those of the Slavic states by annexation of Bosnia-Herzegovina. Within the government the main advocates of a Turko-Slavic bloc in the Balkans were Charykov and Stolypin. Charykov had envisaged such a bloc even before the annexation of Bosnia-Herzegovina.[17] After the annexation he joined forces with Stolypin in opposing Izvol'skii's compensation policy. Together they elaborated a program based on a rapprochement of the Slavic states with Turkey under the auspices of Russia and demanded that the Bosnian question be referred to a conference of the European powers.[18] The prime minister's brother, A. A. Stolypin, was a member of the editorial staff, and the moderate-right *Novoe Vremia* naturally supported these proposals.[19] The Octobrist journals did the same since their party was cooperating with Stolypin.[20] But even the Kadets favored the Charykov-

Stolypin scheme despite their well known opposition to Stolypin's policies. The Kadet newspaper *Rech'*, in particular, recommended a common front of England, France, Russia, and the Balkan states to force Austria-Hungary out of Bosnia-Herzegovina.[21] The Octobrists and moderate right also approved of collaboration with the Entente in the Balkans but wanted to avoid a Balkan conflict or bad relations with Germany.[22] The latter was also the position of Stolypin. He accepted the Entente as the basis of Russian foreign policy and favored diplomatic action to checkmate Austria but strongly disapproved any risk of a war for which Russia was not prepared.[23]

Public anger subsided by November, and this offered Izvol'skii some hope of success in his personal struggle with Stolypin over the control of foreign policy. In early December the foreign minister persuaded the tsar to permit another discussion of foreign policy in the Duma. Then he personally contacted leaders of nationalistic and moderately conservative public opinion in St. Petersburg. The Kadets, being in opposition to the government, were excluded from these consultations. On December 21 and 22 the foreign minister talked at length with A. S. Suvorin, editor of *Novoe Vremia*, and such leaders of the Octobrists and moderate right as A. I. Guchkov, P. N. Balashev, and Prince A. P. Urusov.[24]

In his famous December 25 speech,[25] Izvol'skii again demonstrated his intelligence and skill as a politician. He concurred with the Duma budget commission that the central administration of the foreign ministry needed reform. In fact, he pointed out, a reform project was already under consideration and would soon be submitted to the Duma. Before broaching the subject of the Balkan crisis, the foreign minister sketched broadly Russia's position. War and internal dissension had greatly weakened her, but no one in the foreign office had the slightest intention of renouncing Russia's role as a great power. The entente with England had strengthened her hand in the Near and Far East; good relations with both England and Italy had been useful in the Balkans; and the alliance with France remained the cornerstone of Russian diplomacy. These powers, he emphasized, fully backed Russia in opposing Austria-Hungary's unilateral alteration of the Balkan status quo established by the Treaty of Berlin and in demanding that the annexation of Bosnia-Herzegovina should be submitted to a conference of the European powers. He answered those who had criticized him for not making an immediate and categorical protest to Austria-Hungary by reminding them that no government could ignore previous agreements with foreign powers. Such agreements had been made with Austria-Hungary concerning Bosnia-Herzegovina in the late 1870's (a fact unknown to Izvol'skii himself until November 1908), which effectively prevented any protest. But he assured his audience that the Russian Government was of one mind with the Russian people in its sympathy for Serbia and Montenegro and in its interest in the future of Slavdom. Accordingly, he warmly recommended the establishment of moral and political solidarity among the Slavic states and bringing them closer to Turkey in a common effort to defend their national and economic independence. Here Izvol'skii merely appropriated ideas from Stolypin, Charykov, the Octobrists, and the moderate right. He revealed no details about his discussions with Aehrenthal and still obviously hoped to gain compensations through the support of Great Britain, Italy, and France at a conference of the European powers.

The Octobrists and the moderate right, as had been arranged, moved the approval of Izvol'skii's speech and policy. Octobrist leader Guchkov did express mild regret that foreign policy in Russia, contrary to the practice elsewhere in Europe, still was not included among the questions normally considered by the Duma. And he carefully noted the Duma's sympathy for the Balkan Slavs and its wish that Russian policy would further the just interests of these nationalities. Guchkov probably emphasized sympathy for the Balkan Slavs to warn Izvol'skii that Russian public opinion supported him solely because it expected him to work for a solution of the Bosnian crisis acceptable to the

Slavs of the peninsula. The spokesman of the moderate right, Count V. A. Bobrinskii, following Guchkov's example, approved Izvol'skii's policy and reminded the foreign minister that the Russian people, the "brother people" and "national-liberator" of the Slavs, could not sanction Austria-Hungary's taking over Slavic provinces.[26]

Although Izvol'skii had not discussed foreign policy with Kadet leaders on the eve of his Duma speech, even the Kadet Miliukov, though apprehensive about recent Russian foreign policy, joined the Octobrists and the moderate right and approved in the main the foreign minister's policy.[27] Presumably Izvol'skii's pro-Entente orientation and newly found sympathy for the Balkan Slavs made the liberal Kadets prefer him to some new foreign minister who might share the pro-German views of certain elements close to the court. Moreover, Izvol'skii was sensitive to public opinion and as long as he remained in office the leaders of public opinion might influence foreign policy.

The extreme right and left, on the other hand, sharply criticized Izvol'skii. The Trudovik and Social Democratic left complained that the foreign minister still was not responsible to the Duma and that tsarist policy, seeking Russian hegemony in the peninsula, failed to serve the true interests of both Russians and South Slavs. The extreme right felt slighted because Izvol'skii had excluded them from the consultations with Duma leaders, and it disapproved of irritating Germany by associating Russia too closely with Britain. This faction expressed some sympathy for the Balkan Slavs but pointed to Russia's weakness and the necessity, at the time, of avoiding all foreign policy adventures and international complications.[28] Izvol'skii ignored both the extreme right and the extreme left; these groups constituted but a minority in the Third Duma.

Support from the Kadets, Octobrists, and moderate right in December 1908 strengthened Izvol'skii's hand, but Russia was weak and France and Britain would not risk war to defend her

Balkan interests. Thus when Germany delivered a near-ultimatum
in March 1909, the tsarist government was obliged to capitulate
and recognize Austria-Hungary's annexation of Bosnia-Herzegovina.[29]

Russia's capitulation left Izvol'skii defenseless before his
enemies. Although he remained in office until the fall of 1910,
Stolypin's brother-in-law, S. D. Sazonov, Izvol'skii's eventual suc-
cessor, was appointed assistant foreign minister in May 1909. This
appointment assured Stolypin that the foreign minister could no
longer pursue policies obnoxious to his colleagues in the council
of ministers. And Izvol'skii's former supporters among the leaders
of public opinion abandoned him. The press spoke of a "diplomatic Tsushima" and criticized the foreign minister for the in-
consistency of his policy and for not making full use of the
friendship of Great Britain and France.[30]

Izvol'skii never took the idea of a Balkan confederation including Turkey too seriously. When he endorsed it publicly on
December 25, 1908, he was acting under heavy pressure from
Stolypin and public opinion. By the end of 1909, however, a Balkan confederation and a Turko-Russian rapprochement seemed
less likely than earlier that same year. Both the Kadet press and
D. K. Sementovskii-Kurilo, the Russian Minister in Sofia since
1907 and a long-time advocate of a Serbo-Bulgarian understanding, began to express strong doubts about the feasibility of Balkan
confederation with Turkey, recommending in its place a Slavic
alliance consisting of Serbia and Bulgaria.[31] Izvol'skii sided
with the opponents of Balkan confederation perhaps because he
thought they were right, but no doubt also to gain support in his
struggle with Stolypin for the control of Russian foreign policy.

In October 1909 Izvol'skii scored his first notable diplomatic
success after the Bosnian crisis by arranging a meeting between
the tsar and the king of Italy at Racconigi. Here Izvol'ski and
Italian Foreign Minister Tomasso Tittoni exchanged letters out-
lining a program of Italo-Russian cooperation in the Balkans and

the Mediterranean. They agreed to defend the status quo and the principles of nationalism and noninterference by major powers in the Balkans. Russia further agreed to support Italian interests in Tripolitania and Cyrenaica, and Italy promised to support Russian interests in the Straits.[32] These agreements were clearly directed against the Ottoman Empire and clashed with Stolypin's and Charykov's policy of rapprochement with Turkey. Neither Tittoni nor Izvol'skii, however, contemplated immediate action. Russia, in fact, actively continued to seek Turkish friendship until early 1910, and then again during the fall of 1911.

Until the Bosnian crisis Izvol'skii ignored nationalism and the common interests of Slavdom; paramount were Russia's strategic and economic interests in the Black Sea and the Straits. Entente with England, cooperation with Austria-Hungary, and the sacrifice of the Slavs of Bosnia-Herzegovina were the constituent elements of a policy rationally calculated to defend these interests. Ironically, Izvol'skii not only failed to defend them but was soon obliged by the indignation of the public and of his own colleagues to espouse the cause of Slavic solidarity. At the same time, the critical attitude of the public convinced the government that it could no longer take political leaders and newspaper editors into its confidence concerning foreign policy. Henceforth no Russian Foreign Minister even approached the degree of frankness with which Izvol'skii had outlined his policy on December 25, 1908. Izvol'skii himself was not permitted to interpret current questions of foreign policy in his last appearance before the Duma on March 14, 1910, and as he left the chamber Miliukov denounced the "unsuccessful policy of our foreign minister."[33]

Yet public opinion undeniably influenced the formulation and conduct of Russian foreign policy during these years. Sazonov, as foreign minister from the fall of 1910 to mid-1916, not only strengthened Russia's ties with the Entente but also sponsored the Serbo-Bulgarian alliance. His assistant A. A. Neratov, who administered the Foreign Ministry between March and December 1911 while Sazonov convalesced from a serious illness in Switzerland, was on several occasions influenced by the press in dealing with Montenegrin and Turkish crises. Neither Sazonov nor Neratov seriously consulted leaders of public opinion; nevertheless they hesitated to follow policies repugnant to the Octobrists, Kadets, and moderate right.

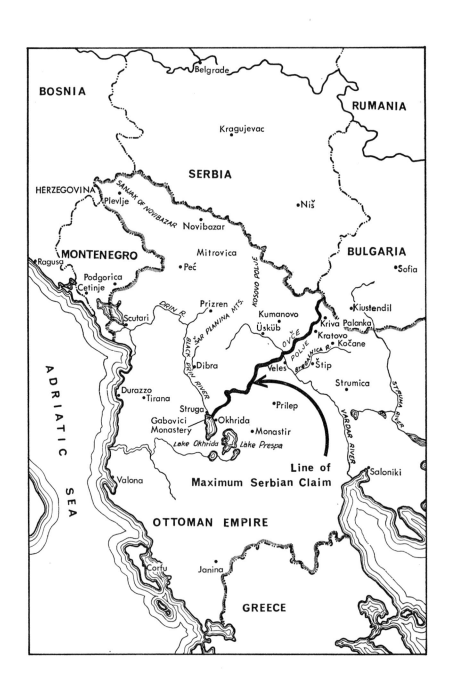

BOSNIA

RUMANIA

Belgrade

Kragujevac

SERBIA

HERZEGOVINA

SANJAK OF NOVIBAZAR

Plevlje

Niš

Novibazar

MONTENEGRO

Mitrovica

BULGARIA

Ragusa

Peć

Sofia

Podgorica

Cetinje

DRIN R.

Prizren

SAR PLANINA MTS.

KOSOVO POLJE

Kiustendil

Scutari

BLACK DRIN RIVER

Kumanovo

Üsküb

OVČE

Kriva Palanka

Kratovo

Kočane

ADRIATIC SEA

Dibra

Veles

BREGALNICA R.

Štip

Durazzo

Tirana

Strumica

STRUMA RIVER

Struga

Prilep

Gabovici

Monastery

Okhrida

Monastir

Lake Okhrida

Lake Prespa

VARDAR RIVER

Valona

Line of

Maximum Serbian Claim

Saloniki

OTTOMAN EMPIRE

Corfu

Janina

GREECE

Chapter 1

THE MONTENEGRIN CRISIS OF 1911

Self-interest had generally motivated Russia's sporadic support of the Balkan Christians. In the name of Orthodox Christianity, Peter the Great's agents appealed to Montenegrins to join his crusade against Turkish tyranny. The Montenegrins responded enthusiastically, proclaiming themselves "one people and one faith" with the Russians, but they received little aid, particularly after the Turks defeated Peter on the Pruth in 1711.[1] This same pattern repeated itself on occasions during the eighteenth and early nineteenth centuries, not only in connection with the Montenegrins but also the Greeks and Serbs. Catherine II and Alexander I, in particular, used discontent and unrest among Greeks and Serbs to serve Russian policy, but eventually abandoned them to the mercy of the Turks.[2]

Nicholas I, the pillar of established authority, feared that Russian encouragement of the Slavs would result in rebellions not only against the sultan but also against his brother monarchs of Prussia and Austria.[3] During the last years of his reign, however, Nicholas did seek to persuade Balkan Christians to join in his war against Turkey and the Western allies. Though not successful, these efforts did much to establish contacts between Russian officials and Balkan leaders.[4] Alexander II and his advisers encouraged further contacts and at home permitted discussion of Slavic issues and the founding of Slavic welfare committees. They also supported Prince Michael of Serbia during the 1860's in his efforts to form a Balkan alliance against Turkey.[5]

Panslavism was further stimulated by the Eastern crisis of 1875–78. Journalists, writers, and orators were then freer to discuss burning public issues than ever before. The Slavophile Ivan Aksakov delivered fiery speeches before the Moscow Slavic Benevolent Committee; the journalist Michael Katkov wrote emotional editorials in his *Moskovskiia Vedomosti* (Moscow News); and to his *Diary of a Writer* Dostoevskii confided dreams of Russia's acquiring Constantinople and asserting moral guardianship over the Orthodox world.[6] Not even high officials were immune to the contagion, and such sentiment no doubt contributed to Russia's declaration of war on Turkey in 1877. Although officials welcomed Panslavist support of the war effort, the government's realistic assessment of Russian power interests in the peninsula and Europe soon became apparent. When Panslavists criticized official policy, especially concessions forced by the exigencies of European politics at the Congress of Berlin, officialdom silenced them, and for many years they had little influence on the bureaucracy and educated public opinion.[7] Official policy returned to its traditional European and power-political orientation, and the public quickly forgot the Balkan Slavs while turning to more pressing internal problems.

After the Revolution of 1905, public opinion and Panslavism again became factors in Russian foreign policy. In the past, St. Petersburg had used the Balkan peoples as instruments of its policy; now, however, it could no longer completely ignore popular feelings, and the South Slav states had the opportunity of using Russia as an instrument of their policy. The Turkish-

Montenegrin crisis of 1911 furnishes one example of an attempt to do just this.

Possessing but scanty natural and human resources, Montenegro could strengthen herself only through external expansion. From the very beginning of his reign in 1860, Prince Nicholas of Montenegro (King after 1910) had dreamed of reconstructing the ancient Serbian empire of Stephen Dušan, the medieval tsar of the Serbs who ruled at Prizren.[8] When Nicholas was still young, his chances seemed good. His family, the Petrovici, had ruled over the free Serbs of the Black Mountain for more than two hundred years; the Karadjordjevici and Obrenovici had ruled in Serbia only a few generations. Moreover, before 1903 Nicholas was certainly a more impressive ruler than the weak and dissolute Obrenović kings. He had led his victorious troops against the Turks in the 1870's and was an outstanding poet in Serbo-Croatian whose lines "Onward, onward, let me see Prizren —For it is mine, I shall come to my home" became, in the words of a British journalist, Mary Edith Durham, "a national song for all the Serbian race." [9]

But with the Karadjordjević restoration, Nicholas of Montenegro found himself increasingly eclipsed by Serbian King Peter I. Serbia, though still relatively backward, was large and wealthy in comparison with Montenegro; economic, political, and social progress around and after 1900 attracted a large percentage of Serbs outside of Serbia—including many of Nicholas' own subjects. The Montenegrin ruler made considerable effort, given the limitations of his own horizons, to increase his country's productivity and improve its laws and institutions. But Montenegro remained, as an English sympathizer wrote, "cramped and confined": "it has no proper port; its territory is still largely barren rock, its products insignificant, and its warriors are not keen to devote themselves to labour or trade. All these defects would be remedied by an extension of its borders which would give the Kingdom richer land, inhabitants more adapted to the pursuits of peace, and harbours which would secure fuller and easier communications with Europe." [10]

In 1910 King Nicholas looked covetously in the direction of northern Albania. At the time, there was much dissatisfaction with Turkish rule throughout that country. An Albanian nationalist movement had come into existence during the latter part of the nineteenth century; a handful of intellectuals formed committees within the country and abroad and demanded more autonomy. The Young Turk Revolution of 1908 was at first received with enthusiasm, which soon cooled, however, with the centralizing and chauvinistic policies of the Young Turks. Efforts to replace the Latin alphabet with Arabic, the use of Albanian taxes and troops outside the country, and disarming of Albanians without paying a promised indemnity—all alienated and antagonized the inhabitants. And in northern Albania, where a large part of the population was Catholic, King Nicholas of Montenegro did his utmost to persuade the Malissori of this region that they should turn to him for protection.[11]

According to the accounts of both the Austro-Hungarian Minister in Cetinje, Baron Giesl, and the British journalist, M. E. Durham, before the Malissori revolted early in 1911 King Nicholas had promised them arms and refuge for their families.[12] When Ottoman troops took the heights of Mount Dečin near the Montenegrin border on May 16, 1911, the defeated insurgents were freely admitted into Montenegro. The Turkish Government then notified Cetinje that although its troops might cross the frontier in pursuit, this should not be construed as a hostile act. The Montenegrin Government in turn warned that such action could lead to armed conflict because of the inflamed feelings of its citizens.[13] Indeed, the Serbian minister in Cetinje informed his Russian colleague a few days later that General Mitar Martinović, a confidential adviser of King Nicholas, had confided that the king was determined to provoke a war with Turkey in the belief that Russia, in the final analysis, would be obliged to support him.[14]

Nicholas had some grounds for optimism. Had not Alexander III once toasted him as "my unique and loyal friend, Prince Nicholas of Montenegro"? [15] And his two daughters, married to Russian grand dukes in St. Petersburg, constantly and vigorously intrigued to further the interests of their father's small mountain kingdom.

Russian military and monetary aid to Montenegro dated back to the time of Peter the Great. And as early as 1907 staff officers in St. Petersburg had discussed the advisability of a military convention. On December 15, 1910, after prolonged discussion in St. Petersburg, a military convention was signed in which Russia promised a yearly subsidy of 600,000 rubles[16] and military instructors, equipment, and arms. Montenegro committed herself to place all of her armed forces at the disposal of Russia whenever requested to do so and agreed not to conclude any offensive alliance with a third power without Russian consent. It was also agreed that the Russian Government could suspend the subsidy and the delivery or supplies upon any infraction of the agreement by Montenegro.[17]

Although this convention seemingly insured effective control over Montenegrin policy, the threat of suspending subsidy payments could not be used with impunity: the Montenegrins might turn to Austria-Hungary. And because of public sympathy for the Balkan Slavs, firm Russian action in restraint of Montenegro would be highly unpopular unless the need for it could be clearly established. Demonstrating the need was difficult as long as King Nicholas refrained from mobilizing and continued to profess his desire to live in peace with Turkey. Ruling for more than fifty years, Nicholas had observed that neither Panslav opinion nor unsupported court intrigues had determined Russian foreign policy. He therefore felt his way forward with care.

On May 22 the Montenegrin King requested the powers to guarantee his country against possible Turkish attack. Fear of aggression, he explained, had convinced him of the necessity of distributing arms to reservists and preparing for mobilization. These measures, however, would not be carried out if the powers would give his country adequate assurances against Turkish aggression.[18] Such competent foreign observers at Cetinje as Baron Giesl, the Austrian Minister, S. Arsen'ev, the Russian Minister, and Colonel Potapov, the Russian military attaché, felt that Nicholas, not the Turks, was the one likely to start trouble, and during May and June 1911 the Turks followed a generally conciliatory policy in northern Albania.[19] Obliged to resort to other tactics, on June 19, 1911 the king sent a special Montenegrin mission, headed by former Montenegrin Foreign Minister Lazar Mijušković, to St. Petersburg to assure the Russian Foreign Ministry that Montenegro would observe strict neutrality in regard to the Malissori rebellion.[20] A few days later the king invited the representatives of the powers in Cetinje to discuss possible ways and means to bring about a pacification of the rebellion on the Turko-Montenegrin border.[21]

Although the powers understandably had no desire to enter into serious negotiations with a country as small and insignificant as Montenegro, the maneuvers of King Nicholas were partly successful. His professions of peaceful intentions had moved the Russians by the latter part of May to try to assure the Ottoman Government of his good will and to suggest that the Porte make an unequivocal statement of its peaceful sentiments toward Montenegro.[22] In June, while the Mijušković mission was in St. Petersburg, the nationalistic newspaper *Novoe Vremia* praised King Nicholas for his efforts to find an acceptable solution to the Albanian question.[23] On June 30 Deputy Foreign Minister Neratov wrote to Emperor Nicholas II that, judging by Mijušković's comments, Montenegro would scarcely undertake provocative action.[24]

Neratov's optimism was not shared by Russia's representatives in Cetinje. By mid-June military attaché Potapov feared that King Nicholas would incite a war with Turkey to "save face" before the Albanians.[25] On June 16, after an interview with the king, Russian Minister Arsen'ev concluded that Nicholas was only waiting for a convenient pretext. The minister felt that Nicholas counted on the aid of Bulgaria but was moving cautiously until he received the payment of the military subsidy due in the latter part of June.[26]

When the subsidy was deposited in the account of the Russian mission in the Bank of Montenegro, Arsen'ev and Potapov requested that St. Petersburg allow them to release only 500,000 of the 1,014,000 crowns. The balance, they argued, should remain in the account until "relative calm" had been established in the country. Although Arsen'ev and Potapov received Neratov's permission on June 28, the acting foreign minister apparently was not convinced that the situation was as grave as the Russian representatives claimed.[27]

On July 2 Nicholas ordered that Montenegrin reservists be armed and prepared to move to Podgorica, in the vicinity of the Turkish frontier. When Potapov learned of the king's act from Montenegrin Minister of War Djurović, he warned the latter that any troop concentration near Podgorica was contrary to the objectives of the Russo-Montenegrin military convention. Potapov added that it was no longer possible, for fear of alarming the Turks, to have a Russian colonel in the vicinity of the Turkish frontier; he could not continue his supervision of the training of the Montenegrin army. Djurović should warn the king that Russia might not (through the subsidy) pay for the concentration at Podgorica.[28]

Furious at this attempt to influence his actions, King Nicholas declared that he had no need of pecuniary aid, that Russia had no right to interfere, and that he would send troops to the area the next day.[29] On July 4, two days later, the king ordered the mobilization of troops at Podgorica. Although Nicholas asserted that he wanted no war and that the concentration was necessary for the security of his country,[30] the Russian Foreign Ministry was not reassured. Neratov, however, did not immediately take new measures to curtail King Nicholas. Apparently he counted on financial difficulties caused by the presence of Albanian refugees in Montenegro and the withholding of one-half of the subsidy. Financial pressure alone, however, scarcely sufficed.

When friction developed on the Turko-Montenegrin frontier in May, only Russia considered the situation serious enough for token diplomatic action. She reassured Turkey concerning Montenegro's intentions, suggested that the Porte affirm Turkey's "pacific sentiments," and asked the other powers to take similar action in Cetinje and Constantinople.[31] But publication of Russia's request that the Porte declare "pacific sentiments" toward Montenegro, argued Charykov, now the ambassador at Constantinople, seemed to many Turks a demonstration of enmity and could only play into the hands of anti-Russian publicists.[32] And the Russian naval attaché at Constantinople wrote that publication of Charykov's instructions had discredited the ambassador's work of many years' standing.[33] During the following months Charykov repeatedly emphasized the necessity of restraining King Nicholas to avoid antagonizing the Turks and forcing them into closer relations with Austria-Hungary and Germany.[34]

Great Britain displayed surprisingly little concern about driving Turkey into the arms of the Germans. The unrelieved tension on the Turko-Montenegrin frontier, the inability of the Turks to pacify northern Albania, and an active campaign by English humanitarians on the behalf of the Christian Malissori persuaded the Foreign Office that some sort of action was unavoidable.[35] On June 21 Sir Edward Grey, the Foreign Secretary, proposed that Austria-Hungary, Italy, and Russia, the powers most directly interested, act together at Cetinje and Constantinople in order to avoid war.[36] Five days later Grey proposed that all the great powers recommend granting acceptable social, economic, and nationality reforms to the Malissori.[37]

None of the other powers found Grey's proposal completely acceptable. The French government, preoccupied with Morocco, pointed out that Grey's proposal would encourage the Malissori and that the Turks would consider it as an intervention in their internal affairs.[38] Germany, especially interested in cordial relations with Turkey, notified Grey that his proposal was tantamount to interference in Turkish internal affairs.[39] Despite fears that London's formula would be acceptable to neither the Malissori nor the Porte, Neratov offered to act in the sense proposed if the other powers approved.[40] Austria-Hungary, in turn, feared that Grey's proposed action would be impractical because of the lack of unanimity among the powers. Aehrenthal recommended action by Italy, Austria-Hungary, and Russia; the Italian ambassador in Vienna assured Aehrenthal at the time of Italy's willingness to cooperate.[41]

Austria-Hungary was especially interested in asserting her influence in Albania. Austrian Catholics had long been active as priests and teachers among the Catholic Malissori, and Albania was also important for the expansion of the dual monarchy's trade and economic power in the western Balkans. An autonomous Albania would gravitate naturally in the direction of Vienna. It was therefore to the interest of Austria-Hungary to have Albanian ties with Constantinople loosened.[42] At the same time, Vienna had every reason to oppose King Nicholas' territorial ambitions, and the longer unrest on the frontier continued, the more likely was Montenegro to profit from Turkey's difficulties.

On July 12 Austria-Hungary formally proposed that the three powers discuss common action. Russia and Italy accepted, and the three governments agreed to concentrate on persuading the Turks and Montenegrins to settle their dispute peacefully. They treated the Malissori question as an internal Turkish affair, but made clear to the Porte that failure to find a satisfactory solution could easily lead to complications and foreign intervention.[43]

In mid-June the Turks had announced an armistice and given the Malissori ten days to accept their terms. When the insurgents refused, the Turks repeatedly extended their deadline, first by fifteen and then by ten and twenty days. But the Malissori, partly because of encouragement from Montenegro, demanded the right to bear arms and political, linguistic, educational, and social reforms in addition to the amnesty and economic assistance offered by the Turks. They also demanded that the implementation of these reforms be guaranteed by the powers.[44] But no Turkish government could stay in power while allowing the powers to guarantee the rights of one of the nationalities living within the Ottoman Empire. On July 20, however, as a result of the Austro-Italian-Russian pressure, the Porte offered not only amnesty but also educational and economic reforms, the right to carry arms, military service limited to Albania, and reduced taxes. Montenegro was promised a minor border adjustment in the neighborhood of Lake Scutari. Finally, the Turkish Government requested that Russia prevent the Montenegrin Government from interfering with the return of the insurgents to Albania.[45]

Turkey had now offered acceptable terms, and her own internal weakness obliged her to act in a spirit of moderation.[46] Montenegro, on the other hand, continued to advise the Malissori not to accept any offers not guaranteed by the great powers —a guarantee that King Nicholas promised to obtain.[47] Russian diplomats were convinced that King Nicholas was bent on war, especially after having been informed in mid-July that the Montenegrin Foreign Minister had sounded the Serbian Minister as to the attitude of his government in the event of hostilities.[48] With the three most interested powers determined to act in concert, however, the king was obliged to submit. On July 26, 1911, S. Arsen'ev, the Russian Minister at Cetinje, transmitted to King Nicholas the demand of the Porte that Montenegro allow the return of the insurgents and warned that all Russian moral and material support would be withheld unless Montenegro complied. The king replied that he needed no Russian subsidy and was glad that he could now conduct his own foreign policy. Arsen'ev again asked Nicholas if he would cooperate in facilitating the return of the Malissori. Finally, after much vacillation, the king promised to inform the Malissori chiefs of Turkey's concessions and find some way to comply with Turkey's demand. Several hours later he summoned Arsen'ev and categorically affirmed that he would in no way obstruct the return of the insurgents.[49]

As he had promised, King Nicholas then urged the Malissori to come to terms with the Turks and even threatened to disarm them and cut off all food supplies unless they accepted the terms offered. The insurgents were still reluctant to accept any offer without a guarantee of the powers, but finally the British journalist M. E. Durham, a woman highly respected and trusted by the Albanians, persuaded them that they had no other alternative. On August 3 they accepted the Turkish terms, and by August 14 there remained in Montenegro only fifty Malissori who absolutely refused to return to Albania.[50] This marked the end of the Malissori affair of 1911. By mid-August Russian military experts apparently considered that relative calm had returned to Montenegro, and on August 14 A. A. Polivanov, the assistant to the Russian Minister of War, requested that the Russian Government resume regular payments of Montenegro's military subsidy.[51]

In general, Russian policy in Montenegro was handled with skill in 1911 and 1912. The foreign ministry not only restrained Montenegro but even managed to strengthen the ties between Cetinje and St. Petersburg. And King Nicholas followed Russia's advice to do everything in his power to maintain peace. For almost a year following the Malissori crisis he tried to restrain the northern Albanians, even threatening to close the frontier and refuse entry for a single Albanian refugee.[52]

Russia's success in Montenegro, however, did not solve the major issue raised by the crises of 1911. In both Albania and Tripoli, Turkey's weakness had been unmistakably demonstrated. Declining Turkish power and disintegrating political order within the Ottoman Empire inevitably opened questions of vital international importance not only in the Balkans but also in the Straits and on the Black Sea.

Chapter 2

CHARYKOV AND THE STRAITS

By the late summer of 1911 the Balkan states were becoming increasingly restless, as indicated by serious alliance discussions between Belgrade and Sofia, and Athens and Sofia, in the first part of 1911. And the consolidation of French control in Morocco was almost bound to be followed by Italian action against Tripoli; Italy was determined to maintain her relative power position in the Mediterranean and had made agreements concerning Tripoli with France in 1902 and with Russia in 1909. Many Russian diplomats, aware of the connection, anticipated a Turko-Italian war which would weaken Turkey and tempt the Balkan states.[1] If these states succeeded in reconciling their differences and forming an alliance, Russia had little alternative but to endorse the principle of Balkan unity. But officials in St. Petersburg desired peace in the Balkans as long as Russia remained militarily unprepared for war, at least another four or five years.[2] Montenegro had sought to force Russia's hand and in so doing demonstrated St. Petersburg's distaste for Balkan adventures. At the moment the tsarist government was only willing to act negatively in the Balkans; more than anything else it wished to restrain the Balkan states, to avoid diplomatic complications and a major crisis in the peninsula.

Though a Balkan confederation including Turkey had been intensely discussed during late 1908 in the Russian press, Duma, and council of ministers, the initiative in negotiations was taken by the Balkan states themselves. Montenegro, Serbia, and Turkey first discussed the subject toward the end of 1908. Montenegro and Serbia, however, wanted an alliance against Austria-Hungary, while Turkey wanted support against Bulgaria. The government in Sofia had used the Bosnian crisis to terminate residual Turkish rights prescribed by the Treaty of Berlin and to proclaim an independent kingdom (tsarstvo). Refusing to pay Turkey compensation for lost tribute and railway rights, Bulgaria seriously prepared for an armed showdown at the end of 1908 and early in 1909.[3]

The Turks were demanding 125 million francs, while the Bulgarians refused to pay more than 82 million. At first Russia and Britain ineffectually admonished Serbia to avoid any agreements directed against Bulgaria and futilely urged Bulgaria and Turkey to reconcile their differences.[4] Finally, however, in January 1909, Russia proposed to excuse forty of the seventy-four war indemnity annuities Turkey still owed from the war of 1877–78; these forty annuities represented an obligation of around 125 million francs, the same amount demanded by Turkey from Bulgaria. The Bulgarians, in their turn were to pay Russia 82 million francs as a long-term loan with four to five per cent interest. The discrepancy of 43 million francs was to be waived by Russia, but the government in St. Petersburg could scarcely have expected to receive all the payments from Turkey. At no cost to herself, Russia thus created good will in both Sofia and Constantinople, and by May 1909 Bulgarian independence had been recognized by Turkey and the great powers.[5]

The settlement of the Turko-Bulgarian dispute greatly improved the chances of Stolypin's and Charykov's Balkan confederation scheme. Charykov himself was named ambassador to

Turkey in May 1909 and assumed his duties at Constantinople in July.[6] Upon his arrival in the Turkish capital the chances of success seemed particularly good. Late in 1908 and early in 1909 a pro-Entente orientation of the Young Turks encouraged even the British. Seeking to bring the Turks and the Christian Balkan states together into an alliance or political agreement,[7] Charykov did his utmost to persuade the Turks of the advantages of good relations with Russia, the Entente, and the Balkan states. In August 1909 his efforts culminated in negotiations for a meeting between the tsar and the sultan. The Turks, however, disappointed in how little the Entente could do for them, dropped these negotiations and inclined more and more toward Germany. Although Russia did not abandon the idea until early in 1910,[8] a Balkan confederation including Turkey was dead.

At Constantinople, however, Charykov never seems to have despaired about the prospects of such an understanding. The one time the state of Turko-Russian relations troubled him seriously was early in 1911, when Turkish military actions on the Persian frontier and plans for railway and naval construction seemed to threaten the security of the Russian empire.[9]

Turkey had shortly before ordered two dreadnoughts in Great Britain. And negotiations had been going on since the late summer of 1909 with the American Chester syndicate and since March 1911 with the French entrepreneur Sallandrouze de Lamornaix about concessions for railway lines running from north central Anatolia to the Black Sea at Samsun and to eastern Anatolia near the Russian and Persian frontiers. The dreadnoughts challenged Russian naval supremacy on the Black Sea, and the railways promised to reduce considerably the time needed to send troops to the Caucasian frontier.[10]

The St. Petersburg foreign ministry proposed to meet this challenge by opening the Straits for warships so that Russia could reinforce her Black Sea fleet.[11] The general staff of marine affairs, on the other hand, feared that opening the Straits would permit other naval powers on the Black Sea and recommended seizing and fortifying the upper Bosphorus.[12] As both the foreign ministry and General V. A. Sukhomlinov, the minister of war, pointed out, however, Russia lacked the military and naval power for such a venture.[13] Sukhomlinov also warned that Russia could only maintain her strategic advantages in the Caucasus through improvement of the railway network on the Russian side of the frontier.[14] And extensive railway construction was then out of the question for financial reasons. The Russian Government was thus obliged to rely primarily on diplomatic persuasion.

After a meeting of the tsar and kaiser at Potsdam in October 1910, Germany and Russia had engaged in protracted discussions about Persia and the Berlin-to-Bagdad railway. On October 15, 1911, a few days before a final Russo-German agreement concerning Persia was signed, Germany formally renounced any intention to construct railways in northeastern Anatolia.[15] During these same months the Germans had also unwittingly rendered the Russians a service by inducing Turkey to postpone consideration of concessions to the American Chester syndicate.[16] Meanwhile, the French agreed, with certain reservations, not to build railways in the area covered by a Russo-Turkish railway accord of 1900 [17] without first obtaining Russian consent. Although the French insisted on continuing with plans to build a line between Samsun and Diabekir via Harput,[18] Russia had general French support in bargaining with the Turks about revision of the 1900 accord.

During the summer of 1911, Turkey had displayed a conciliatory attitude toward Montenegro and the Albanian insurgents. And the decision of the Porte on July 29 to permit the French Compagnie Jonction-Salonique to proceed with preparatory work for a Danube-Adriatic railway seemed to indicate that Turkey was again ready to consider a rapprochement with her Balkan neighbors and Russia. In any case, such a conclu-

sion seemed inescapable to Charykov when he commented on
the Franco-Turkish agreement in early August.[19] Acting Foreign
Minister Neratov was similarly optimistic several days later, on
August 7, when he suggested to Minister of Finance V. N. Kokovtsov that Turkey might be persuaded to open the Straits in
exchange for approval of railways in the area designated by the
Russo-Turkish agreement of 1900.[20] Little is known concerning
the discussions of Russian government leaders in August and
September about the Straits and Turkish railways in Anatolia.
Kokovtsov, who became premier in September, saw no "organic
connection" between Anatolian railways and the Straits and
recommended caution in discussing with the Porte the complex
and undefined Straits question.[21] Kokovtsov's objections seem to
have persuaded the Russian Foreign Ministry to modify Neratov's formula, for Charykov was later instructed to keep the
two issues separated—indeed to limit himself initially to discussion of Anatolian railroads.[22]

Turkey's seemingly friendly attitude, however, convinced
St. Petersburg that it should at least explore the possibilities
of rapprochement. Too, Italy's attack on Turkey in late September 1911 necessarily caused some Turks to question the wisdom
of continued friendship with Germany, an ally of Italy in the
Triple Alliance. Three years earlier rapprochement with the
Balkan states and the Entente had seemed attractive when another member of the Triple Alliance had disregarded Turkish
rights. Perhaps Turkey would turn again to the Entente and
seek to improve relations with the Balkan states.

On September 26 Izvol'skii, now the ambassador to Paris,
wrote to Neratov and emphasized that Russia should not confine herself to a passive policy in the Balkans but should use
every opportunity to turn the course of events to her own advantage.[23] The hypothesis that Neratov was then Izvol'skii's
tool [24] once seemed plausible because Izvol'skii specifically mentioned in this letter both the Straits and the construction of railways in Asia Minor. These subjects, however, had been dis-

cussed in St. Petersburg as early as August 1911. Moreover, Izvol'skii's letter arrived in St. Petersburg on October 1, 1911,[25] two days after Neratov had wired Charykov that special instructions concerning negotiations with the Porte would be sent[26] and one day before Neratov actually sent them. The detailed instructions must have taken a number of days to prepare, so it is highly unlikely that Izvol'skii's letter of September 26 was an important consideration when they were drawn up.

It is also unlikely that the acting foreign minister was carried away by the combined arguments of Izvol'skii and Charykov. On September 30 Charykov sent a dispatch and two letters to St. Petersburg in which he outlined his ideas on possible negotiations concerning the Straits and railways in Turkey.[27] Since these letters and the dispatch were sent on September 30, it is practically impossible that they could have reached St. Petersburg in time to influence the formulation of the instructions forwarded to Charykov only two days later. Charykov's letters and dispatch of September 30, however, are more important for the historian than the communication sent by Izvol'skii four days earlier. Izvol'skii in Paris was only on the sidelines as far as the Straits negotiations of 1911 were concerned, while Charykov played an essential role. The thoughts he expressed at this time are valuable for the light that they cast on his subsequent actions.

In his letters and dispatch of September 30, Charykov emphasized above all that Russia should arrive at a preliminary understanding with the other great powers before entering into direct negotiations with Turkey. It was especially important, he pointed out, to obtain Italian and French recognition of Russian interests in the Straits region.[28] Charykov did not speak of a Balkan confederation including Turkey at this time, nor did he particularly emphasize Turko-Russian friendship. Instead, he wrote: "Russia should be the master of the Bosphorus and the Dardanelles and use them for her warships on a basis of equality with Turkey as long as this nation continues to exist and then alone when Turkey disappears."[29] In the meantime, he considered it wise to encourage the Balkan states to come to an understanding and avoid fighting among themselves in the event of a Turkish collapse.[30]

Already at war with another European power, the Porte was scarcely in a position to deny Russia important concessions. On this point Izvol'skii, Charykov, and the Russian Foreign Ministry were in substantial agreement in late September 1911. Neratov's instructions of October 2 referred to this factor, and attached were four draft agreements concerning railway construction in Turkey, the Straits, agreement for increasing Turkish customs duties, and the transfer to Russia of the contracts for the dreadnoughts ordered in Great Britain. The draft on the Straits offered Russian support for the preservation of the status quo in the Bosphorus and the Dardanelles, including adjacent territories, in exchange for the free passage of Russian warships. Neratov, however, instructed Charykov to begin with discussion of revision of the Turko-Russian railway agreement of 1900. The importance of the Straits was not emphasized in the original instructions, probably because of disagreement in St. Petersburg as to the advisability of raising this question at that particular moment. Charykov was to discuss the Straits, customs duties, and the dreadnoughts only after the Turks had demonstrated themselves well disposed in the matter of railways in Asia Minor.[31]

The ambassador probably had these instructions in his hands by October 6 or 7.[32] And on the 6th Neratov sent a telegram urging Charykov to lose no time in opening negotiations. The following day Neratov wired to Constantinople the emperor's approval of the proposed negotiations and assured the ambassador that the thoughts in his letter of September 30 had been carried out.[33]

The telegrams sent to Charykov on October 6 and 7 could only give him the impression that action was urgent. If he acted imprudently during the following days, certainly Neratov was vaguer than he should have been when he assured the ambassador that the thoughts expressed in his letter of September 30 had been carried out. Charykov's letter of September 30 was long and expressed many ideas; apparently Neratov only meant that the Russian Foreign Ministry had informed the French and Italian governments of its intention to begin discussions in Constantinople. Charykov, however, interpreted the telegram as an assurance of French and Italian approval for opening the Straits to Russian warships.[34] And the ambassador had indeed stated explicitly in his letter of September 30 that he considered the preliminary approval of France and Italy essential to the negotiations. Neratov's failure to send more precise instructions at this crucial moment justifies Charykov's observation of 1928 that it was a "piece of ill luck" for Russia that the regular foreign minister, Sazonov, was then absent from St. Petersburg because of illness.[35] Indeed, Neratov's vagueness and hesitation in handling Charykov during October and November 1911 demonstrate that he lacked the self-confidence and diplomatic skill to deal successfully with such delicate and complicated matters as the Straits and Russo-Turkish relations.[36]

The day after Neratov sent his telegram notifying Charykov that the latter's ideas had been carried out, the ambassador reported (October 8) that he had taken "preliminary steps" to raise the question of the Straits with the Turks. He added that he had discussed the matter with Bompard, French Ambassador at Constantinople, who considered the situation favorable for discussions.[37] On October 9 Charykov also proposed a new article for the draft agreement concerning the Straits: "The Russian Imperial Government also takes upon itself to employ its good offices to facilitate the establishment—on the basis of the status quo—of firm, good-neighborly relations between the Imperial Ottoman Government and the Balkan states."[38] On October 11 the ambassador wired that he could no longer wait for a response to his letter of October 9; "local circumstances" made it necessary to communicate the Russian proposals before the opening of the Turkish parliament. He also suggested a Russian offer to discuss the capitulations. In order to avoid alarming the Turks, the ambassador proposed to start the negotiations with a personal letter from himself to the grand vizier.[39]

Charykov's communications of October 8, 9, and 11 made it clear in St. Petersburg that he was on the verge of exceeding his instructions, and Neratov promptly wired him to proceed with extreme caution. Above all, the ambassador was not to mention the capitulations or rapprochement with the Balkan states.[40] These instructions, however, apparently arrived after October 12, the day Charykov handed over his "personal" letter to the grand vizier.[41]

Neratov was partly responsible for the precipitate action of the ambassador in Constantinople, but much of the responsibility must be placed on the shoulders of Charykov. His memoirs[42] reveal a cultivated, refined, well-educated, and sensitive gentleman. But this did not make him an effective diplomat. Izvol'skii had attended school with Charykov, had served with him on different occasions in the diplomatic service, and therefore knew him well. Upon hearing that he had discussed the Straits with French Ambassador Bompard, Izvol'skii guessed that Charykov had begun action in Constantinople and, with "characteristic impetuosity," had already "spoiled the whole affair." [43] Charykov's precipitate actions of the second week of October 1911 as well as his acts during the ensuing month and a half justify this observation and the judgment of Baron Taube in 1928:

> [Charykov] was a great worker and even an erudite, but without diplomatic suppleness, without a "sense of perspective" which distinguishes . . . the essential from the secondary. Very often he lost himself in details to the extent of having earned the rather severe *mot* of his chief in Berlin (Count Shuvalov); "Charykov loves to administer enemas to flies." In a word, very conservative, very immovable in his opinions and biases, stolid and even obstinate with, from time to time, plunges into the unknown, unexpected and little motivated, based on some combination . . . jealously guarded in his mind.[44]

Neratov had to wait approximately a week before he knew exactly what Charykov had communicated to the Porte. Only on October 14 did the ambassador attach a copy of his letter to Said Pasha to a dispatch[45] Neratov probably received around October 20. Neratov feared that Charykov's efforts to bring about a rapprochement between Turkey and the Balkan states might complicate Russia's role as the protector of Bulgaria and Serbia.[46] The two states were then discussing the formation of a Balkan alliance which would be logically directed against Turkey. Neratov was only acting foreign minister, however, and Charykov one of the senior members of the Russian foreign service at that time. Thus although Neratov mildly criticized the ambassador for having exceeded his instructions, he accepted the text of Charykov's letter as a point of departure for the negotiations. Now he considered discussion of the capitulations admissible and felt that discussion of a rapprochement between Turkey and the Balkan states *would be* permissible once Turkey had accepted the other conditions proposed by the Russian government.[47]

Developments in Turkey at this time seemingly justified Charykov's *démarche*. The government of Hakki Pasha had fallen because of the war with Italy. The new cabinet formed under Said Pasha seemed in favor of a pro-Entente orientation and inclined to abandon the Young-Turk program of "Ottomanization" in the Balkans. Toward the end of the second week of October the new Turkish Foreign Minister, Assim Bey, asked Charykov to help him in his efforts to encourage a rapprochement with Russia. Assim Bey also mentioned the sultan's wish to send a mission to Livadia to visit the Russian Emperor in the near future.[48] In Said Pasha's speech of October 19 before the Turkish parliament, the grand vizier declared that Turkey could no longer maintain her neutrality and must reach an understanding with one group or another of the powers in order to defend her vital interests. The Turkish parliament gave Said Pasha a vote of confidence (125 to 60). This vote was a defeat for the Young Turks who a little later declared they would abstain from

47

all interference in the government and would not cause difficulties for the cabinet of Said Pasha. Moreover, the Young Turks agreed to accept a rapprochement with the powers of the Triple Entente if Said Pasha judged this expedient, even though they preferred the Triple Alliance.[49]

By the end of October the possibility of a basic reorientation of Turkish foreign policy was a popular subject for discussion in Russia. On October 24 *Novoe Vremia* approved the rumored *pourparlers* in Constantinople, commenting that Russian diplomacy should seize this opportunity to prove to the Young Turks the error of their past flirtations with the Triple Alliance.[50] Another St. Petersburg newspaper, the liberal *Rech'*, even engaged in polemics with the Turkish newspaper *Tanin. Tanin* had shortly before urged an alliance with Russia. *Rech'* considered an alliance acceptable only if the Turks granted autonomy to Albania and Macedonia and ceased encroaching on Persian territory (i.e., threatening Russian military security in the Caucasus). Rapprochement, however, was another matter. It would be to the advantage of both countries to iron out some of their differences in negotiations comparable to those Russia had conducted several years earlier with Great Britain and Japan. A satisfactory understanding concerning the Straits and the Black Sea, for example, could assure the free passage of Russian warships through the Straits and give Turkey the security she needed to cut down on heavy naval expenditures that she really could not afford.[51]

Between October 27 and November 8 *Rech'* also discussed rumors in Constantinople and Bulgaria of a Balkan confederation including Turkey. *Rech'* noted that such a confederation had appeared feasible when Izvol'skii had recommended it several years before. At that time the Young Turks seemed willing to decentralize the administration of the Ottoman Empire. This, however, had proved not to be the case, and the necessary condition for a Balkan confederation, *Rech'* insisted, was still decentralization of the Ottoman administration, especially autonomy for Albania and Macedonia.[52]

Around the beginning of November, Neratov had fewer reservations than *Rech'*. On October 30 he reminded Bulgaria that Russia desired only a Serbo-Bulgarian treaty based on the status quo in the Balkans, and on November 4 he wired Nekliudov and Hartwig, the Russian ministers in Sofia and Belgrade, that any Serbo-Bulgarian treaty of alliance should not exclude the possibility of the eventual adherence of Turkey.[53] In a word, by November 4 Neratov, though he remained somewhat skeptical,[54] had decided to give Charykov's pet scheme a fair trial.

If a genuine rapprochement had taken place between Turkey on the one hand and the Entente and the Balkan states on the other, and if the powers had agreed to special rights for Russia in the Straits, then Charykov would have indeed won a brilliant diplomatic victory. France, he reasoned in late September, was obliged to Russia for support during the Moroccan crisis. Great Britain, dependent on French naval power in the Mediterranean, could hardly object to Russian reinforcements for the French Mediterranean fleet. Italy, too, would certainly support Russia because of the special understanding on Mediterranean questions. Only Germany and Austria-Hungary might raise serious objections, but Charykov felt that their acquiescence could be obtained if they received compensations.[55]

But Germany, contrary to Charykov's expectation, was more receptive than Britain and France to Russia's wishes concerning the Straits. On October 13 Italy promised to act in the sense of her earlier understanding with Russia,[56] and little more than a month later Germany assured St. Petersburg that she would not oppose the opening of the Straits. Kiderlen-Wächter, the German Foreign Secretary, hoped to weaken the Triple Entente by supporting Russia and letting France and Great Britain defend the status quo.[57] Only Austria-Hungary among the powers of the Triple Alliance actively opposed Charykov. Aehrenthal, irritated at the cordiality of Russo-German relations since the Potsdam meeting of 1910, argued with the Germans about the wisdom of permitting egress for Russian warships[58] and advised the Turks to reject Charykov's proposals. But he did not want to alienate Russia and therefore, late in November, expressed willingness to recognize Russia's interests in the Straits whenever a satisfactory understanding could be reached concerning the status quo in the Balkans and the Mediterranean. Aehrenthal's answer was really a polite "no," for he certainly knew that Russia would not purchase Vienna's support at the price of guaranteeing its position in the Balkans.[59]

As Kiderlen-Wächter had anticipated, Britain and France were embarrassed by Charykov's initiative. Although unwilling to give Russia a free hand in the Straits, they felt obliged to appear helpful. Accordingly in mid-October France gave general assurances of support,[60] and toward the end of October Sir Edward Grey told Benckendorff, the Russian Ambassador in London, that Great Britain would consider the question with "sympathy." Benckendorff was not entirely sure how he should interpret Grey's words, but he felt that Britain would welcome a rapprochement of the Porte with the Entente and the Balkan states.[61]

General expressions of sympathy naturally did not satisfy St. Petersburg. On November 2 Neratov instructed Izvol'skii to inform the French Government that Russia desired assurance of "full liberty of action" in the Straits.[62] But France was in no mood to give a *carte blanche* at this time. Russia had finally backed France in Morocco in 1911, but the French were resentful that firm support had not been given more promptly.[63] Moreover, St. Petersburg had not defined precisely to what regions the projected Russian guarantee of the status quo in the proximity of the Straits was to be extended. French Foreign Minister de Selves therefore insisted that his government should know this as well as the attitude of Sir Edward Grey before replying officially.[64]

Great Britain, as William C. Askew has remarked, "held the key to the success or failure of Charykov's dreams." [65] When the

Turks hinted that they wanted better relations with the Entente, they had in mind especially friendship with Britain. In fact, at the end of October they even offered to conclude an alliance with the British. Grey, desiring to maintain friendly relations with Italy,[66] declined to discuss an alliance as long as hostilities continued between Turkey and Italy. But the Foreign Secretary encouraged the Turks to believe that an alliance with Britain was feasible once the war had ended.[67] He informed both the Russian and French Ambassadors about Turkey's overtures and stated that Britain, though she wished to remain neutral in the Italo-Turkish war, considered Anglo-Turkish friendship as a means of eventually bringing about a general rapprochement of the Entente with Turkey.[68]

But Benckendorff was wrong in assuming that the British would actively work for a Turko-Balkan rapprochement in the fall of 1911. To be sure, they had encouraged the formation of a Balkan confederation during the Bosnian crisis. Since then, however, they had lost faith in the Young Turks as reformers. Earlier in 1911, for example, Britain had supported the Albanians when they demanded social, economic, and political reforms. And during the fall of 1911 British diplomats did not take seriously Charykov's words and rumors emanating from Sofia and Constantinople. As the foreign office commented late in December 1911: "A Balkan Federation is as yet very far distant. They [the Bulgarians and the Serbs] distrust not only Turkey but each other."[69]

The Foreign Secretary's attitude in early November 1911 reassured neither Benckendorff nor Neratov. The ambassador was disturbed by Grey's reference to a previous memorandum of 1908, which had made British approval of free passage for Russian warships through the Straits contingent upon Turkish acceptance and the granting of similar rights to all the powers.[70] Equally disquieting for Benckendorff, both Paul Cambon, the French Ambassador in London, and Arthur Nicolson, the permanent undersecretary at the Foreign Office, raised the question whether the guarantee of the inviolability of the Straits and Turkish territory envisaged by Charykov was compatible with Russian neutrality during the Italo-Turkish war. Though Anglo-Russian friendship had developed very satisfactory since 1908, Benckendorff and Neratov realized it would be difficult to win British support for Charykov's proposals. If Turkey did not consent to these proposals, Neratov concluded, British support was especially unlikely.[71]

These surmises of early November 1911 were essentially correct. In December Grey summarized his position in a telegram to the British Ambassador at Constantinople: "As to opening the Straits to ships of war, I had promised Iswolsky in 1908 that we would not oppose the raising of this question, if Russia wished to raise it. But, in so far as this opening would require an alteration of Treaties, it was a question which must be discussed with the powers who were parties to the Treaties." [72] In early December Grey had made every effort to ascertain Turkey's attitude in regard to Charykov's proposals. Certainly Turkey's resistance at the time to diplomatic pressure applied by Charykov was an important consideration for Grey in deciding against changing the Straits policy he had formulated in 1908.[73]

French preoccupation with Morocco, the secondary importance of Russian interests in the Straits for France, and reluctance to offend an ally explain the long delay in answering Russia's request, made early in November 1911, for "full liberty of action." On January 4, 1912, the French Government finally informed Russia that it was ready to exchange views with Russia "if new circumstances made necessary an examination of the Straits question." [74] By this time Charykov had already been disavowed by the Russian Foreign Ministry and there was nothing to discuss.

Since the attitude of Britain and France was already apparent early in November 1911, it became all the more important for Russia to know exactly how she stood with Turkey. By November, however, Turkey no longer had much reason to court

St. Petersburg. After Italy's annexation of Tripoli without official protest by the great powers, Said Pasha could gain little by hinting at eventual Turkish adherence either to the Triple Alliance or to the Triple Entente.[75] Nor was Italy able to effect a crushing victory over the Turks and force them to sue for peace. Thus the Porte judged it expedient to follow a policy of watchful waiting, for the war was proving more onerous for Italy than for Turkey.[76]

Charykov perceived neither the change in Said Pasha's policy nor the failure of Russian diplomacy to win over Britain and France. He persisted in interpreting all he heard and saw in much too optimistic a manner. On November 6, for example, when Said Pasha requested an extension of fifteen days to reply to the Russian Ambassador's letter, Bompard, the French Ambassador, correctly interpreted the move as "purely dilatory," while Charykov considered it a "good augury." [77] A few days later Bompard informed Paris that Charykov, having learned of the conversations between Benckendorff and Grey, was convinced that Great Britain had approved the Russian project concerning the Straits.[78] Daeschner, French chargé d'affaires at London, wired the French Foreign Ministry in this connection on November 11, pointing out that Charykov had attached too much importance to the Foreign Secretary's remarks. Grey, according to Daeschner, had replied in a general but favorable manner in order not to discourage Russo-Turkish negotiations that could be resumed and studied *after* the end of hostilities between Italy and Turkey. No other significance, he emphasized, should be attached to Grey's remarks.[79]

Daeschner and Bompard were not the only ones to doubt the chances of success for Charykov's plan. The Russian ministers in Belgrade and Sofia, Hartwig and Nekliudov, began to campaign vigorously against the plan after they had received instructions from St. Petersburg that any Serbo-Bulgarian alliance should not exclude the possibility of the eventual adherence of Turkey. It was clear to the two ministers on the spot that Bulgaria and Serbia had no interest in a rapprochement with Turkey, but only in an offensive alliance and a division of Turkish possessions in Europe.[80]

These warnings of its representatives in the Balkans, together with the obvious reluctance of the Turks, French, and British to commit themselves, indicated to the Russian Foreign Ministry that Charykov had little hope for success. The first concrete indication of a change in attitude on the part of Neratov was during the visit paid to the Russian Emperor in Livadia by a special Turkish delegation in mid-November 1911. Charykov had suggested that the tsar pronounce himself in favor of a rapid and positive conclusion of the Turko-Russian pourparlers.[81] Neratov, however, troubled by Said Pasha's delay in replying to Charykov's letter of October 12, recommended that the Turks be allowed to take the initiative at Livadia.[82]

Not at all influenced by Neratov's caution, Charykov once again, on November 27, presented to the grand vizier, with only minor modifications, the same proposals he had made six weeks earlier, this time in the form of an *official* communication from the Russian Government. In a dispatch of November 30 informing Neratov of his "official" action, Charykov explained that the *démarche* was a natural consequence of the return of the Turkish mission from Livadia on November 23.[83] Ten days previously, as Charykov had already informed Neratov, Said Pasha had told the ambassador that official negotiations could begin as soon as the Turkish mission had visited the Russian Emperor. Since Charykov had the impression that this mission received a favorable reception, he initiated negotiations shortly after it returned.[84] Charykov may also have considered this moment especially opportune because of rumors of Italy's intention to extend hostilities from Tripolitania to the Straits and other parts of the Ottoman Empire.[85] Only two days before, however, Assim Bey, the Turkish Foreign Minister, had sounded the British Ambassador at Constantinople as to the possibility of British aid if Russia demanded the opening of the Straits.[86]

Charykov and the Straits

Neratov seems to have communicated to Charykov neither his own and Benckendorff's fears about British policy nor the criticisms made by Hartwig and Nekliudov. Nor does he seem to have informed Charykov of French reluctance to give Russia full liberty of action. During the second half of November, when British and French hesitation about supporting Russia was becoming increasingly evident, Neratov apparently sent no warnings to Constantinople. With regard to British and French attitudes, Charykov has written:

> I feel it my duty to say that I had always insisted to the Foreign Office that our plan of opening the Straits could only succeed with the help of France and England; and in the beginning of my negotiations I received a telegram from our Foreign Office informing me that help had been secured. I leave it to those who sent that telegram to decide whether this assertion was a voluntary or involuntary delusion.[87]

Many of Neratov's telegrams could be easily construed to mean that some sort of action was necessary. On November 21 and 25 he informed Charykov that it was inadmissible, according to the London agreement of 1871, that Turkey should close the Straits, even if the Italo-Turkish war spread to the Aegean Sea.[88] And on November 17 Neratov wrote Charykov that Vienna had no objections to free passage of Russian warships through the Straits and, as the ambassador in St. Petersburg had assured him, Germany still followed Bismarck's policy of recognition for Russia's special interests in the Straits.[89] Since Charykov included in his "official" proposals of November 27 the article on rapprochment between Turkey and the Balkan states, it is also very unlikely that Neratov had forwarded to him the comments of Hartwig and Nekliudov.

In a minute to Charykov's dispatch of November 30, Neratov strongly disapproved of the ambassador's action and was especially worried lest Charykov's text give rise to the "fiction" that other powers had the right to control the negotiations. Finally, he commented that the "forced character of the beginning of these negotiations presaged nothing good." [90] When Neratov replied to Charykov on December 6, however, he expressed no direct criticism and merely reminded the ambassador of his instructions of October 2 as well as the necessity of submitting "all our further steps" to St. Petersburg for the judgment of the council of ministers. Neratov also asked Charykov to telegraph Assim Bey's answer and any comments of the British and French ambassadors at Constantinople. Article IV of the "official" proposal should also be changed to avoid interference by other powers in Russo-Turkish negotiations concerning the Straits.[91] Apparently Neratov was waiting for Sazonov to return and take further action on Charykov's case. He did not have to wait long, for on December 9 an interview with Sazonov appeared in the Paris *Matin*. The foreign minister bluntly disavowed Charykov's negotiations: "having demanded nothing, Russia had not undertaken any negotiation, has not made any diplomatic *démarche*." [92]

Charykov was recalled from Constantinople in March of the following year and appointed senator. His recall surprised no one, and he himself considered it justified:

> I [undertook these negotiations] . . . on my own initiative but with positive instructions from the Foreign Office, given unfortunately in the absence of Sazonoff, who was on sick leave. When the Minister resumed his functions he decided, as was his right and duty, that under the then existing circumstances the negotiation should not be proceeded with. And as I had voluntarily acted on my own personal responsibility so as to shield my Government in case of unsuccess, I was naturally recalled from Constantinople in March 1912, and appointed Senator.[93]

Although Sazonov had practically no alternative but to disavow his ambassador and salvage what he could of Russian diplomatic prestige, he was in one sense very much indebted to Charykov. For the ambassador had given a fair test to the hypothesis that Russia might further her interests through friendship with Turkey. The Porte's conciliatory policy in Albania and Monte- negro, approval of the Danube-Adriatic railway, and rumors of Balkan-Turkish rapprochement made it seem to many officials in St. Petersburg that Russia should re-examine her attitude toward Turkey. Thus, in late July and early August, the Russian govern- ment supported the Turks in their dispute with Montenegro and, during the ensuing months, seriously considered the idea that Russia might gain concessions in regard to the Straits and rail- way construction in Asia Minor in return for supporting a Turkey torn by internal crisis and menaced by foreign aggression. And a Balkan confederation including Turkey offered the pleasant pros- pect of assuring Russian influence in both the Black Sea region and the Balkans. The Turks did not respond positively to Chary- kov's overtures, however, and it was finally clear that friendship with Turkey could not be used to defend Russian interests in these areas.

Chapter 3

RUSSIA AND BULGARIAN-SERBIAN RAPPROCHEMENT

After 1870, thanks to rapidly expanding economies and the development of education and political leadership, the Balkan states succeeded where the Turks failed, i.e. they achieved a degree of internal cohesion that enabled their political leaders to mobilize popular support. But while these Balkan models of the West European national state utilized national resources and energies much more efficiently than did the multinational and politically backward Ottoman state, individually they were still too weak to defeat Turkey. And until the second decade of the twentieth century, dependence on the great powers and differences among themselves repeatedly frustrated a rapprochement among the Balkan states.[1]

Macedonia represented the main apple of discord. A Turkish firman of 1870 permitted the Bulgarian church to extend its jurisdiction over areas outside of Bulgaria proper upon the vote of two-thirds of the inhabitants. The Serbs were not given similar rights at the time, but as early as the 1880's and 1890's generously subsidized Serbian and Greek patriotic societies were actively founding schools and disseminating propaganda in Macedonia. Nevertheless the Bulgarian exarchate won a large proportion of the Slavs in Macedonia and Thrace for the Bulgarian national cause.[2]

The situation was further complicated by internal developments in Macedonia. Unlike many other Balkan Slavs, the Macedonians had not benefited in any way from the Treaty of Berlin of 1878. The Turks continued to rule, and the chiflik system, which stifled peasant initiative by requiring them to deliver a substantial share of their crop to Moslem landowners and officials, greatly hindered the economic and social development of Macedonia.[3] Article xxiii of the Treaty of Berlin, it is true, obliged the Turks to introduce reforms and permit a degree of political autonomy to European Turkey analogous to what had been done in Crete in 1868,[4] but the Turks never honored this obligation.

Macedonian leaders realized that their people had no future as long as this situation remained unchanged. Furthermore, many of them felt that a separate revolutionary movement had to be formed if Macedonians were to avoid being partitioned by their neighbors. The slogan "Macedonia for the Macedonians" was used as early as 1885,[5] and by 1893–94 the Inner Macedonian Revolutionary Organization was active. Imro caused considerable difficulty for Turkish officials by the beginning of the twentieth century, but it overestimated its own strength and the sympathy of the great powers when it staged the disastrous Ilinden uprising in 1903.[6] After this failure, imro drifted under the influence of the rival Macedonian Supreme Committee (Makedonski Verkhoven Komitet). This committee, founded in 1895 at Sofia by Macedonian refugees, had a pro-Bulgarian orientation,[7] and after 1903 Greeks and Serbs tended to equate imro with the idea of a Bulgarian Macedonia. Serbian and Greek revolutionists therefore actively opposed imro in Macedonia, which led to bitter vendettas in the disputed province.[8]

The Serbs were particularly active in the strategically important region around Üsküb (Skoplje). At the same time the

Bulgarians wanted Üsküb (promised them by the Treaty of San Stefano) as a junction for their planned Bulgaro-Macedonian railway.[9] Such a railway would have established economic control over the Vardar River valley and the entire region lying between Sofia and Saloniki. The Serbs, of course, were interested in the Üsküb region for similar reasons. And if they could not connect Belgrade with Saloniki, they wanted this area for the alternate access it offered to the Adriatic across northern Albania.[10] Greece, too, had designs on part of the Vardar valley, hoping to obtain southern Macedonia as a hinterland for a Greek-controlled littoral on the northern Aegean. Both Greece and Serbia favored partition of Macedonia, while the Bulgarians preferred an autonomous Macedonia under nominal Turkish suzerainty until some future time when it could be annexed to Bulgaria.[11]

In 1903 and 1904 the bloody and unsuccessful Ilinden uprising in Macedonia, the murder of pro-Austrian King Alexander Obrenović of Serbia, and the establishment of Russophile governments in Belgrade and Sofia temporarily united Serbia and Bulgaria. They signed treaties of friendship and alliance in 1904 and a tariff agreement in June 1905. The honeymoon was short, however, and the wedding annulled by a change of government in Sofia, renewed rivalry in Macedonia, and Austro-Hungarian diplomatic pressure.[12]

The Balkan states repeatedly sought outside assistance for their respective national causes, occasionally even Turkish assistance. As long as the Christians of European Turkey lacked leaders and nationalism, policies favoring one national group could have a bearing on the final outcome of the competition of the Balkan states in Thrace, Albania, and Macedonia. The Bulgarians benefited first with the Bulgarian exarchate in Macedonia, and Premier Stephen Stambolov's (1887–94) rapprochement policy with Turkey won several additional Macedonian bishoprics.[13] The Bulgarian government of I. E. Geshov paid lip service to the principle of good relations with Constantinople as late as 1911, shortly before Bulgaria decided to join Serbia in an aggressive alliance directed against Turkey.[14] The Turks soon realized, however, that a Bulgarian majority in Macedonia and Thrace could very well jeopardize their European interests; they therefore frequently cooperated with the Serbs and Greeks during and after the 1880's. But the Porte was reluctant to grant significant concessions to anyone, so these interludes of cordial relations with Serbs, Greeks, and Bulgarians were brief.

The other principal outside sources of assistance for Balkan nationalism were Austria-Hungary and Russia. These two powers never completely ceased their rivalry. Even during their period of Balkan entente from 1897 to 1908, they carefully observed each other's actions in the peninsula. In 1902, for example, Russia concluded a defensive military convention with Bulgaria in answer to an Austro-Rumanian treaty of alliance of April 17, 1902. Although never ratified by the Bulgarian Sobranie, the military convention did illustrate both Russia's Balkan ambitions and the existence of Russophiles who advocated furthering Bulgarian national interests through friendship with Russia.[15] But Russophobes in Sofia argued that Austria-Hungary could do more for Bulgaria, especially in Macedonia, than Russia could.[16] Russophobe and Russophile governments succeeded one another periodically, creating considerable uncertainty about Bulgaria's intentions. This uncertainty encouraged Vienna and St. Petersburg to hope for success in courting Sofia.

Similarly, Russophiles and Austrophiles competed for power in Belgrade. Between 1878 and 1903, until the Obrenović dynasty was overthrown, Serbia generally looked to Vienna for support. But after 1889 the Russophile Radicals, under the leadership of Nikola Pašić, were in power on several occasions. They did much to revive memories of Russo-Serbian friendship and, through personal contacts in St. Petersburg and Moscow, to win friends for Serbia.[17] The Radicals were the dominant party after the murder of Alexander Obrenović in 1903; their influence and public opinion assured a consistently pro-Russian orientation of Serbian policy until the country was overrun in 1915.[18]

After the Ilinden uprising, Austria-Hungary and Russia demanded reform of the Ottoman administration in Macedonia under the supervision of their own civil agents. Although the reforms neither eliminated the social, economic, and political grievances of the Macedonians nor ended the activities of armed bands, Austria-Hungary (mainly because of Russia's difficulties in the Far East) strengthened her influence in areas of northern Macedonia and Albania coveted by Serbia. At the same time the dual monarchy sought to force Belgrade to cooperate economically during the so-called pig war (an embargo on imports from Serbia). The Serbs reacted by seeking new markets in Western Europe and, especially after the annexation of Bosnia-Herzegovina in 1908, by intensifying nationalistic agitation in both Macedonia and the southern provinces of Austria-Hungary.[19]

After the annexation, the Serbs considered their future in the Balkans jeopardized and between 1908 and 1911 became the principal advocates of Balkan unity. Serbian efforts to create a Balkan bloc were supported by both Russia and Great Britain, especially in the form of a rapprochement between the Balkan states and Turkey. Although Bulgarian ambitions in Macedonia stood in the way of such a bloc, after the Young Turk Revolution of 1908, all the Balkan peoples felt increasingly threatened by the Young Turks' program of transforming Turkey into a modern national state and curtailment of the activities of Slavic and Greek nationalists.[20] Bulgarian leaders, fearful that they would not fall heir to the Ottoman lands in Europe, and aware of their own growing strength as contrasted with the continuing disorder within Turkey, decided by the fall of 1911 that the time was ripe for common action.

Neratov had yielded somewhat to pro-Slav sentiment when he asked the Turks to assure Montenegro of their peaceful intentions. Soon, however, he not only acted firmly to restrain Montenegro but did so in close cooperation with Austria-Hungary, Italy, and the other European powers. Especially noteworthy was his willingness to cooperate with Austria-Hungary, the nation so often described by Russian publicists as the hereditary enemy of all Slavs. In a word, by 1911 much of the resentment Russian diplomats had felt for Austria-Hungary during the Bosnian crisis had subsided. A Balkan alliance was still regarded as desirable, but not as necessary for curtailing further Austrian expansion as it had been three years before.

In the absence of Sazonov from St. Petersburg, Neratov did not actively encourage a Balkan alliance. In April and May even unmistakable signs of revived Serbian and Bulgarian interest in an agreement did not cause St. Petersburg to act more energetically in the Balkan capitals. And when the Russian Minister at Belgrade requested permission to go to Sofia to give "new impetus to the negotiations between Serbia and Bulgaria," [21] Nicholas II and Neratov vetoed such a trip.[22] Similarly in August Neratov rejected the advice of Russia's diplomatic and military representatives in Sofia who urged renewing negotiations for a Russo-Bulgarian military convention. The tsarist government had discussed the subject with the Bulgarian Government on a number of occasions during 1909–10, but had waited in vain for concrete Bulgarian proposals. Now Neratov felt that Sofia should take the initiative in this matter. Not knowing Bulgaria's real attitude, Neratov decided that it would be a mistake to give the impression that Russia was especially eager to conclude a military convention.[23]

Despite Neratov's caution, Nekliudov and Hartwig, the Russian Ministers at Sofia and Belgrade, encouraged Serbia and Bulgaria in their negotiations for a Balkan alliance. Nekliudov and Hartwig clearly worked at cross purposes to Charykov, for the projected Serbo-Bulgarian alliance was directed above all against Turkey. Until Sazonov's return to St. Petersburg in December, however, Balkan confederation including Turkey was never definitely rejected by the Russian Foreign Ministry.

Few Russian diplomats welcomed the prospect of war with Germany and Austria-Hungary; they generally sought at least to postpone the outbreak of any war in the Balkans, for Russia in 1911 still was a number of years away from achieving the stabilization of her economy and the reorganization of her army. Officials in St. Petersburg realized that a purely Balkan alliance presented many serious risks: Once they had settled their differences, the Balkan states would be tempted to force Turkey out of Europe. And Russian sponsorship of a Serbo-Bulgarian alliance would place the tsarist empire in an extremely dangerous position *vis-à-vis* Austria-Hungary and Germany, for such an alliance was intolerable for Austria-Hungary in the long run and Germany was bound by treaty to support her ally.[24]

Perhaps the best solution was the one proposed by Prince L. V. Urusov while chargé d'affaires at Sofia in May 1911. He suggested that Russia offer the Balkan states generous material and military assistance. This, if properly handled, would serve to restrain them from undertaking military action contrary to Russian wishes.[25] In a word, he envisaged an arrangement similar to that provided by the Russo-Montenegrin military convention. But the Balkan states had no intention of allowing Russia to restrict their freedom of action, and they did not always take official warnings too seriously, for they believed that St. Petersburg's vested interests in the Balkans and pro-Slav public opinion would oblige Russia to save them, if need be, from the wrath of the Turks and Austrians.[26] Furthermore, to bribe the Balkan states into accepting counsel and leadership would have taken more money than Russia could afford at that moment. And to subject them to Russia's will without generous expenditures would have placed impossible demands on diplomatic skill and adroitness.

Neratov scarcely displayed even diplomatic skill during the fall of 1911. Generally, he confined himself to commenting on ideas originating in either Belgrade or Sofia and admonishing the Balkan states to avoid mention of aggressive intentions in drafts of their treaty to alliance. When Nekliudov suggested that the projected Serbo-Bulgarian alliance should have "the immediate goal of the maintenance of the status quo in the Balkans," [27] Neratov approved the suggestion by return telegram on October 4 [28] and during the following months frequently reiterated that a treaty should be based on the status quo. Neratov's flirtation with Charykov's plans made him all the more eager to persuade the two Balkan states to draft a defensive, not an offensive, alliance.[29] On November 10 he criticized a draft treaty for mentioning the partition of Macedonia and offensive military operations. Serbia and Bulgaria, he noted, should limit their aspirations in Macedonia to a definition of spheres of cultural influence.[30] Such a desire was understandable but not realistic; Bulgarians and Serbs would be satisfied only with a pure and simple annexation of the disputed province.

The absence of a firm hand in St. Petersburg naturally tempted Russia's representatives at Constantinople, Belgrade, and Sofia to impose their own views on the foreign ministry. Charykov was the first to try; his initial success and ultimate failure have already been described. Meanwhile, Hartwig and Nekliudov opposed Charykov's plans and sought to give Russian Balkan policy a more pro-Serbian or pro-Bulgarian orientation. During the ensuing months they occupied a central position on the diplomatic stage; their personalities and attitudes, therefore, deserve analysis as part of any serious discussion of Russian policy in the Balkans during 1911 and 1912.

Nicholas Genrikovich Hartwig, Russian Minister to Serbia between 1909 and 1914, was a capable and experienced man who possessed a logical mind and more than his share of energy and personal ambition. His driving energy and ambition were such that he could not easily be content with the customary activities of a diplomat in the only two posts he occupied outside of Russia, minister to Persia and Serbia. In Persia his energetic and even ruthless defense of Russian interests between 1906 and 1909 brought him into bitter conflict with the British Minister in Tehran. After several years, Hartwig's relations with his British colleague deteriorated to the extent that the two men no longer spoke and hardly even bowed when they met.[31] As a result, Hartwig was transferred to Belgrade where he soon became very popular among the Serbs. He was a confidant of Pašić, and on one occasion Hartwig's intervention seems to have been decisive in keeping the premier in power.[32] A Russian journalist, who obviously admired Hartwig, has vividly, though with some exaggeration, described his position at Belgrade:

> The King, Prince Alexander, Paschitch, none of these made any decision without first consulting him. He had cleverly instilled in the minds of all the Serbian parties a love for Russia. I have seen him at his work, having been his guest for some time at Belgrade in 1912. Every morning his study was besieged by Serbian statesmen who came to get advice from him, but as usual the saying that a prophet is not without honor save in his own country held true, and Iswolsky and Sazonoff, possibly fearing a successor in Hartwig, took it upon themselves to paralyze his actions and nullify his work. When Hartwig warned our ministry that the first Balkan War was inevitable, Sazonoff sent him a note with orders to advise a moderate course to the Serbian government. One day when our minister had read one of these innumerable notes sent by Sazonoff to M. Paschitch, the old Serbian statesman said to him, "Have you finished, mon cher ami? All right! C'est bien. Nous pouvons maintenant causer sérieusement!" [33]

If Izvol'skii and Sazonov did not always follow his advice, it was not because Hartwig did not make every effort to gain foreign ministry approval of his views. Indeed, the Serb Božin Simić, who knew him well, wrote that Hartwig would not even hesitate to falsify facts in order to impose his views on others and to slander anyone who dared to oppose him on any important issue.[34]

Despite his German name and grandfather, Hartwig was an extreme Russian nationalist. As a young man he had been a correspondent for the chauvinistic *Novoe Vremia,* and his later

66

actions in Persia and Serbia and the reports he sent from Belgrade reflected an intense preoccupation with Russian national interests and with what he described as Russia's "secular task" in the Balkans. Like so many other Russian nationalists who reached maturity around the time of the Russo-Turkish War of 1877–88, Hartwig was an outspoken and self-proclaimed friend of the "brother Slavs." As Nekliudov wrote:

> Having spent all his life (with the exception of two short visits to Montenegro and Burgas) in the offices of the Asiatic Department specializing in the Slav question, Hartwig had gained a knowledge not only of Balkan questions and records, but up to a point of the people themselves. To him were sent all the Slavs who came on missions, young princes and princesses educated at the expense of the Court in privileged schools and institutions, etc. Amongst all these people, whom he received with good-nature and in whose favour he interceded with his chiefs, "Nicolas Henricovitch" was deservedly popular. He found himself at once amongst old acquaintances when he took up his post in Belgrade, where he had access to everything, and where he might flatter himself that his advice would be listened to and followed. On this score he experienced a few disappointments. But with the innate adaptability of his nature he appropriated those very ideas which it was his duty to fight, and made himself their authorised champion; so that they often were approved of by our Foreign Office, where he had left a few fervent friends and some devoted admirers. But one must allow that in order to have his support, every cause had to bear the stamp of very orthodox Slavophilism, *i.e.* of hostility to Austria and devotion to Russia.[35]

During the five years Count V. N. Lamsdorf was foreign minister (1901–6), Hartwig's competence, incessant activity, and authority as director of the Asiatic department made him one of the most influential figures in the foreign ministry. The close relations of his wife with high-ranking figures at court and the position he had gained by his own efforts gave him good reason to hope that he would succeed Lamsdorf. But upon becoming foreign minister Izvol'skii, possibly fearing Hartwig as a dangerous rival, had him sent to Tehran.[36] The chagrin that Hartwig felt as a result of having been sent away from St. Petersburg must have made him all the more determined to score personal diplomatic victories. These were especially feasible during the years in Belgrade, for he served there at a time when Russia was beginning to concentrate her diplomatic efforts more and more in the Balkans.

During the first years Hartwig was in Belgrade, his interest in a Serbo-Bulgarian entente was shared by D. K. Sementovskii-Kurilo, Russian Minister to Bulgaria. Sementovskii-Kurilo died at the beginning of 1911, however, being replaced in May by Nekliudov, a somewhat more cautious man. And Neratov did not actively encourage the formation of a Balkan alliance. Thus Hartwig alone continued to work for a purely Balkan alliance during most of 1911. Opposing Charykov's plans, Hartwig argued that the concept of a Balkan confederation including Turkey was contrary to the spirit of traditional Russian policy in the Near East. This policy, according to Hartwig, should properly pursue two objectives: (1) encouragement and support of the Slavic nations in the Balkans and the division of Turkey's European possessions among them; and (2) realization of the "secular task" of Russian diplomacy, i.e. establishing Russian control over the shores of the Bosphorus, the gateway to the "Russian sea." [37]

Hartwig also differed from other Russian diplomats in his fervent espousal of the national cause of Serbia. Again and again he urged St. Petersburg to favor Serbia over Bulgaria. Serbia, Hartwig insisted, should serve as Russia's advanced post in the Balkans.[38] Bulgaria's geographical position was already sufficiently strong, he claimed, and it was therefore in Russia's interest to support Serbia, whose geographical and political situation was considerably weaker.[39] Hartwig believed that Serbia was necessarily more dependent on Russia than Bulgaria, whose stronger position permitted her to act more independently.

But Russian favoritism toward either Serbia or Bulgaria was likely to push the other power into the arms of Austria-Hungary.

This was especially the case if Serbia were favored, because Bulgaria, as Hartwig's own arguments implied, enjoyed more freedom of action and could more easily turn to Austria-Hungary for assistance. Certainly Hartwig's manifestly pro-Serbian agitation and activities in Belgrade caused Bulgarian misgivings.

There was hardly a more outspoken and extreme Austrophobe among Russian diplomats than Hartwig. He considered the Balkan peninsula "one of our future bases for operations" in the "imminent catastrophe," for which reason he argued that it was imperative for Russia to prevent Austria-Hungary from gaining any position of advantage in the Balkans.[40] It did not, however, necessarily follow that Hartwig wanted an immediate armed showdown. He seems to have been aware of the military weaknesses of both Serbia and Russia and perhaps hoped to postpone the "imminent" conflict for several years. Such was the opinion of the Austrian Minister to Serbia, Baron Giesl, in whose study Hartwig died of a heart attack on July 10, 1914. According to Giesl, Hartwig, had he lived, would have postponed the outbreak of World War I by persuading the Serbs to comply with all of Austria-Hungary's demands.[41]

Whatever Hartwig might have done in July 1914, his presence in Belgrade before that time was a constant thorn in the side of the dual monarchy. His Austrophobia was shared by influential people inside of Russia, and this must have made him seem all the more of a menace. For example, when Nicholas Giers, the Russian Ambassador at Vienna, was in Russia in March 1912, he noted with alarm that many generals were speaking openly of a war with Austria-Hungary. Such talk, Giers pointed out, was unfortunate, for it coincided with troop concentrations in the Ukraine and therefore could only arouse fears in Vienna. Hartwig's activities in Belgrade, he added, made this talk seem all the more dangerous:

> One speaks the same bellicose language at Belgrade thanks to the incurable Austrophobia of Hartwig. He would do better to pursue only and above all the interests of Russia.

I would prefer to see him as minister at Bucharest, where he would do less harm. Also, this legation is more advantageous. At Belgrade there should be a more balanced representative so that our action . . . would be more in conformity with the instructions of our august master and that my efforts would not be paralyzed.[42]

Sazonov, too, felt that Hartwig compromised Russia with his overtly anti-Austrian attitude and agitation in Belgrade, complaining that Hartwig did not sufficiently restrain the Serbs and "interpreted Russian policy in Belgrade according to his own taste, and thereby greatly added to my difficulties."[43] Yet Hartwig was not removed from his post in Belgrade, perhaps because he had many influential friends in St. Petersburg. And as long as he remained in Belgrade, he naturally continued his efforts to impose his own views on the Russian Foreign Ministry. Clearly, it was not always considerations of *Realpolitik* that determined his anti-Austrian and pro-Serbian activities but more often the frustration and boundless energy of an ambitious and competent man who was, as Simić remarked, very much like an "encaged lion in the small diplomatic circle of Belgrade."[44]

Anatole Vasil'evich Nekliudov, the Russian Minister in Sofia, was a more moderate and balanced man than Hartwig. He was, judging by his memoirs and diplomatic reports, well-educated, urbane, and honest. But he certainly was Hartwig's inferior in energy and probably also native intelligence, for his diplomatic career was rather ordinary and uneventful. Prior to his appointment as minister to Bulgaria, he had spent seventeen years as secretary in the legations at Sofia and Belgrade and as counsellor at the embassy in Paris. In Bulgaria he failed to gain the confidence of King Ferdinand and, apparently for this reason, was transferred to Stockholm as ambassador.[45] In June 1917 he was made ambassador to Spain, which post he resigned three months later.

From the very beginning of the Serbo-Bulgarian negotiations, Nekliudov agreed with Neratov concerning the need to restrain the Serbs and Bulgarians from an offensive alliance.[46] He especially feared that Austria-Hungary would use any disturbance in the Balkans as a pretext for occupying the Sanjak of Novibazar and Old Serbia.[47] If this happened, general war would probably break out in the Balkans, and Russia would "have to submit to many disagreeable things if she does not wish to be drawn into the fray."[48] Such an eventuality could only be avoided, he emphasized, if Russian diplomacy displayed the same skill that it had previously with France. When the Franco-Russian Alliance had been signed seventeen years before, many Frenchmen had viewed it primarily as a means of obtaining *revanche* for their defeat in the Franco-Prussian War. Now, Nekliudov claimed, such sentiment was no longer an important consideration, and the alliance had become a source of strength for both Russia and France. He optimistically reasoned that skillful Russian diplomacy could also prevent the Balkan states from undertaking provocative actions until some future time when Russia would be in a better position to defend her vital interests.[49]

Nekliudov did not believe that the status quo in the Balkans could be maintained indefinitely. Indeed, he predicted that it would not be too long before the Turkish empire would collapse. At such a time, he pointed out, there would be no way to prevent Serbia and Bulgaria from realizing their territorial aspirations in Macedonia and elsewhere.[50] For the same reason Nekliudov, like Hartwig, opposed Charykov's plan for a Balkan confederation including Turkey. Serbia and Bulgaria were the potential enemies, not allies, of Turkey.[51]

Nekliudov's position was much less dogmatic and rigid than Hartwig's. In his memoirs Nekliudov criticized Hartwig for often allowing "an apt syllogism" to take the place of the "inexorable logic of facts."[52] The "inexorable logic" of the Balkan situation

71

for Nekliudov was that for a number of years Russia would not be in a position to profit from the collapse of Turkish authority. Hence the sensible thing was to arrange a modus vivendi with Austria-Hungary in the Balkans based on the status quo and the territorial integrity of the Ottoman Empire. He trusted Vienna no more than Hartwig did, but he considered the dual monarchy too weak to act aggressively in the Balkans as long as Turkey remained intact and Russian diplomacy prevented the Balkan allies from attacking her prematurely.[53]

Nekliudov customarily gave the Bulgarian point of view in the reports he sent to St. Petersburg. Russia, he warned, could not remain neutral in a Balkan war and should make every effort to keep Bulgaria from joining Austria-Hungary.[54] Accordingly, as will be pointed out in the next chapter, Nekliudov almost invariably backed Bulgaria during the months of wrangling with Serbia over the division of Macedonia. He did, however, support Serbian demands on one occasion,[55] and his commitment to Bulgaria's interest was not as unqualified as that of Hartwig to Serbia's.

The support Nekliudov did give to Bulgaria's special wishes could only arouse the anger of Hartwig, since the granting of special Bulgarian requests would have tended to give a new pro-Bulgarian orientation to Russian Balkan policy. This Hartwig was not willing to accept passively, for he had always insisted that Russia's true interests in the Balkans could only be served by making Serbia Russia's preferred and most trusted ally in the peninsula.

By 1911 considerable progress had been made in improving relations between the Balkan states. The Bulgarian and Greek churches and private groups in Belgrade and Sofia now took Balkan cooperation much more seriously than they had for a number of years. There was also action on the governmental level. In the latter part of 1910 and in 1911, Greece and Bulgaria discussed an alliance,[56] and the new Russophile cabinet at Sofia (March 1911) of S. Danev and I. E. Geshov improved the chances for Serbo-Bulgarian cooperation. In April Serbian Foreign Minister M. G. Milovanović proposed to the Bulgarian Minister at Belgrade, A. Toshev, that their two countries should prepare for an imminent Balkan crisis by forming an alliance. Toshev discussed the subject with Milovanović and Nikola Pašič, the Serbian Premier, on several other occasions, but Bulgarian reluctance to accept division of Macedonia again proved an obstacle to serious negotiations.[57]

The coalition Geshov-Danev government followed a pro-Turkish policy throughout the spring and well into the summer of 1911. The Bulgarians hoped for an understanding with the Porte that would safeguard Bulgarian interests in Macedonia without concessions to Serbia. Geshov, who was both prime minister and minister of foreign affairs, therefore took a number of measures to improve relations with Turkey. He sent Bulgarian princes Boris and Cyril to visit Constantinople in April 1911 and took steps to hinder the passage of terrorist bands from Bulgarian territory into Macedonia. The alliance discussions with Serbia and Greece were suspended, and Geshov began negotiations with Assim Bey, Turkish minister at Sofia, for a Turko-Bulgarian entente.[58]

Despite weakness and internal problems, however, the Porte refused any concessions that would have significantly improved the position of the Bulgarian element in Macedonia, and the Young Turks continued to demand centralized government and the suppression of all opposition.[59] In May a Bulgarian officer, a Captain Georgiev, was killed by Turkish soldiers on the frontier. Bulgarian nationalists were also infuriated by rumors of the massacre of peaceful villagers in Macedonia. And in June the Macedonian chetnici held a secret meeting at Kiustendil to consider reprisals against the Turks. At Sofia Geshov's political opponents accused him of "criminal weakness" because of his conciliatory policy.[60]

In his book on the Balkan alliance, Geshov commented that it was impossible for him to ignore this public indignation: "My manifest duty was to examine how Bulgaria could best be enabled to stop these excesses. Among the various methods that suggested themselves, the most important consisted in an understanding, not with Turkey who had rejected our advances, but with our other neighbours." [61] The imminence of a Turko-Italian war may also have contributed to his decision to open negotiations with Serbia. Tension between Italy and Turkey mounted during the summer of 1911 as Turkey resisted Italian efforts to establish a privileged position in Tripoli. Italian newspapers waged a violent campaign against Turkey, and Turkish protests were curtly rejected by the Italian Foreign Ministry.[62]

It was certainly not coincidental that the Bulgarian Minister in Rome, Dimitŭr Rizov, returned to Sofia on vacation in the early part of September 1911. Before mid-September it was decided that Rizov should go to Belgrade to arrange an interview for Geshov with Milovanović. This interview was to take place after Geshov's return from Vichy, where he proposed to go after the general elections in Bulgaria. On September 20, three days after the elections, Geshov left for Vichy. He was still there when the Tripolitan War broke out on September 29 and immediately departed for Paris where he sounded French Foreign Minister de Selves.[63] Meanwhile, Rizov conferred with Milovanović, Pašić, and Hartwig at Belgrade. The Bulgarian plenipotentiary arranged the interview and also touched upon the main points concerning a Balkan alliance that Geshov would want to discuss.

On October 6 Rizov left for Vienna, where he met Geshov and Dimitŭr Stanchov, the Bulgarian Minister to France.[64] The three worked out a memorandum which contained the Bulgarian conditions for the proposed alliance. The Serbo-Bulgarian treaty of 1904 was considered as the point of departure; Macedonia was to be divided if it proved impossible to establish an autonomous province. Montenegro was to be permitted to join the alliance, and Russian approval was referred to as a *sine qua non*.

The *casus foederis* was to arise (1) if Serbia or Bulgaria were attacked by a third power, (2) if Turkey attacked any Balkan power, (3) if Austria-Hungary attempted to occupy Macedonia or Albania, (4) if internal troubles in Turkey threatened the peace or tranquillity of the Balkans, or (5) "when the interests of Bulgaria and Serbia demand that the question should be settled." [65]

While in Austria, Geshov talked with both Aehrenthal and King Ferdinand of Bulgaria, who was then paying one of his periodic visits to the Austrian capital. Geshov assured Aehrenthal of Bulgaria's peaceful intentions and tried to find out as much as he could about the attitude of Austria-Hungary to the Turko-Italian war. In his audience with Ferdinand, he gave a full account of the negotiations he was about to open in Belgrade and, having obtained the king's approval, left Vienna for Belgrade on October 11. [66]

In order to ensure the secrecy of the negotiations, [67] an unidentified Bulgarian traveled through Belgrade and on to Sofia under the name of Geshov. Geshov, himself, arrived incognito at the Belgrade railway station in the evening of October 11. There a special Serbian coach was attached to the train, and for the next three hours, while the train traveled between Belgrade and Lapovo, Milovanović and Geshov discussed the terms of a possible agreement. First of all, Milovanović warned that the time was not ripe for action because the great powers wanted to localize the Tripolitan War and to avoid complications in the Balkans. Consequently, he reasoned, the Serbs and Bulgarians should remain quiet and await the end of the war. But before they did anything else, they had to obtain Russian support; "without this support one cannot and should not undertake anything." [68]

Milovanović proposed a definition of the *casus foederis* closely resembling the one worked out by Geshov, Rizov, and Stanchov in Vienna. Each ally was to be committed to come to the other's assistance if it were attacked by a third power. They were to offer military resistance to the attempt of any power to occupy Macedonia or Old Serbia. And point three of Milovanović's definition referred to military action against Turkey with the aim of "liberating Macedonia and Old Serbia in circumstances deemed favourable to both countries" and "of putting an end to the anarchy or massacres in the Turkish provinces where the vital interests of either contracting party are at stake." [69]

Milovanović insisted that the provinces liberated as the result of a victorious war against Turkey should be partitioned between the two allies. He reserved the area north of the Šar Planina for Serbia and the one around Adrianople for Bulgaria. But he opposed drawing any definite line of demarcation in Macedonia at that particular moment:

By adopting that course you will spare yourselves the criticisms of having consented to a preliminary repartition of Macedonia. Later on, when your compatriots have secured the lion's part, no one would think of protesting that a small part of Macedonia has been awarded to Serbia by the Russian Emperor, under whose patronage and high sense of justice this great work will have been accomplished. Ah yes! If the "winding-up" of Turkey coincides with the crumbling of Austria-Hungary, matters will be enormously simplified. Serbia will get Bosnia and Herzegovina, while Roumania receives Transylvania, and we shall then have no reasons for apprehending a Roumanian intervention in our war against Turkey.[70]

The Bulgarians had long been reluctant to discuss the partition of Macedonia. Now, however, without such an understanding with Serbia, Bulgaria could scarcely hope to take advantage of the weakened position of Turkey. After several months of negotiations and bickering over various small points, the two parties finally narrowed their differences to a small disputed area, the division of which, assuming a victorious war against the Turks, was to be decided by the Russian tsar.[71]

From the very beginning of these negotiations Serbian and Bulgarian political leaders insisted on the importance of Russian support. They needed Russia as the arbiter of their own differences, and St. Petersburg's diplomatic support was essential to prevent the great powers from nullifying any gains at the expense of the Ottoman Empire. The question of what attitude the Russian Government would take toward the projected alliance was therefore a pivotal one for Serbian and Bulgarian statesmen in the fall of 1911.

Although Sazonov had continued to approve Serbo-Bulgarian rapprochement until his illness in March 1911, his assistant Neratov gave little encouragement to the talks begun by Milovanović with Toshev at Belgrade in April of that same year. Neratov especially had misgivings about the Bulgarian government's attitude toward Russia. In August, for example, he advised against haste in resuming negotiations for a Russo-Bulgarian military convention.

Despite these reservations, Neratov did not reject a Serbo-Bulgarian alliance when he first heard of Rizov's negotiations with Milovanović and Pašić in the early days of October 1911.[72] The tsarist government could not permit the Balkan states to form an alliance independently of its guidance without jeopardizing Russian prestige and vital interests in the peninsula. Too, rumors in the fall of 1911 concerning Austria-Hungary's intention to reoccupy the Sanjak of Novibazar must have made the conclusion of a Balkan alliance seem important and necessary.

The Russian Foreign Ministry was bombarded by warnings from Sofia and Belgrade. Nekliudov pointed out that Austria-Hungary had been an unsettling factor in Balkan politics since 1908 and would probably seize the first opportunity to move into the Sanjak, Old Serbia, and even Serbia proper as a base for further expansion to Saloniki. He did not, however, attach much importance to talk about King Ferdinand's close ties with Vienna and alleged interest in a pro-Austrian orientation of Bulgarian policy.[73] Hartwig, in Belgrade, did believe this, ascribing the slow pace of the Serbo-Bulgarian negotiations to Ferdinand's pro-Austrian sentiments.[74] In the fall of 1911 Hartwig was particularly alarmed about a concentration of Austro-Hungarian troops in Bosnia-Herzegovina. He sought to convey to St. Petersburg the atmosphere of fear and apprehension in Belgrade and emphasized that troop movements in Bosnia-Herzegovina were incompatible with Aehrenthal's professions of peaceful intentions.[75] Sazonov shared this concern when Nekliudov talked with him in the early part of October at Davos, where the foreign minister was still convalescing:

> At Davos [Nekliudov later wrote] I had the pleasure of finding M. Sazonoff really on the road to recovery, and the next day I was able to relate and discuss with him the overtures recently made to me by M. Todorov [Bulgarian Finance Minister]. M. Sazonoff listened most attentively. "Well," said he, when I had finished, "but this is perfect! If only it could come off! Bulgaria closely allied to Serbia in the political and economic sphere; five hundred thousand bayonets to guard the Balkans—but this would bar the road for ever to German penetration, Austrian invasion!"[76]

Actually, Aehrenthal, seeking to preserve the status quo in the Balkans,[77] considered it expedient to let Balkan political leaders believe that the dual monarchy would use any disturbance of Balkan peace by a Slav nation as a pretext for military action.[78] It was, however, difficult for Russia to form a correct opinion of Austro-Hungarian intentions. The Russian ambassador at Vienna, N. N. Giers, felt that it was unlikely that Austria-Hungary would move into the Sanjak at the time.[79] Neratov also had doubts but was disturbed by what seemed to be Austro-Hungarian intrigues in the Balkans.[80] Only in December 1911, after Conrad von Hötzendorf was dismissed as chief of the Austro-Hungarian general staff, was Giers able to provide convincing evidence of Aehrenthal's peaceful intentions.[81]

Conrad had long considered Serbia and Italy the principal threats to the security of the dual monarchy. He had argued in 1909 and again in the fall of 1911 that conditions were favorable for a military decision in the Balkans. In 1911 he wanted to concentrate troops on the Italian and Serbian frontiers and move against the southern neighbors if the proper occasion presented itself. Aehrenthal, however, demanded that Hötzendorf confine himself purely to military affairs; Franz Josef agreed, and on November 29, 1911, Conrad resigned as chief of staff.[82]

A lull followed the Milovanović-Geshov discussion of October 11, and toward the end of the month Hartwig became very impatient. It was high time, he wrote Neratov, to change from words to acts; in an epoch of rapid and kaleidoscopic changes, two weeks of inactivity in regard to something as important as the Balkan alliance was inadmissible.[83] On October 30, however, Miroslav Spalajković, the Serbian Minister in Sofia, left for Belgrade to obtain new instructions from Foreign Minister Milovanović.

Before departing Spalajković had an interview with Nekliudov who reminded the Serbian diplomat that Russia desired an alliance based on the status quo and that she hoped the Balkan allies would refrain from willful actions. Spalajković, of course, assured Nekliudov of Serbia's intention of following Russia's advice and declared twice during the interview: "Nous considérons . . . la Russie comme le dépositaire et le garant de l'alliance."[84] That same day Nekliudov proposed to Neratov that Russia guarantee the rights of Serbs and Bulgarians living in the Ottoman Empire as an inducement to Serbia and Bulgaria to accept the status quo. Turkey, according to Nekliudov, should be allowed to keep her possessions in Europe for the time being, but Russia should try to obtain more autonomy for the Slavs.[85] Neratov, however, apparently fearing that such a guarantee represented a dangerous commitment, does not seem to have given serious consideration to Nekliudov's proposal.[86]

Spalajković returned to Sofia during the first week of November with a draft of the treaty of alliance. The third and fourth articles envisaged the possibility of an offensive war against Turkey for the purpose of realizing the national aspirations of the two countries. If the two Balkan powers could not agree concerning the advisability of war at a given moment, they were to refer the matter to the judgment of the Russian tsar. The Serbs also proposed that the tsar arbitrate the division of the vilayets of Monastir and Saloniki between Serbia and Bulgaria after a successful war against Turkey.[87]

Nekliudov immediately informed Spalajković of Russia's disapproval of the draft; his government could only approve of a defensive treaty based on the status quo.[88] The Bulgarians, too, were not happy about the Serbian proposals; they had long considered the vilayets of Monastir and Saloniki as completely within Bulgaria's legitimate sphere of influence.[89] Spalajković was therefore obliged to get new instructions from Belgrade.

On November 7, Spalajković submitted a revised draft of the third and fourth articles. The new draft provided that no offensive military operations were to be undertaken without the preliminary agreement of Russia.[90] It was problematic, however, whether St. Petersburg could exercise much control if Serbia and Bulgaria should decide that it was expedient to attack Turkey.

The Bulgarians were no more satisfied with the revision than they had been with the original version. Now the Serbs proposed a threefold division of Macedonia: a Serbian zone including the vilayet of Scutari and the northern part of the vilayet of Kosovo; a Bulgarian zone including the vilayets of Adrianople and Saloniki and the southern part of the vilayet of Kosovo; and a third zone to be arbitrated by the Russian tsar. As Geshov pointed out, the draft made no mention of autonomy for Macedonia and failed to allot to Bulgaria parts of Macedonia which the Bulgarians considered rightfully theirs.[91]

Milovanović and King Peter made an official visit to Paris during the latter part of November. The Bulgarian Minister in Rome, Rizov, who was on good personal terms with Milovanović, was sent to Paris for the express purpose of talking with the

Serbian Foreign Minister. Rizov and Stanchov, the Bulgarian Minister at Paris, had a lengthy conversation with Milovanović at the Bulgarian legation on November 19 and apparently convinced him that Serbia would have to make further concessions.[92] Both Serbia and Bulgaria, however, remained remarkably intransigent during the next several months, bickering over minor towns and villages and small river valleys.

Another factor delaying the conclusion of an alliance was the attitude of the Russian Government during November and early December 1911. Despite the warnings of Hartwig and Nekliudov that Serbia and Bulgaria would only be interested in the division of the Turkish heritage in Europe, Neratov continued to insist that the Balkan states confine themselves to a delimitation of spheres of cultural influence in Macedonia.[93] And as late as December 6 he still recommended that the possibility of Turkish adherence to the alliance should not be excluded.[94] This position could only discourage the Balkan states. The Bulgarians in particular feared that Russia might sacrifice their interests in her efforts to obtain special rights in the Straits.[95]

Though no letters have been published, it is probable that there was some correspondence between Sazonov, who was still in Western Europe, and the Russian Foreign Ministry during November and December. Nevertheless, Neratov apparently wanted to delay important decisions until his chief returned to St. Petersburg. The few communications sent to Hartwig and Nekliudov during the month preceding Sazonov's return on December 15, 1911 merely reiterated what had been said previously concerning the status quo, spheres of cultural influence, and the need to leave open the possibility of Turkish adherence to the alliance.[96] The foreign minister's statement of December 9 in Paris decided the fate of Charykov's plan, however, and by the beginning of January it was apparent that he was bent on active encouragement of the Serbo-Bulgarian negotiations.

Chapter 4

BULGARIAN-SERBIAN
AGREEMENT

Sazonov's inadequacy as foreign minister has often been exaggerated. "Devoid of authority and experience," wrote Luigi Albertini, he "vacillated irresolutely between the promptings of his former chief and the pacific tendencies of the Tsar" and was "no match for the events that were soon to take place." [1] Baron Taube considered Sazonov a "Slav feminine spirit," "unceasingly variable in his impressions and 'intuitions.'" [2] Maurice Paléologue, French Ambassador at St. Petersburg between 1914 and 1917, complained that Sazonov lacked "a sense of reality and objectivity." [3] And such observers as Hans Kiendl, Miliukov, and Taube have agreed that Sazonov was Izvol'skii's inferior in intelligence and lacked independent ideas and a broad conception of Russian Near Eastern policy.[4]

Actually, as Otto Bickel has correctly noted, Sazonov was a diligent and capable, though cautious, diplomat and administrator.[5] True, he did not possess the intellect and imagination of an Izvol'skii; but common sense, prudence, and psychological finesse were then qualities more needed by Russia than Izvol'skii's personal ambition and erratic brilliance. Certainly it is misleading to emphasize Sazonov's irresolution and deficient "sense of reality and objectivity." To the contrary, he firmly asserted his leadership immediately upon resuming his duties as foreign minister in late 1911 by disavowing Charykov.

There is little reason to believe, as did Langer in 1928, that Sazonov dreamed in 1910 and early 1911 of "smashing the Ottoman Empire by means of the Balkan League." [6] The work of I. V. Bestuzhev in Soviet archives shows that shortly before he became foreign minister Sazonov favored Charykov's project of a Balkan confederation.[7] He did try to impress on Serbia and Bulgaria the need for a rapprochement and in September 1910 even used a rumor of a Turko-Rumanian military convention (never actually concluded) to emphasize this point.[8] But these actions in themselves did not necessarily mean a reorientation of Russian policy. For Serbo-Bulgarian understanding did not rule out the possibility of good relations with Turkey.

After Turkey's negative reaction to Charykov's proposals, however, the foreign minister realized that Russia's only alternative was to strive to maintain her prestige and influence in the Balkans by urging a speedy conclusion of the Serbo-Bulgarian alliance. Once the alliance was concluded, he consistently worked to restrain Sofia and Belgrade from precipitate actions and Bulgaria from dangerous commitments in her negotiations with Greece during the spring of 1912. Although he ultimately failed to control the Balkan allies, the difficulty of exercising such control was no secret to Sazonov and other Russian diplomats. Meanwhile, Russia's repeated friendly advice in the name of Balkan peace and tranquillity kept open lines of communication with Sofia and Belgrade and helped create the impression in Europe that Sazonov was a man of peace and good will.

Sazonov desired a speedy conclusion of the Serbo-Bulgarian alliance partly because of intensified Austro-Hungarian diplomatic and financial activities in Bulgaria and Montenegro during the winter and spring of 1911–12. Bulgarian loyalty to Russia had always seemed a little doubtful, and Montenegro, in addition to the explosive nature of Montenegrins, was a most unreliable ally because of irritation with the role Russia had played in thwarting her ambitions in Albania in the summer of 1911. Too, the Russian Ambassador in Vienna feared that Aehrenthal had won only a Pyrrhic victory over Conrad von Hötzendorf.[9] Franz Ferdinand, the heir apparent, sympathized with Conrad and would certainly break with Aehrenthal's peace policy as soon as the aged Franz Josef died.[10]

In 1909 and 1910 the Austro-Hungarian Government made it possible for Bulgaria to obtain money from banks in Vienna.[11] In April 1911 Franz Josef conferred the order of the Golden Fleece upon King Ferdinand, which greatly flattered the Bulgarian ruler's ego.[12] In June 1911 the Vienna government renounced capitulations in Bulgaria (extraterritorial privileges surviving from the period of Turkish rule),[13] and in March 1912 signed a commercial treaty.[14] Although the Serbo-Bulgarian alliance negotiations during the fall and winter of 1911 represented a serious setback for Austria-Hungary, many Russian diplomats still feared that King Ferdinand might suddenly give a pro-Austrian orientation to Bulgarian policy. In November 1911, Ferdinand again visited Vienna and had an audience with Franz Josef. Sazonov was fairly certain that Austria-Hungary had sought to drive a wedge between Bulgaria and Serbia by offering Sofia a free hand in Macedonia.[15] Such thoughts must have made Sazonov all the more determined to hasten the conclusion of the Serbo-Bulgarian alliance as insurance against unpleasant surprises.

Another possible source of unpleasant surprises for Russia was King Nicholas of Montenegro. In mid-October 1911 the rumor circulated in Cetinje that Vienna had assigned Scutari and Berane (to the south and southeast of the mountain kingdom) to Montenegro in the event that Austria-Hungary should occupy the Sanjak.[16] And at the beginning of November Nicholas even offered to conclude a secret treaty or convention with Austria-Hungary. He promised to heed without exception the advice and instructions of the dual monarchy if Vienna would recognize his claim to northern Albania should circumstances,

84

"perhaps against the will of Montenegro and Austria-Hungary," bring about the "liquidation of Turkey."[17] Both the Austro-Hungarian Minister at Cetinje, Baron Giesl, and the Ballhausplatz believed that Nicholas only wanted to play off Austria-Hungary against Russia.[18] Nevertheless, Vienna decided to show Montenegro special favor. First of all, a loan of three and one-half million crowns was made available through the Boden Credit Anstalt in Vienna and ratified by the Montenegrin Skupština on December 17, 1911. One million crowns of the loan were to be used to cover the deficit in Montenegro's budget for 1911, one and one-half million for agricultural loans, and one million to construct highways.[19]

About the same time Vienna also decided to send two experienced Austro-Serbian jurists to Montenegro to assist in raising the standards of the judicial system. Montenegro, however, wanted full control over their activities, and when Vienna finally (in April 1912) named two Dalmatian jurists, Montenegro replied that the jurists had not been requested and should not be sent.[20]

When the Russian Minister and military attaché in Cetinje learned that the Skupština would ratify the Austrian loan, they suggested that Sazonov warn Montenegro that ratification could easily result in Russia's cutting off the military subsidy.[21] Although the foreign minister did not follow this advice, he was nonetheless concerned about Austro-Hungarian activities in Cetinje.[22] In a report to Emperor Nicholas II, he pointed out that a mortgage bank like the Boden Credit Anstalt could easily gain control of the Montenegrin economy.[23] Sazonov considered the planned Austrian assistance for Montenegro's court system an attempt to control an important branch of the internal administration. Such control, he instructed the Russian chargé d'affaires in Cetinje to inform the Montenegrin Government, "will paralyze the true development of the kingdom which Russia has always sincerely encouraged."[24] But influential, pro-Russian figures, in Cetinje, e.g., the head of the Montenegrin cabinet, Lazar Tomanović, profoundly distrusted Austria-Hungary. The warnings of Tomanović and others finally persuaded King Nicholas to decline the Dalmatian jurists.[25]

Early in 1912 Sazonov felt that a Serbo-Bulgarian alliance sponsored by St. Petersburg would give Russia some control over events and help defend her interests in the Balkans. He wrote later:

> We could only endeavour to lessen the acuteness of the situation by taking an active part in bringing about a *rapprochement* between the various Balkan States. We hoped that by showing a united front they might reduce the risks attendant on their inevitable struggle with the Young Turks over the Balkan problem, and perhaps with Austria-Hungary also, in the event, always to be reckoned with, that the latter should attempt a fresh hostile move.[26]

Without a Serbo-Bulgarian alliance Russia could never be sure that Bulgaria would not be enticed at such a time into the camp of Austria-Hungary and Germany. Both Belgrade and Sofia had not only kept Russia informed about details of the negotiations but also modified the alliance in accordance with suggestions from St. Petersburg. The deference these two powers seemed to show to Russian wishes certainly must have reassured Russian diplomats. As Sazonov commented in his memoirs: "Our participation in the conclusion of an alliance between Serbia and Bulgaria gave us the right to control the activities of these allies, and to veto any decision on their part which did not accord with Russian policy." [27]

An alliance excluding Montenegro would also isolate King Nicholas and discourage him from provoking a premature war with Turkey. From the Russian point of view, Sofia and Belgrade were considerably more reliable than Cetinje. Russia therefore opposed Montenegrin membership in the alliance.[28]

Although Serbo-Bulgarian agreement seemed the most promising answer to Russia's problems in the Balkans at the beginning of 1912, the complicated Macedonian question had to be resolved to the satisfaction of both parties. Apparently neither knowing nor caring too much about the complexities of Macedonian ethnography, history, and geography, Sazonov became increasingly impatient with Serbian and Bulgarian intransigence about minor towns and rivers.

Although the Serbian Government reconsidered its position after the Milovanović-Rizov-Stanchov conversations at Paris in the latter part of November, it was still unwilling to make major concessions in Macedonia. The Serbs were particularly interested in the predominantly Slavic region between Dibra and Lake Okhrida. They believed possession of this area would make it easier in the future for Serbia to control and absorb hundreds of thousands of Albanians to the north in Old Serbia. In addition, they considered this region an essential hinterland south of the projected Danube-Adriatic railway. Accordingly, at the beginning of December the Serbian Government proposed a new line of demarcation which passed through Kratovo to the west and ran southeast across the Vardar in the direction of Struga.[29]

Although the Bulgarian Government waited more than two weeks before replying, the only reservation it made was that Kriva Palanka in northeastern Macedonia should be included within the Bulgarian sphere of influence.[30] Through their minister to Bulgaria, Nekliudov advised the Serbs to conclude the alliance as soon as possible and not to demand any more concessions. He also wired Hartwig, asking him to support this recommendation in Belgrade.[31] Hartwig, however, indignantly refused, commenting that he would decide for himself what sort of advice he wanted to give the government to which he was accredited.[32]

Probably because of Hartwig's encouragement, the Serbian Government ignored Nekliudov's advice. On December 28 it informed Bulgaria that it would waive Kratovo and Kriva Palanka only in return for part of the Ovče Polje. The Serbs emphasized that this "concession" represented the last one they could make. If Sofia was not willing to accept these terms, the government at Belgrade proposed Russian arbitration.[33] The Serbs did, however, accept at this time the Bulgarian view that the possibility of autonomy for Macedonia should not be excluded in the projected Serbo-Bulgarian treaty of alliance.[34]

As was to be expected, Hartwig supported the new position and even sent a letter to Nekliudov defending the justice of Serbia's demands.[35] And he transmitted to Sazonov by telegram Milovanović's request that Russia intervene at Sofia in favor of the proposal. Hartwig gave three reasons why Russia should act as requested: (1) Pašić and other leaders of the Radical Party opposed the "concessions" already made in Macedonia, and the personal prestige of Milovanović was at stake; (2) the small section of the Ovče Polje demanded was of minor importance for Bulgaria, but for Serbia an indispensable natural defense for Üsküb; and (3) from the Russian point of view, Bulgarian acceptance of the Serbs' proposal was highly desirable considering the importance of Serbia as the "advanced post" of the tsarist empire in the Near East.[36]

On January 1, 1912, seeking a rapid conclusion of the alliance, Sazonov wired Nekliudov that Russia hoped that the treaty would be signed in the near future on the basis of Serbia's last proposal.[37] Nekliudov had already informed the Russian Foreign Minister on December 29 that he found the latest Serbian proposal not only reasonable but also satisfactory for Bulgaria.[38] But he was mistaken in assuming that the new line of demarcation proposed by the Serbs would be acceptable.

Previous Serbian references to Struga had been vague, but at the beginning of January 1912 Bulgarian political leaders learned that the Serbs wanted Struga included within their sphere of influence. Geshov told Nekliudov that Bulgaria had assumed in good faith that the Serbian government had long since assigned Struga to Bulgaria.[39] For strategic reasons, military circles at Sofia demanded that any alliance with Serbia should guarantee Bulgaria's possession of half of Struga and the left bank of the Black Drin at its mouth in Lake Okhrida.[40]

At this stage Lieutenant Colonel Romanovskii, Russian military attaché in Bulgaria, traced a line giving Bulgaria several kilometers of the left bank of the Black Drin at its mouth, leaving Serbia the right bank and half of Struga. On January 11, 1912, Nekliudov asked Sazonov to lend his support in Belgrade to Romanovskii's suggested line,[41] but five days later wired that the Serbs had rejected the Romanovskii project and categorically demanded acceptance of their proposal of December 28. Serbia's stand, wrote Nekliudov, meant the end of all Serbo-Bulgarian negotiations.[42]

Extremely disturbed by Nekliudov's telegram, Emperor Nicholas II wrote on its face: "Impossible!—Tsarskoe Selo, January 18." [43] On January 19 Sazonov notified Hartwig that he considered it expedient to advise Serbia to accept the Romanovskii line; it would be a pity if the Balkan alliance could not be realized because of a consideration of secondary importance.[44] In a return telegram the following day, Hartwig gave a number of examples of Serbian concessions during the negotiations. The latest Bulgarian demand for half of Struga, he argued, was merely a caprice, while this town was of vital importance for Serbia. Support of Bulgaria could only make an extremely unfavorable impression on the Serbs, "who always had felt the inequality of the favors accorded by Russia to the Slavic monarchies." [45] But the Belgrade government, Hartwig assured Sazonov, was willing to accept Russian arbitration.[46] He doubtless hoped to suggest that Serbia, in contrast to Bulgaria, trusted Russia. Three weeks later Hartwig bluntly stated that Bulgaria feared arbitration because she knew that Russia, in the final analysis, would realize that Serbia's point of view was not only justified but also in conformance with Russian vital interests in the Balkans.[47]

Sazonov wavered and on January 25 informed both Hartwig and Nekliudov that the Romanovskii line was not to be interpreted as an official Russian proposal.[48] Apparently he feared support of Bulgaria would cause difficulties for Pašić who was then weathering a serious cabinet crisis.[49] On February 16, however, Nekliudov transmitted the request of the Bulgarian Government that St. Petersburg intervene at Belgrade in favor of the Romanovskii line.[50] Russian suspicions had been aroused when King Ferdinand visited Vienna in mid-February,[51] and Sazonov, wanting to keep Bulgaria on the side of the Slavic states, sent Hartwig the appropriate instructions on February 17.[52]

Although Bulgaria had stated that she was ready to sign the treaty provided Russia *secretly* promised Struga to Bulgaria,[53] Sazonov, noting the indignant reaction of the Serbs,[54] decided to alter the line by assigning the town to Serbia. On February 24 he informed Hartwig that Bulgaria would agree if the Serbs admitted the possibility of altering the frontier through Russian arbitration at a later date. Sazonov confided to Hartwig that he was not too concerned about such details, the important thing being that the two powers should make haste.[55] At the same time, he told Nekliudov that both sides should be reassured concerning Russian arbitration. He made no reference in the telegram to Sofia to a Russian commitment concerning Struga, though he crossed out the comment that Russia could make no promises to Bulgaria.[56]

Hartwig apparently sensed, or knew, that mention of altering the frontier at a later date meant that Bulgaria sought some sort of secret understanding with Russia. Lengthy arguments had not influenced St. Petersburg, but perhaps he could prevail upon Nekliudov to use his influence in Sofia. On February 24, 1912, Hartwig sent a strange letter to Nekliudov. It had been written on January 6, but, as Hartwig noted on the margin of his rough copy, was "not sent until February 24 on account of the prolonged absence of a suitable occasion." [57] In early January both Sazonov and Nekliudov supported Serbia's position.

In this letter Hartwig took exception to what Nekliudov had written him on December 31, 1911. The minister at Sofia had maintained that the Serbo-Bulgarian rapprochement in September was not (as Hartwig claimed) the direct result of uninterrupted Russian diplomatic efforts at Belgrade, but that only the advent of the Danev-Geshov cabinet in Sofia had made rapprochement possible. Moreover, he doubted Hartwig's claim that St. Petersburg supported his policy re the partition of Macedonia and the *casus foederis,* pointing out that Neratov had undoubtedly sent the same instructions to the legations in Belgrade and Sofia.[58] Nekliudov "sinned" against the memory of his predecessor at Sofia (Sementovskii-Kurilo) if he pretended that the negotiations of September had been initiated by Geshov and Danev. To the contrary, Hartwig wrote, these negotiations were the result of three years' work on the part of Russian diplomacy, as illustrated by the visit of King Ferdinand at Belgrade in 1909, the stay of King Peter of Serbia at St. Petersburg in 1910, and the two trips of Milovanović to Sofia in the course of the same year. Concerning the text of the proposed treaty of alliance, Hartwig ignored the crux of Nekliudov's arguments by simply stating that Neratov had of course sent the same instructions to Belgrade and Sofia. He somewhat condescendingly reminded Nekliudov that their instructions were always couched in general terms and that Russian diplomatic representatives abroad were entitled to a certain liberty in the interpretation of their orders. In conclusion, he enjoined his colleague at Sofia to adhere more closely to archival facts in the future.[59]

Nekliudov replied in a polite but firm manner. He again declared that the cabinet of Danev and Geshov had reanimated the Serbo-Bulgarian conversations in September. As to the instructions of the foreign ministry, Nekliudov emphasized that the disputed point was Hartwig's allegation that Neratov had accepted *his* view on the disputed articles in the draft treaty of alliance. At the same time, Nekliudov asked his colleague to cooperate in terminating their "regrettable quarrel," the continuation of which would make them both appear ridiculous.[60] Since it was plain that the moment was not well chosen to win over Nekliudov and Sazonov, Hartwig temporarily abandoned his efforts to gain acceptance for his pro-Serb policy. It was only later that the conjuncture of events from the fall of 1912 to 1914 permitted Hartwig to play a more prominent role in influencing the conduct of Russian Balkan policy.

On February 27 Nekliudov wired Sazonov that the Bulgarians would sign an agreement only if Russia guaranteed them possession of the eastern half of Struga.[61] Fearing the collapse of the Serbo-Bulgarian negotiations, Sazonov instructed Hartwig on March 1, 1912, to explain to the Serbs that Russia considered herself morally committed by promises made at the time of the Treaty of San Stefano to give Struga to Bulgaria. That same day Nekliudov received orders to declare orally to Geshov that Russia would take into consideration Bulgaria's desires concerning Struga and the future demarcation between Serbia and Bulgaria in Macedonia.[62]

These instructions show that Sazonov had accepted the pro-Bulgarian policy advocated by Nekliudov. A too active support of Belgrade and the resultant confidence in Russian backing against Austria-Hungary would have encouraged Serbian extremist activities in Bosnia-Herzegovina. Under these circumstances, the Russian Foreign Minister considered ties with Serbia already close enough. Thus, in April, he rejected two Serbian requests, one for permission to send a Serbian military mission to the spring maneuvers of the Russian army, the other that a special Serbian delegation[63] present a copy of the Serbo-Bulgarian treaty to Tsar Nicholas. The emphasis of Sazonov's policy during the late winter and spring of 1912 was on closer relations with Sofia. This policy was indeed timely in view of the conclusion of the Austro-Bulgarian commercial treaty of March 1912. Russia's intervention at Paris in favor of a French loan to Bulgaria,[64] support of Bulgaria's claims in Macedonia, a three million-franc personal loan to King Ferdinand, and a conference in Livadia (scheduled for May) between Sazonov and Danev to discuss Bulgaria's vital interests in the peninsula[65]—all contributed to Bulgarian adherence to the Slavic bloc in the Balkans.

Once Russia had promised Struga to Bulgaria, all that remained to be done was the preparation of the final draft of the treaty of alliance. Spalajković, the Serbian Minister, and Geshov put the finishing touches on such a draft in Sofia at the beginning of the second week of March.[66] Spalajković then brought it to Belgrade, where it was signed by Milovanović and King Peter on March 11.[67] And on March 13 Geshov and King Ferdinand added their signatures in Sofia.[68]

The agreement consisted of a treaty of friendship and alliance and a secret annex. The seven articles of the treaty defined the general character of the alliance. The two countries exchanged mutual guarantees of "their sovereign independence and the integrity of their territory" and promises of military aid if one of them were attacked by a third power. Article II, which provided for military assistance if either Bulgaria or Serbia felt threatened by an attempt of a great power to occupy or annex any part of European Turkey, effectively assured Serbia of Bulgarian support in the event that Austria-Hungary should occupy the Sanjak of Novibazar. Both contracting parties agreed that neither would conclude a separate peace without the knowledge of its ally in time of war. The treaty was to remain in effect until January 13, 1921. A military convention was to supplement the treaty. Finally, no other state, besides Russia, was to learn of its existence without the preliminary approval of both contracting parties.[69]

The secret annex spelled out the details concerning Russia's participation in the alliance and the division of Macedonia. Article I, which defined the *casus belli* and described Russia's role, was in some ways influenced by the counsel Neratov and Nekliudov had given Bulgaria and Serbia during the fall of 1911. For example, the words "maintenance of the status quo" were included in the text of the annex. The Balkan leaders, however,

93

gave the phrase a new meaning by stating that internal troubles in Turkey which threatened the status quo could be considered by either Serbia or Bulgaria as a *casus belli*. They agreed, however, to consult Russia before embarking on such a war. Should both powers favor war, they would commence hostilities *if Russia did not oppose* such action. If only one of the two powers favored war, St. Petersburg's decision would be obligatory for both Serbia and Bulgaria. If Russia preferred to make no decision, one Balkan nation could remain neutral but must mobilize and render assistance to its ally in case a third power should enter the war on the side of Turkey.[70]

Though the definition of the *casus belli* had been modified in accordance with the criticisms of Neratov and Nekliudov, the alliance remained an aggressive one directed primarily against Turkey. Precisely for this reason, Serbia and Bulgaria periodically reassured Russia that they would make every effort to preserve peace in the Balkans. When King Peter signed the treaty on March 11, he gave Hartwig "the most positive assurances that he would under no circumstances decide on an active policy without the preliminary agreement of Russia."[71] Geshov made almost exactly the same statement to Nekliudov a little later.[72] Hartwig, no doubt for his own reasons, accepted such declarations pretty much at face value; Nekliudov and Sazonov did not. In the reports he sent to St. Petersburg during the spring and summer of 1912, Nekliudov repeated his earlier warnings: that Bulgaria would soon find a convenient pretext to attack Turkey.[73] Sazonov confided to Nekliudov similar concern about the warlike attitude of the Balkan powers.[74] The foreign minister also cautioned Danev, when the latter visited the tsar in Yalta at the beginning of May, that Russia would disapprove of any irresponsible acts or provocations; too, it was doubtful that Bulgaria had anything to gain from a Balkan war.[75] Sazonov assured France at the end of April that the secret promise of the Balkan states not to make any offensive moves without first consulting Russia enabled the tsar to exert influence over the actions of both Serbia and Bulgaria.[76] But did Sazonov believe this himself?

Article II of the annex concerned the division of the spoils in the event of a successful Balkan war. Although no mention was made of Adrianople, which Nekliudov had persuaded the Bulgarians to eliminate from the treaty a number of months earlier, King Ferdinand reminded Nekliudov of Bulgaria's interest in this town during the conversation on the day the treaty was signed. Nekliudov indicated that Russia could hardly approve of such a claim since she had no interest "in seeing Turkey disappear as the guardian of the Straits." [77] Danev also raised the question of Adrianople when he talked with Sazonov in early May 1912. Sazonov replied that Adrianople had not been awarded Bulgaria by the Treaty of San Stefano. The realization of Bulgaria's other national aspirations would transform Turkey into a second-rate power; under such circumstances, Adrianople would, of course, lose its former importance.[78]

The one reference to autonomy for Macedonia was in a negative sense: i.e. if the two powers found it impractical to establish an autonomous Macedonia, they would partition the province. Certainly Bulgarian faith in the possibility of autonomy had almost disappeared by the spring of 1912. Hence the persistent bargaining to limit the extent of Serbia's maximum claims in the area south of the Šar-Planina, for such claims only applied in the event that an autonomous Macedonia was not established. The line marking the maximum claims of Serbia was basically the same one the Serbs had proposed on December 28, 1911. Kratovo and Kriva Palanka went to Bulgaria, whereas part of the Ovče Polje was included within the Serbian sphere of influence. Bulgaria agreed to accept this frontier if the Russian tsar would decide a later alteration in her favor.[79] Struga was not specifically mentioned in Article II, though the termination of the western end of the line of maximum Serbian claims near the Gabovici Monastery on Lake Okhrida seemed to assign this town to Serbia. Romanovskii reported to the quartermaster division of the general staff on March 13, 1912, however, that Bulgaria had only signed the Serbo-Bulgarian treaty that same day on the condition that Russia recognized Bulgaria's right to Struga.[80]

Nor was there any specific mention of a contested zone. The secret annex merely referred to the indisputable right of Serbia to the area north and west of the Šar-Planina and of Bulgaria to the region east of the Rhodope Mountains and the Struma River. True, there was a zone between the limits of Serbia's indisputable and maximum claims, but Bulgaria agreed, if recommended by the Russian tsar, to accept Serbia's maximum claims. Insistence that Struga should be secretly promised to her indicates that Bulgaria expected no modification of this line other than a slight one in Bulgaria's favor at its western extremity. In effect, this meant that no contested zone remained for Russia to arbitrate inasmuch as the only disputed part of the line of maximum Serbian claims had already been assigned to Bulgaria.[81]

Article III of the secret annex specified that a copy of the treaty and the secret annex should be jointly presented to the Russian Government; Article IV that St. Petersburg should be the final arbiter of any differences that might arise in regard to the interpretation and execution of the treaty, the annex, and the projected Serbo-Bulgarian military convention; and Article V that the contents of the annex should be kept secret and not communicated to any other state without the preliminary understanding of the two contracting parties and the approval of Russia.[82]

Though kept informed of the progress of the negotiations for a Serbo-Bulgarian military convention,[83] Russia had little direct influence on the actual drafting of its fourteen articles. It was signed two months after the alliance, on May 12, 1912, by Geshov, Milovanović, and generals A. Nikiforov and R. Putnik. The convention obliged Bulgaria to furnish 200,000 soldiers and Serbia 150,000. At least 100,000 men from each army were to be sent to the Vardar front. If Austria-Hungary should attack Serbia, Bulgaria promised to send 200,000 soldiers to the aid of her ally. Similarly, Bulgaria was assured the support of 100,000 Serbian troops in the event of a Rumanian attack on Bulgaria.[84]

Article xiii of the convention specified that the Bulgarian and Serbian chiefs of staff should immediately begin discussions concerning the disposition and movements of their respective armies in Macedonia during a Balkan war. Such discussions continued until July 2, 1912, when generals R. Putnik and I. Fichev signed an agreement at Varna that outlined a joint plan of operations.[85]

The Serbs were sufficiently well informed to convince themselves during September that Austro-Hungarian intervention in a Balkan war was highly unlikely.[86] They could not, however, be completely sure and always had to allow for the possibility of a war on two fronts. Serbia's caution very much irritated General I. Fichev, the Bulgarian chief of staff, when he was in Belgrade at the end of August 1912 to arrange the final details of military cooperation. To Fichev's chagrin, the Serbs showed little desire to discuss final arrangements, but instead wanted to revise the military agreement of July 2, 1912. They no longer agreed that the Maritsa Valley would be the principal theater of operations, but now insisted that the entire Serbian army, supported by one Bulgarian division, be concentrated for an attack through the Vardar Valley. Fichev interpreted this demand to mean that the Serbs did not want to wage war seriously against Turkey and would concentrate on obtaining territory in Old Serbia and Macedonia.[87]

After the death of Foreign Minister Milovanović in July, Pašić had temporarily stepped aside as premier. In the interim Marko Trifković headed the government. It was generally assumed in Belgrade that the Trifković cabinet would be replaced by a new one headed by Pašić as soon as a final decision had been made for opening hostilities against Turkey.[88] On September 12 Pašić formed a new cabinet in which he also served as foreign minister,[89] but he was too astute a politician to hasten events without first obtaining a few additional concessions. On September 21 the Bulgarians arranged a meeting between Danev and Pašić in a railroad car traveling between Lapovo and Niš. At this time Pašić demanded that Serbia should not be required to fight against Turkey if Austria-Hungary mobilized. Danev of course took violent exception to this demand, but did succeed in getting Pašić to agree to mobilize, though the Serbian Premier made no definite commitment to declare war on Turkey.[90]

A few days later, however, the Turks detained twenty carloads of war materials en route from France to Serbia. And all the Balkan states were disturbed by Turkey's decision of September 22 to call up 100,000 Redifs (Turkish reservists) for maneuvers in Thrace.[91] Although the Turks had enough trouble without aggressive action against the Balkan states, Bulgarian leaders treated the planned maneuvers in Thrace as a deliberate provocation and insisted on a general mobilization of the Balkan states in accordance with their treaties of alliance. Pašić still hesitated and haggled over details, but on September 26 finally agreed to mobilize by the end of the month.[92]

On September 28 the Bulgarian and Serbian chiefs of staff signed the final agreement at Sofia. The Vardar Valley was not referred to as such, but the designation of Macedonia up to the line of Üsküb-Veles-Štip as the theater of operations for practically the entire Serbian army[93] meant that Bulgaria had accepted the plan proposed by the Serbian general staff several weeks earlier. Sofia was too eager to take advantage of Turkey's current difficulties to bicker and in the final analysis put its trust in Bulgarian military strength. The Serbs felt much the same way but prudently took the precaution of arranging the physical presence of the Serbian army in disputed areas.[94] In 1913, with their army in the Vardar Valley, the Serbs first demanded alterations in the Serbo-Bulgarian treaty and then forced the Bulgarians out of Macedonia except for a strip on the eastern fringe.

Chapter 5

GREECE, MONTENEGRO, AND THE OUTBREAK OF WAR

Informal discussion of a Greco-Bulgarian alliance had taken place as early as the fall and winter of 1910. In April 1911, through J. D. Bourchier, the London *Times* correspondent and a *persona grata* in both Sofia and Athens, the Greeks proposed a defensive alliance. The Geshov government was following a conciliatory policy toward Turkey, however, and did not want to get involved in the Greco-Turkish dispute over Crete.[1] Russia does not seem to have been informed about these discussions between Athens and Sofia.

The Bulgarian Government nevertheless let the Greeks know through Bourchier that it was not adverse to future discussion of an entente.[2] During the remainder of 1911 remarkably friendly relations, considering previous enmity, were maintained between the two countries. In the spring of that year a group of Bulgarian students visited Athens, where they were received with great enthusiasm.[3] In May the Greek patriarch joined the Bulgarian exarch and other leaders of Eastern Christendom in making a joint representation to the Porte in defense of the rights of the

Christians living in the Ottoman Empire.[4] And the bitter rivalry and terrorism between Bulgarians and Greeks in Macedonia abated during these months.[5]

The Tripolitan War made a Bulgarian entente seem all the more urgent to Greek Premier Eleutherios Venizelos. On October 16, 1911, he had the Greek Minister at Sofia, D. Panas, renew the proposal for an alliance. The Bulgarian cabinet and King Ferdinand now accepted the idea in principle,[6] but negotiations for a treaty dragged out over a period of six months, apparently because Bulgaria wanted to be sure of the Serbian alliance before entering into a formal agreement with Greece. It was also difficult to reach agreement on such matters as autonomy for Macedonia and the extent of Greece's sphere of influence in European Turkey.[7]

On October 19, only three days after Panas had reopened the matter, Geshov told Russian chargé Urusov about the Greco-Bulgarian negotiations. Urusov's immediate reaction was general approval; he quickly added, however, that Bulgaria should be particularly circumspect because of the dangerous implications of the Cretan question.[8] After the outbreak of the Tripolitan War, twenty-seven deputies to the Cretan Parliament proclaimed an election for a special revolutionary assembly from which deputies to the Greek National Assembly in Athens were to be selected. Such an election actually took place on November 13 despite the opposition of the great powers. For a number of months thereafter the powers busily intercepted would-be Cretan delegates on their way to Athens.[9] Nekliudov repeated Urusov's advice several days later and recommended rejection of the Greek proposal. But Geshov insisted that an agreement with Greece, in one form or another, was highly desirable. There was good reason to believe that Vienna was seeking to entice Greece into an anti-Slavic bloc of Albania, Rumania, and Austria-Hungary. Greece, he concluded, would certainly be tempted to join such a bloc if isolated diplomatically.[10]

At the end of October Geshov asked for an official statement from the Russian Government. Nekliudov, believing that a Greco-

Bulgarian alliance would add unnecessary complications to Russian Balkan policy, commented in English to Neratov: "It is not handy."[11] Accordingly, he requested a statement that St. Petersburg could only approve of a Greco-Bulgarian treaty based on maintenance of the status quo.[12] This request conformed to the Balkan policy then pursued by the Russian Foreign Ministry, and several days later Nekliudov received permission to make an official communication to Geshov.[13]

Although Nekliudov's words may have temporarily discouraged Bulgaria, friendly relations with Greece continued into 1912. In February the participation of Greek Crown Prince Constantine in the festivities marking the majority of Bulgarian Crown Prince Boris made a most favorable impression in Sofia. At the same time, the Bulgarian Government made significant concessions to its Greek minority, approving Greek parish schools and seriously considering restoration of a number of Greek churches previously appropriated.[14]

When the negotiations were resumed in February 1912, the Bulgarians did not inform the Russians. Before the British journalist, Bourchier, left Sofia early in February, immediately after the celebration of the majority of Crown Prince Boris, Geshov told him "Our relations with Greece are excellent, but we wish to strengthen them and to render them still more intimate. We consider that the proposals which have been made to us through your agency furnish a suitable basis for an arrangement, and we should be glad if the Greek Government would now transmit them to us through its Minister, M. Panas."[15] Panas commenced official negotiations with the Bulgarian Government in the last week of February.

For almost two months Russia's representatives in the Balkans could only speculate as to what was going on in Sofia. On February 24 Nekliudov erroneously believed that formal proposals still had not been made and that no official discussions had taken place.[16] A little more than a week later the Russian chargé d'affaires in Athens made the same incorrect assumption.[17] At the end of March Geshov finally informed Urusov of a few

101

specific details.[18] On April 30 Nekliudov received somewhat more detailed information,[19] but only on May 14 was he given a reasonably complete and accurate version of the full French text proposed by Greece. Nekliudov gave a résumé in the following words:

> Article 1: The two contracting parties commit themselves to bring assistance with all their strength in case of a direct Turkish attack or . . . flagrant and systematic violation by Turkey of rights resulting from treaties or of fundamental principles of the law of nations. Article 2: reciprocal collaboration of the two contracting parties to safeguard the recognized and acquired rights of the congeneric populations in Turkey, and this as the best means of conservation of the status quo. Articles 3 and 4: secret character of the treaty from 3 to 5 years at the option of Bulgaria. A special annex stipulates that the affairs of Crete would not constitute . . . a *casus foederis*.[20]

The final protocol, signed two weeks later, conformed to Nekliudov's résumé in all important respects, though the Bulgarians chose to have the treaty remain in effect for three years.[21]

Both Nekliudov and Sazonov felt that Article 1 had dangerous implications.[22] Sazonov in particular questioned whether the limited military aid Greece could furnish (about 120,000 troops) justified the Bulgarian commitment to defend something so vague as Greek treaty and human rights.[23] Geshov admitted the dangers, but assured Nekliudov that Bulgaria would not permit Greece to give a "dangerous interpretation" to the alliance.[24] The treaty was signed on May 29, 1912, and its final text was basically the same one to which St. Petersburg had objected earlier. Geshov later explained that he could not have changed the text because this would have delayed the conclusion of the alliance. And, King Ferdinand had insisted on the conclusion of the alliance as soon as possible.[25] Although the Bulgarians seem to have been much more concerned about having autonomy for Macedonia mentioned in the treaty than in avoiding "dangerous interpretations,"[26] they did not want to postpone signing by protracted wrangling with the Greeks over Macedonia which was not mentioned in the final text.

About the same time (May 1912) that Sazonov warned Danev against enlisting Montenegro in a Balkan alliance, Bulgarian representatives broached the subject with King Nicholas. Discussions took place in the Vienna Hofburg between June 8 and 19, 1912, right under the noses, so to speak, of Austrian Foreign Minister Count Leopold von Berchtold and Franz Josef, who had invited King Nicholas to pay his respects at the Austrian court. Montenegrin General Mitar Martinović told Danev (on his way home from Russia) and Rizov (who was on intimate terms with many Montenegrin leaders and had come from Rome expressly for this meeting) that Montenegro would attack the Turks at any time if Bulgaria subsidized her army. The Bulgarians agreed in principle but could not commit themselves definitely until the alliance arrangements with Greece and Serbia were completed.[27]

Since the military convention between Greece and Bulgaria was not signed until October 5, 1912,[28] King Nicholas found it expedient to avoid border incidents along the Turkish frontier. In May the Turks had decided to renew annual subsidy payments that had been made to Montenegro prior to 1908; in the early part of June, Nicholas actually received 10,000 liras.[29] On June 11 a joint commission signed a Turko-Montenegrin protocol that provided for rectification of certain frontier irregularities which had embittered relations since 1878.[30] The Turkish government, however, delayed ratification, allegedly in order not to antagonize the tribes of northern Albania with the prospect of incorporation into Montenegro at a time of general unrest in this area.

King Nicholas told the Russian representative in Cetinje that he would have to resort to drastic measures,[31] and around mid-July and early August 1912, a series of border incidents occurred on the frontier.[32] On August 10, after having attacked Turkish positions on several occasions, the Montenegrin Government officially requested the powers to draw a new boundary.[33] According to the Russian military attaché in Cetinje, Nicholas planned to raze the whole line of Turkish blockhouses on his eastern frontier. Armed support to Slavic insurrectionists in the Sanjak of Novibazar was apparently intended as a prelude to such action.[34]

Alarmed by these incidents, the Russian Foreign Ministry made diplomatic representations at Cetinje, Constantinople and the major European capitals.[35] Efforts to keep the peace were frustrated, however, because the Montenegrin situation developed in close connection with events elsewhere in the Balkans.

General Balkan tension had increased with the Kočane massacre and the success of a new series of Albanian uprisings that had begun in the spring of 1912. In reprisals after revolutionists exploded a bomb in the Kočane market place, the Turks killed or wounded several hundred Macedonians on August 1.[36] All the Balkan states feared that the Albanians might eventually gain control over large parts of Macedonia and Old Serbia, and the Kočane affair was of course fully exploited by Bulgarian extremists pushing for war with Turkey.

Early in July representatives of IMRO had asked the Bulgarian Minister of War, A. Nikiforov, for arms for a general uprising.[37] Geshov's government could only fear the close connections between the Macedonian revolutionists and opposition political leaders in Bulgaria. The latter hoped to force Geshov and Danev out of office by insisting on the liberation of Macedonia and a more vigorous conduct of Bulgarian foreign policy. The one way for Danev and Geshov to counter this tactic was to persuade Bulgarians that only the government in power could provide the leadership and statesmanship required for the liberation of Macedonia. As Geshov later wrote it was necessary to take the Macedonian question "out of the hands of the Macedonian Revolutionary Committee, as Cavour took the question of Italian unity out of the hands of the Italian revolutionists." [38] Nikiforov therefore told the IMRO representatives that they should postpone their uprising until September. Premature action would cause difficulties in the negotiations Bulgaria was then conducting with the other Balkan states. When these negotiations were completed, however, he promised that Bulgaria would provide the arms and declare war against Turkey.[39]

The opposition in Bulgaria seized upon the Kočane massacre, accusing the Geshov-Danev government of cowardice and inability to defend the interests and rights of Bulgarians in Macedonia.[40] Throughout August numerous protest meetings were organized by the opposition and IMRO, and it seemed that public opinion might push Bulgaria into war at any moment.[41] Of one of these meetings and a congress of Macedonian revolutionists held on August 24, 1912, Geshov later wrote that both "voted resolutions to the same effect: Bulgaria must immediately mobilize her army and demand autonomy in favour of Macedonia and Thrace, failing which, she must declare war on Turkey. Otherwise the country was threatened with troubles, bringing in their wake incalculable consequences." [42]

Additional pressure was put on Geshov to act when Berchtold addressed a note to the powers on August 13, proposing that they encourage the Porte to decentralize administration and introduce other reforms in European Turkey.[43] Bulgarians viewed the proposal as part of an Austrian plan to support Albanian aspirations to territory as far as the Vardar River. An autonomous or independent Albania extending to the Vardar, Bulgarians reasoned, would serve as a means for Austria-Hungary to control the route to Saloniki.[44]

The presence of armed bands of Albanians in the Vardar Valley in mid-August 1912 particularly worried Balkan publicists and politicians. The Turks seemed on the verge of granting the Albanians important concessions and a privileged position in the vilayets of Scutari, Kosovo, Janina, and Monastir. On August 12 a force of 15,000 Albanians entered Üsküb, the principal city of northern Macedonia.[45] These Albanian advances disturbed all the Balkan states. The Montenegrins approached Serbia about the danger of Albanian autonomy and Austrian intrigues, suggesting as early as the second part of July and again in early August common action against Turkey.[46] Though they also found the prospect of Albanian autonomy distasteful, the Serbs distrusted King Nicholas and hesitated to risk war, so they replied evasively to the Montenegrin inquiries.[47] The Greek Government, too, fearing that the Berchtold note would encourage the Albanians to make further demands detrimental to its interests, asked Belgrade, Sofia, and Cetinje to exchange views on the problem.[48]

Montenegro, especially eager for war with Turkey, pressed Bulgaria to conclude the agreement discussed several months earlier at Vienna. Geshov felt that he had to give King Nicholas a definite answer, and the Bulgarian Minister at Cetinje, A. Kolushev, was therefore summoned to Sofia in the latter part of August to make a detailed report and receive instructions.[49] While Kolushev was in Sofia the Bulgarian cabinet met daily.[50] At his hunting lodge near Cham Koriia, on August 26, Ferdinand presided over a crown council consisting of Geshov, Teodorov, and General Nikiforov. Here it was decided that the allies should immediately demand that Turkey carry out reforms in Macedonia in accordance with Article xxiii of the Treaty of Berlin. Apparently none of the Bulgarian leaders believed that the Turks would comply with this demand, and refusal would be used as a pretext for war. At the same time definite proposals for Montenegro were drawn up.[51] The die was cast; the cabinet of Geshov and Danev had irrevocably decided on war.

By mid-September Bulgaria and Montenegro had agreed on the final draft for a military convention. Both powers were committed to engage all their military forces in a war against Turkey. Montenegro would begin hostilities not later than September 28, and Bulgaria within a month thereafter. Bulgaria agreed to pay Montenegro 700,000 francs during the war. And, finally, Serbia was to be informed of the agreement and decision to begin war.[52]

Although the military convention was never formally ratified by the Sobranie,[53] the Bulgarian Government seems to have considered itself bound. On September 28 the Bulgarian Minister at Cetinje was instructed to inform King Nicholas that Bulgaria approved of Montenegro's beginning military hostilities and would fulfill her promises as soon as Greece and Serbia entered the war.[54]

Montenegro, however, had little prospect of military success in the Sanjak and Old Serbia without Serbian support. Early in September King Nicholas wrote King Peter of Serbia, urging a military convention with Montenegro. A reply to Nicholas' letter was delayed by the ministerial crisis at Belgrade.[55] Pašić formed a new government on September 12, however, and by September 25 the Serbian Government had notified Cetinje that it would send a general staff officer to Switzerland to meet with Montenegrin representatives.[56] It was assumed that Austro-Hungarian agents would be less likely to discover negotiations in Switzerland.[57] On September 25 two Montenegrin delegates left for Italy on their way to Switzerland,[58] and by October 2 had agreed on texts for a political and a military convention.[59] The military convention specified the operational areas for the two armies and provided that both powers should declare war on Turkey no later than October 14, 1912. In the political convention, they also agreed to use all of their forces against Austria-Hungary if that power invaded any part of European Turkey. The agreements became effective October 6, 1912 upon signature by the two governments.[60]

On September 13 King Nicholas told Kolushev, the Bulgarian Minister, that Montenegro was prepared to commence hostilities on September 27. Geshov quickly had Nicholas informed that the negotiations between Bulgaria, Greece, and Serbia still had not been completed and that Montenegro should therefore wait a little longer.[61] But war was in the air and its imminence made King Nicholas increasingly intransigent in his dealings with the Porte. When the Turkish chargé d'affaires in

Cetinje requested on September 21 that Montenegro discontinue material and moral aid to insurgents in northern Albania, King Nicholas peremptorily refused to negotiate on the subject.[62] Shortly thereafter, he announced to the Russian Minister in Cetinje that it had become necessary for Montenegro to engage in a duel with Turkey, even though she was perfectly aware that Russia would not come to her aid in the impending struggle.[63]

Toward the end of September the governments in Belgrade, Athens, and Sofia began to prepare their collective note demanding reforms for the Christians in European Turkey.[64] The three Balkan allies and Montenegro mobilized on September 30 and October 1, 1912. King Nicholas not only mobilized the Montenegrin army but also heaped reproaches on the representatives of the powers at Cetinje for their lack of action on the Turko-Montenegrin border question. Because of this inaction, he declared, Montenegro would have to occupy several Turkish border points as a sort of collateral for the final settlement of this question.[65] Although the Balkan allies kept in close contact with King Nicholas and consulted him concerning the note, his impatience soon led him to break with the other Balkan states as to the timing of the attack. Both Greece and Serbia advised that Nicholas wait at least a week before beginning hostilities, but on October 6 Montenegro broke off diplomatic relations with the Porte and declared war two days later.[66]

Bulgaria approved of Montenegro's premature action.[67] Serbia and Greece, however, apparently felt that the allies should first draw up their collective note, present it to the powers and Turkey, and then commence hostilities. On October 13 representatives of the three countries presented identical notes to the powers and the Porte, demanding that Turkey accept and implement a comprehensive program of reforms. The Porte failed to answer these notes and, on October 15, recalled its representatives in the Balkan capitals. On October 17 Bulgaria, Greece, and Serbia declared war against Turkey.[68]

Chapter 6

THE BALKAN ALLIES
AND EUROPE

"This is the first time in the history of the Eastern question," wrote the French chargé d'affaires at St. Petersburg in October 1912, "that the small states have taken a stand so independent of the great powers and have felt so capable of getting along without them and even taking them in tow." [1] The Triple Entente and the Triple Alliance had temporarily minimized their differences to maintain peace in the Balkans. The Balkan allies, however, successfully diverted the attention of the powers, skillfully exploited the rivalry between them, and thus frustrated common action.

Ironically, on the same day the Greco-Bulgarian treaty was signed Nekliudov expressed to Sazonov the hope that Russia would not only postpone a Balkan crisis but would even manage to direct the course of events in the peninsula.[2] But the Serbo-Bulgarian military convention was drawn up pretty much without Russian participation. And Sofia kept Russia in the dark about the details of the negotiations for a Greco-Bulgarian alliance; Russian advice was ignored, and Russia had to wait three weeks after May 29 before she learned that the treaty had been signed. Later in 1912 Montenegro was included in the alliance despite expressed Russian opposition, and the final military agreements and conventions in the fall of 1912 were worked out without consulting St. Petersburg.

During the summer of 1912, Nekliudov and Romanovskii repeatedly warned that Bulgarian leaders would seize upon the first appropriate pretext to begin a war against Turkey.[3] A telegram Nekliudov sent on July 4 so disturbed Sazonov that he took up the subject with the British and French Embassies.[4] Nothing resulted from these discussions because Nekliudov's British and French colleagues in Sofia argued that Bulgaria had undertaken no concrete measures for war and therefore no reason existed for formal diplomatic action of the powers at Sofia. The French Minister to Bulgaria, H. A. de Panafieu, feared that such action would undermine Geshov's government, which would be unfortunate in view of Geshov's moderation and common sense.[5] And many people in St. Petersburg took Nekliudov's warnings lightly. Nekliudov has commented in his memoirs in this connection: " 'Have you read Nekludoff's hysterical telegram?' the heads of departments and the young secretaries of Sazonoff's set were constantly asking each other. Alas! This telegram proved to be *historical,* not hysterical!" [6]

Izvol'skii and V. Krupenskii, Russian chargé d'affaires at Rome, also sent warnings. On June 6 Izvol'skii wrote to Sazonov about a conversation with the Bulgarian Minister of Finance, T. Teodorov, who had been in Paris briefly for discussions about a loan. Teodorov told Izvol'skii that Bulgaria would be making a serious mistake if she did not take advantage of the Tripolitan War to realize her "historical goals" in the Balkans.[7] Krupenskii reported in a similar vein about a month later concerning a conversation with Dimitŭr Rizov, the Bulgarian Minister at Rome. Rizov had told Krupenskii that the time was almost ripe for Bulgarian action against Turkey: Macedonia eagerly awaited liberation; Bulgaria was militarily prepared, while Turkey had been weakened by her conflict with Italy. But this favorable situation could soon change to the detriment of Bulgaria unless

she struck while the iron was hot. "If we do not attack the Ottoman Empire now and wrest Macedonia from her," Rizov concluded, "then the realization of our sacred dreams will be postponed for a long time." [8]

Sazonov did not dismiss Nekliudov's warning as frivolously
as some of his subordinates did. He refrained, however, from
immediate and direct pressure on Bulgaria for fear of provoking
resentment toward Russia. Nekliudov was therefore simply instructed on July 8 to keep St. Petersburg informed concerning
the development of war sentiment in political circles. Gentle persuasion rather than intimidation was to be used; Nekliudov should
let the Bulgarians know that, according to a reliable source, direct
peace negotiations between Turkey and Italy were imminent.
As Sazonov pointed out, Bulgaria was likely to stand alone
against Turkey.[9]

By August the Russian Foreign Ministry began to use firmer
and more unequivocal language. As early as July Krupenskii had
told Rizov in Rome that Bulgaria could not count on Russian
support if she attacked Turkey.[10] But Krupenskii seems to have
merely expressed his own personal opinion, for Neratov, then in
charge of the foreign ministry while Sazonov was on vacation,
opposed official warnings.[11] On August 5, however, alarmed by a
series of incidents on the Turko-Montenegrin frontier, Neratov
notified Serbia, Bulgaria, and Greece that Russia considered action against Turkey "entirely inopportune" and that they could
not expect support from Russia.[12]

Geshov's skill in posing as "the most fervent partisan of
peace in the Balkans" [13] no doubt had much to do with Russia's
long delay in delivering a strong warning. Geshov's government
constantly assured St. Petersburg of Bulgaria's loyalty and determination to avoid dangerous actions.[14] In early July, Geshov
contrasted his peace policy with the prevalent bellicosity in
Athens and Belgrade and even promised Nekliudov that he would
resign if his colleagues should cease supporting this policy.[15] In
mid-July the Bulgarian Minister at Constantinople, Sarafov, com-

plained to his Russian colleague, M. Giers, about Turkey's failure to complete a railway between Kumanovo and Kiustendil. Bulgaria had already finished her part of the line, but the Porte, despite promises, had done nothing. Geshov had recently been sharply attacked by the opposition for his allegedly pro-Turkish policies, and Turkish fulfillment of promises made two years before was necessary to justify his peace policy.[16] Russia then urged the Porte to proceed with the construction of the line,[17] but Turkey apparently took no action; the main result of Bulgaria's diplomatic maneuvers was to strengthen the image of Geshov as a man of peace in the eyes of some Russian diplomats.

A. I. Guchkov, the former president of the Duma, visited the Balkan capitals during July 1912, ostensibly as the representative of a Russian insurance company. He was a garrulous and gregarious individual who fervently believed in Slavic solidarity, and in his presence the Bulgarians talked freely. Guchkov soon repeated the substance of these conversations to his many acquaintances in the Russian diplomatic corps at Sofia, Belgrade, and Vienna. War was to begin in September. By then Bulgaria would have reached agreement with Greece and Serbia concerning the final details of their military cooperation, and the military preparations of the Bulgarian army would be completed. Reservists would also join the colors more willingly after they had gathered the harvest. Finally it was anticipated that the French would grant the 180 million-franc loan by the beginning of September.[18]

Nekliudov, too, was able to provide a generally accurate appraisal of Bulgarian policy throughout the summer of 1912. He knew about plans to demand Macedonian reforms. The prevailing confusion and lack of authority in the Ottoman Empire during 1912 made it impossible for any Turkish government to carry out such reforms, and, as he correctly concluded, war was almost unavoidable once Bulgaria presented her demand.[19] Nekliudov also noted Kolushev's arrival in Sofia from Cetinje, Spalajković's departure from Sofia for Belgrade, and the increased frequency of cabinet meetings in Sofia toward the end of August. He assumed that Kolushev came to Sofia with a proposal for common Bulgarian and Montenegrin action, and Spalajković's departure on August 26 meant that an important decision was about to be made in Belgrade. Convinced that this decision would have an important bearing on Bulgarian and Serbian war plans, Nekliudov again warned Geshov that any Bulgarian adventure would be at Bulgaria's own risk and that no help could be expected from Russia.[20] He also emphasized Turkish strength and the likelihood of Rumanian and Austro-Hungarian intervention in the event of a Balkan conflict.[21] Sazonov[22] and Nekliudov waited until the second part of September, however, before they told Bulgaria bluntly and officially that Russia had intended the Balkan alliance to be an "act of mutual defense and recognition of common interests" and would, if the Balkan states attacked Turkey, act exclusively in accordance with her own "direct and immediate interests."[23]

At Yalta in May 1912, Sazonov and Emperor Nicholas had made it clear that Russia was not ready for war and did not want the Balkan alliance used for aggression against Turkey.[24] Despite encouragement from unofficial Russian publicists, there seems little reason to doubt Nekliudov's success in persuading Bulgarian leaders that the Balkan states would have to fight alone and without Russian material aid. Danev has stated that Bulgaria expected only sympathy and some diplomatic support from Russia and the Triple Entente. Even a categorical Russian refusal to support the Balkan states diplomatically, he wrote,[25] could not have overridden other considerations in favor of war —the favorable situation created by the Tripolitan War and confidence in the military superiority of the Balkan states over Turkey, also shared by military leaders in Belgrade.[26]

The very success of Russian diplomats in persuading Bulgarian politicians that they could not count on Russian assistance made it all the more unlikely that Russia could exercise effective influence or control over the course of Balkan events. The Bulgarians had become psychologically conditioned to the idea of fighting without Russia. All that could have restrained them at this point would have been the outright refusal of one or more of the other Balkan states to open hostilities against Turkey.

Despite efforts to restrain the Balkan powers, Russia did not welcome the intervention of the concert of Europe. Counsels of prudence from St. Petersburg helped promote intimate relations with the Balkan allies, thus assuring Russia's preponderance in the peninsula. In the event of a crisis that seemed to imperil the peace of both the Balkans and Europe, St. Petersburg was, to be sure, willing to turn to the other powers but, if at all possible, to France and Great Britain, preferably France alone. Only when her principal Balkan protégés, Serbia and Bulgaria, were not directly involved did Russia voluntarily seek the cooperation of the powers of the Triple Alliance. In July 1911, for example, St. Petersburg was ready to act in concert with Austria-Hungary and Italy to curb King Nicholas of Montenegro, considered more of a nuisance than an asset to Russian policy. And in February 1912 Russia turned to Germany rather than to the Entente with a proposal to ask Italy for her peace terms and then to apply pressure on Turkey to accept them.[27] Although concerned about the effect of the Tripolitan War on the Balkans and on Black Sea trade, St. Petersburg apparently hesitated to approach Britain and France because of their reluctance to put diplomatic pressure on the Porte.

Russia first approached France, about maintaining "the closest contact" in regard to possible new complications in the Near East, at the end of January 1912, slightly more than a month before the signing of the Serbo-Bulgarian alliance. The Russian Government deliberately dissociated this projected exchange of views from the discussions then being conducted by the powers concerning the Tripolitan War. France was asked not to reveal the nature of this exchange of views to any other power, though Sazonov suggested that Britain could be consulted once France and Russia had reached an understanding. Raymond Poincaré, who had become French Premier and Minister of Foreign Affairs on January 5, 1912, naturally wanted to know precisely what Russia had in mind and therefore agreed to enter into such conversations, assuring St. Petersburg that nothing would be revealed.[28]

On February 14, Sazonov indicated that Russia wished an exchange of views in regard to three eventualities: (1) an internal political crisis in Turkey, (2) an "active *démarche*" of Austria-Hungary in the Sanjak or Albania, and (3) an armed conflict between Turkey and the Balkan states.[29] Sazonov's questions disturbed Poincaré, but the French Premier preferred to discuss them rather than risk involvement in a rapid succession of events without having had an opportunity to influence Russia's actions or pose France's conditions. He therefore asked for additional information concerning Russia's intentions and views and instructed the French Ambassador at St. Petersburg to inform Sazonov that French public opinion would not permit France to support Russia over an issue not of primary national importance for France. And France's own "powerful interests" obliged her to insist on the principle of the territorial integrity of the Ottoman Empire.[30]

Poincaré seems to have first learned of the existence of the Serbo-Bulgarian treaty on April 1, 1912, when Izvol'skii informed him that a strictly defensive agreement had been arranged.[31] Several days later he received information from Sofia that led him to believe that the agreement was anything but defensive.[32] Although he pressed the Russians for more details, the text of the treaty was only communicated to the French at the time of Poincaré's visit at St. Petersburg in August 1912.[33]

In his *Au service de la France* Poincaré persuasively stated his version of how he worked to restrain Russia and the Balkan states during the spring and summer of 1912.[34] He also carefully avoided emphasizing the obvious connection between his trip to St. Petersburg in August and his persistent efforts during 1912 to reinforce the ties that bound together Great Britain, France, and Russia in the Triple Entente.

Shortly before Poincaré left for St. Petersburg, negotiations for an Anglo-French naval convention had begun, and on July 16, 1912, representatives of the French and Russian naval general staffs signed a draft Russo-French naval convention.[35] During Poincaré's stay in Russia, the Russo-French naval convention became official through an exchange of letters between the two governments.[36] Judging by Sazonov's account of their conversations, Poincaré was much more interested in discussing military cooperation between the Entente powers than the danger of a Balkan war. Thus he emphasized the importance of improving Russia's railway communications in the western provinces; this subject had been discussed at length during the Paris conference of the Russian and French chiefs of staff in July 1912.[37] Poincaré also confided in Sazonov the nature of secret arrangements with British military leaders that assured France of military and naval support if attacked by Germany. In discussing Anglo-French naval cooperation, Poincaré also suggested that Russia arrange a naval convention with Britain similar to the one she had just concluded with France. Such a convention, he argued, would protect Russian naval interests in the Mediterranean and Black Sea and would improve the position of Russian naval power in the Baltic.[38]

The Balkan question was, however, discussed at some length. During the first six months of Poincaré's premiership, France had warned the Russians on numerous occasions that they could not count on French military support if they attacked Austria-Hungary in order to protect Russian interests in the Balkans. But now, although Poincaré cautioned Sazonov that Russia could not count on French military support in a Balkan war, he promised that France would fulfill her alliance obligations if Germany intervened. The same assurance was made to Izvol'skii in September after Poincaré had returned to Paris. Poincaré also painted for Izvol'skii an optimistic picture of the favorable military situation of the Entente powers at that moment. A recent report of the French general staff had stressed the likelihood of Italy's desertion of her allies in the event of a general war and the probable involvement of large Austro-Hungarian forces in the Balkans.[39]

France, Izvol'skii reasoned, had effectively promised military assistance in the event of a war caused by the Austro-Russian rivalry in the Balkans.[40] In his *Au service de la France,* Poincaré denied having made such a promise,[41] but it is highly questionable whether Izvol'skii would have deliberately falsified Poincaré's statements and intent over a period of months.[42] And Sazonov had two opportunities during the latter part of 1912 to talk with Poincaré at length and check the accuracy of the ambassador's reports. Certainly, as Luigi Albertini has remarked, there was little in the utterances Poincaré made to Russian diplomats between August and November 1912 "of a nature to deter Russia and the Balkan states from risky ventures." [43]

When Poincaré first learned of the conclusion of the Serbo-Bulgarian alliance, he welcomed it in the presence of Izvol'skii as "highly comforting for the powers of the Triple Entente." [44] Several months earlier France and Bulgaria had begun negotiations concerning a French loan of 180 million francs. Paléologue, the French Minister at Sofia, had told Geshov in mid-February that Poincaré would only approve of loans to states which "politically traveled the same road" that France did.[45] After Russia assured France in April that the terms of the Serbo-Bulgarian alliance permitted Russia to exercise effective influence over the action of the Balkan allies,[46] Poincaré immediately approved the Bulgarian loan in principle.[47] Several months later, however, after official visits by King Ferdinand in Berlin and Vienna, the French Premier complained to Izvol'skii that France had been inclined to grant the loan only because Russia had declared that Bulgaria was firmly committed to the cause of the Triple Entente.[48]

Despite reservations about Bulgaria, French diplomats and leaders continued to regard the Balkan alliance favorably during the months preceding the First Balkan War. At St. Petersburg in

August, Poincaré, though very critical of the aggressive character of the treaty that Sazonov then communicated to him for the first time, approved of the alliance as a means of increasing the military potential of the Balkan states.[49] And shortly before the outbreak of hostilities in the Balkans, Panafieu, the French Minister at Sofia, sharply criticized Russia for having warned Bulgaria and Serbia that they could expect no assistance or sympathy. Panafieu gloomily predicted that this action could only accrue to the benefit of Austria-Hungary.[50]

But French financial interests in the Ottoman Empire conflicted with the aims of French diplomacy in Bulgaria.[51] France had long maintained friendly relations with Turkey, and French capital was heavily invested in railways, ports, and banking. By August 1912 it had become abundantly clear that Bulgaria was bent on war, and French diplomats tried to restrain Bulgaria by notifying her that it was no longer possible for French banks to grant the 180 million-franc loan. Thereafter the French Government consistently refused to permit the official listing of any Bulgarian loans.[52] During the late summer and early fall of 1912, France worked more energetically than any other European power to prevent, or at least postpone or localize, war in the Balkans.

Once war broke out in the Balkans, however, France necessarily adopted a somewhat more flexible attitude. The government permitted banks to make advances to Bulgaria for munitions ordered in France.[53] And Paris was now much more inclined than ever before to support Russia in regard to purely Balkan questions. Here Poincaré's main consideration seems to have been the fear that Russia might move closer to Germany unless her vital interests in the Balkans received more whole-hearted support than had often been the case in the past. Statements made in December 1912 by Poincaré, the French Minister of War, Alexandre Millerand, and the deputy chief of staff of the French army even indicated that France was prepared to go to war in support of Russia.[54] At the time a partial mobilization of the Austro-Hungarian army in response to Serbia's demand for an Adriatic port had created a tense situation. Russia, however, showed no inclination to make an issue of the measures taken by Austria-Hungary, and the crisis ended with Serbia's abandonment of her demand for an outlet to the Adriatic.

Great Britain experienced many of the same difficulties that France did in formulating a satisfactory Balkan policy during 1912. Like France, Britain ruled over millions of Moslem subjects and had large sums invested in the Ottoman Empire. British leaders knew, however, that St. Petersburg had been sorely disappointed by the lukewarm support from Britain and France during the Bosnian crisis of 1908–9 and feared that another setback in the Balkans might cause Russia to leave the Triple Entente.[55] Nor could the Foreign Office ignore the Balkan Committee and such influential people as G. P. Gooch, Lord Bryce, Noel Buxton, George Trevelyan, and *Times* reporters J. D. Bourchier and M. E. Durham, who had long been active in arousing public opinion in Great Britain about the plight of the Christians in the Ottoman Empire. Many of these friends of the Balkan countries were better informed than British diplomats, and they exerted considerable pressure on the Foreign Office in 1912.[56]

Aside from Russia, Great Britain knew more about the Serbo-Bulgarian negotiations of 1911 and 1912 than any other major European power. Sir H. G. O. Bax-Ironside, the British Minister at Sofia, reported the Geshov-Milovanović railway conversation to Grey as early as October 23, 1911. From this time until the signing of the Serbo-Bulgarian alliance, he supplied Foreign Office leaders in London with an accurate and fairly complete account of the negotiations that took place between Sofia and Belgrade.[57] Sir Edward Grey approved of Bax-Ironside's efforts to keep London informed but instructed him to avoid giving advice or expressing any opinion concerning the Serbo-Bulgarian negotiations.[58]

Though he declined to give active encouragement to the negotiations of 1911–12, Grey had favored a Serbo-Bulgarian rapprochement since the latter part of 1908. But British diplomats had then viewed a Serbo-Bulgarian understanding as a means of preventing further Austro-Hungarian penetration into the Balkans.[59] Britain, of course, did not favor a Balkan alliance directed primarily against Turkey, but she could not actively oppose their negotiations and still be regarded as a friend by the Balkan states should they drive the Turks out of Europe.

The ambiguous position of Great Britain naturally disturbed Russian diplomats, and Britain's encouragement of an Austro-Russian understanding[60] and obvious reluctance to participate in any joint action of the powers at Constantinople caused further misgivings. Since Austria-Hungary was Russia's principal rival in the Balkans, St. Petersburg understandably hesitated to consider seriously any meaningful form of cooperation and diplomatic action *à deux* with the dual monarchy. During August and September 1912 Russia persistently sought to persuade the Turks that they could avoid catastrophe only by ratifying a frontier agreement with Montenegro, punishing the Turkish officers and soldiers responsible for the Kočane massacre, appointing Christians to important administrative posts in Macedonia, and, generally, by introducing and implementing an acceptable program of reforms in European Turkey.[61] In this way war in the Balkans would be delayed, since the Balkan states would have no reason to attack Turkey if Russian diplomacy could bring them the fruits of victory without bloodshed.[62] France was willing to cooperate with Russia in this endeavor;[63] Great Britain, however, was not.

British reluctance to pressure the Turks into making concessions[64] naturally irritated Russia and made her reluctant to take the British into her confidence. Thus when he visited the British Foreign Secretary at Balmoral in September, Sazonov did not divulge the secret annex of the Serbo-Bulgarian treaty, as he had to Poincaré at St. Petersburg in early August. He did so only on November 5, 1912, as a result of Poincaré's insistence.[65]

British leaders clearly feared that Russia might drift away from the Entente unless fairly confident of support in the event of war, but the realities of domestic politics prevented the Foreign Office from making the iron-clad commitments that would have convinced Russia of the sincerity of Britain's friendship. It was no doubt for this reason that Grey and George v reassured Sazonov at Balmoral in September 1912 concerning Great Britain's readiness to assist France and Russia in case of war with Germany.[66] They made these assurances, to be sure, in a vague and general form and did not commit Britain definitely. Too, during the naval discussions with Russia between 1912 and 1914,[67] Britain signed no formal agreement but she was at least morally committed to assist Russia under a variety of circumstances.

Great Britain was also ready to sacrifice many interests in the Near East for the sake of her Entente relationship with Russia. Such sacrifices were made, for example, in Persia between 1910 and 1912.[68] The Foreign Office viewed the Serbo-Bulgarian negotiations with mixed feelings, for British economic interests were bound to be jeopardized by an alliance directed against Turkey. British diplomats knew of Russia's role in promoting the alliance but avoided reproaches; they fatalistically felt that they could not do much to prevent Russia from creating a possibly dangerous diplomatic situation in the Balkans. As Grey remarked in April 1912:

> We shall have to keep out of this and what I fear is that Russia may resent our doing so: the fact that the trouble is all of her own making won't prevent her from expecting help if the trouble turns out to be more than she bargained for. On the other hand Russia would resent still more our attempting to restrain her now in a matter that she would at this stage say did not concern us.[69]

As early as October 1910 General Fichev had indicated to Colonel H. D. Napier, British military attaché in Serbia, Bulgaria's interest in reaching an understanding with the powers of the Triple Entente.[70] At the beginning of 1912, the progress of the Serbo-

Bulgarian negotiations made such an understanding seem all the more desirable. Thus M. I. Madzharov, a prominent Bulgarian politician who had a good knowledge of both the English language and conditions, was appointed minister in Great Britain for the express purpose of working for closer relations between the Entente and Bulgaria.[71] His activities in London were not intended to be isolated; during these same months King Ferdinand, Geshov, and other Bulgarian leaders and diplomats repeatedly sought to impress on French and British diplomats the value of Bulgarian friendship for the interests of the Entente in Europe.[72]

The Bulgarians also took British and French diplomats partly into their confidence concerning the Serbo-Bulgarian alliance while carefully hiding the fact of its existence from German and Austrian diplomats in Sofia. Although Bulgarian leaders had decided on a pro-Entente policy, they avoided an open break with Vienna; Austrian friendship might again prove useful in the event of a resumption of their rivalry with the Serbs in Macedonia.

Containment of Russia was among the principal objectives of German and Austrian Balkan policy. Though desiring Russian good will, Germany could not afford to forget that any drastic revision of the Balkan status quo would threaten not only the very existence of Germany's only reliable ally but also German economic interests throughout the Near East. Thus German Chancellor Bethmann-Hollweg described the Balkan alliance in his memoirs as "a long stride on the part of Russia towards the domination of the Balkans and the liquidation of Turkey in Europe." [73] From the Austrian point of view, a war of the four Balkan allies against Turkey promised to strengthen Serbia; Vienna also feared that the alliance would serve as a convenient instrument of Russian policy against "everything that was not Russian in the Near East." [74]

Kiderlen-Wächter, German Foreign Secretary, did not initially consider the Balkan alliance a serious danger; unaware of the secret annex, he assumed that the alliance was defensive and that the allies would not undertake any offensive action without first consulting Russia.[75] Indeed, German diplomats were reassured by Russian participation in the alliance negotiations. Their reasoning was that pressing internal problems would oblige Russia to follow a peaceful policy for a number of years. Comments by Emperor Nicholas II, Premier Kokovtsov, and Sazonov at Baltic Port in July greatly reinforced this belief.[76]

Berchtold remained ignorant of the existence of the Serbo-Bulgarian alliance until he visited Berlin toward the end of May 1912. The information Kiderlen then gave him did not especially alarm the Austrian Foreign Minister.[77] Like Kiderlen, he believed that Russia dreaded war in the Balkans every bit as much as Austria-Hungary did.[78] Moreover, Berchtold received repeated assurance from the Austrian Minister at Sofia that conflicting interests practically excluded any meaningful cooperation between Bulgaria and Serbia even if they had signed an agreement.[79]

Both Aehrenthal and Berchtold had sought to persuade Bulgaria of her identity of interests with Austria-Hungary. The news of the Serbo-Bulgarian treaty, although an unpleasant surprise, did not change Berchtold's mind about the desirability of Bulgarian friendship. King Ferdinand was therefore warmly received when he visited Vienna in early June 1912, and the foreign minister refrained from disclosing what he knew of the alliance.[80] Berchtold apparently hoped to keep all possibilities open for a future time when Serbo-Bulgarian relations would again deteriorate. As late as August 10, 1912, he instructed Count Tarnowski, the Austrian Minister in Sofia, to find a convenient occasion to assure Bulgaria that there was no conflict of interest in the Balkans between Sofia and Vienna and that Austria-Hungary would not hinder Bulgaria's historical development once the "fatal hour had struck for Turkey." [81]

Tarnowski carried out these instructions during the last week of August.[82] Had he known of the decisions then being made in Sofia, he would have realized how futile Berchtold's policy was at that particular moment. Here the strict secrecy with which the Serbs, Bulgarians, and Russians kept the details of the alliance paid dividends. It prevented Austria-Hungary from acting effectively on the basis of an accurate assessment of the actual state of affairs. Only Berchtold's ignorance of the extent of Bulgaria's commitment to Serbia and the idea of war permitted him to believe that he could combine cultivation of Bulgarian friendship with insistence on Turkey's territorial integrity until some indefinite future time. Bulgaria was simply no longer interested in Austrian promises of support at some hypothetical future time when Vienna would finally decide that the "fatal hour had struck for Turkey." Furthermore, the stake Russia and the Entente had in the Balkans seemed to oblige these powers, *nolens volens,* to support the cause of the Balkan states, at least diplomatically, in the event of war.[83]

The effective conduct of Austrian Balkan policy was further hindered by a number of other considerations. Kiderlen-Wächter wanted to terminate the leadership of the Triple Alliance Austria-Hungary had assumed under Aehrenthal. He was all the more determined to do so because of the lukewarm support by Vienna during the Moroccan crisis of 1911. Since the Potsdam conference of 1910, Austria-Hungary had resented what seemed to be a German attempt to limit her freedom of action in the Balkans, and the Austro-German misunderstanding became particularly evident in September 1912, when Kiderlen made it plain that Vienna could scarcely expect support unless Germany was adequately informed concerning the dual monarchy's intentions. Austria-Hungary's habit of presenting Germany with *faits accomplis* especially vexed Kiderlen.[84]

A second difficulty was the failure of Italy and Turkey to reach a peace settlement. As long as the war continued, both Austria-Hungary and Germany were in an embarrassing position. Because of growing tension between the Entente and the Triple Alliance, Germany, in particular, wanted to avoid losing Italian friendship. Though the two countries were allies of Italy, Austria-

Hungary to be sure a reluctant one, they also wished to maintain good relations with Turkey. But support of Italy scarcely aided the activities of Austrian and German diplomats in Constantinople and implicitly sanctioned an Italian action that greatly weakened the Ottoman Empire, and the territorial integrity of Turkey was essential for the maintenance of a status quo in the Balkans compatible with the vital interests of Austria-Hungary.[85]

A third difficulty for Austria-Hungary was her internal South Slav problem. In September 1912 Serbian staff officers generally felt that the sympathy of the monarchy's South Slav subjects for Serbia made it unlikely that Vienna would intervene in a Balkan conflict. Even if Austria-Hungary should decide on intervention, it seemed that the monarchy's military operations would be paralyzed by guerrilla operations against bridges, tunnels, depots, etc. Indeed, preparations had already been made for such harassment.[86] Although the events of 1914–15 proved it unwarranted, the existence of such optimism at Belgrade obviously did not strengthen the hand of diplomats in Vienna during the weeks preceding the First Balkan War.

Germany's role in restraining Austria-Hungary in the late summer and fall of 1912 should not be exaggerated. As E. C. Helmreich has observed, "Germany could not be expected to be more Austrian than the Austrians themselves." [87] Indeed, Kiderlen assured the Austrian Ambassador at Berlin on October 10 that Germany had not changed her policy since the Bosnian crisis in regard to the defense of Austrian vital interests in the Balkans.[88] There is no evidence that Kiderlen would have refused to defend such interests if he had been requested to do so. Kiderlen interpreted Berchtold's failure to request German support as a sign that the Austrian Foreign Minister did not know what he really wanted in the fall of 1912.[89]

Such indecision meant that the Triple Alliance would not assert itself. Italy was still at war and in no position to mediate between Turkey and the Balkan allies. And Germany's interests in the Near East were too contradictory to demand an effective and consistent policy. Germany had heavy investments and extensive trade relations with both Bulgaria[90] and Turkey. The extent of German economic and political influence in Turkey made it to Germany's advantage to maintain a strong Turkey in Europe. This interest, however, conflicted with Germany's alliance with Italy.

It is known that Kaiser Wilhelm II was disgusted with Turkey for having bickered over details and prolonged the negotiations for a Turko-Italian peace treaty.[91] The Kaiser also disapproved of any attempt of the powers to prevent the expansion of the Balkan states at the expense of Turkey.[92] But Wilhelm's advisers and German Government leaders were more mindful than he of the complexity of Germany's Balkan interests. Certainly they understood the importance of Austria-Hungary for Germany, and of the Balkans for Austria-Hungary, so sooner or later they would probably have accepted any coherent and realistic plan of action that Berchtold might have developed.

The Austrian chief of staff, General Blasius Schemua, and other military leaders were confident of the chances for success in a war and pessimistic about Turkey's fighting alone against the Balkan allies.[93] Schemua especially favored an invasion of the Sanjak of Novibazar which would have kept Montenegro and Serbia separated. But Berchtold's was essentially a policy of bluff and awaiting events. He did not even feel that Serbia's acquisition of the Sanjak would seriously affect the vital interests of Austria-Hungary; nor did he oppose territorial changes in the Balkans as long as the integrity of Albania was respected and no power received territory along the Adriatic.[94] Clearly, Berchtold no longer believed that it was possible to maintain the famous Balkan status quo; he had apparently lost faith in the possibility of maintaining Turkey in Europe as a means of avoiding changes in the Balkans detrimental to the interests of Austria-Hungary.

Because of Berchtold's lack of a concrete plan, the failure of his one serious attempt to seize the diplomatic initiative was almost a foregone conclusion. His note of August 13, which proposed that the powers encourage the Porte to introduce reforms and further administrative decentralization in the provinces of European Turkey, appears to have been based on little consideration of the European and Balkan diplomatic situation at that moment. He did not bother to inform Germany about his note beforehand, which naturally irritated Kiderlen-Wächter.[95] The latter quickly perceived that Berchtold's suggestion would be construed by the Porte as interference in Ottoman internal affairs,[96] and the Turks did, in fact, react as Kiderlen had predicted.[97] Although Berchtold had intended his *démarche* as a means of strengthening Turkey's position in the Balkan crisis,[98] he did not take the elementary precaution of feeling out the Porte in advance. Moreover, he did not understand that raising the question of Ottoman decentralization at a time of Albanian revolutionary successes in Macedonia would necessarily alarm both Russia and the Balkan states.

The apprehension Berchtold's note aroused in both Turkey and the Balkan states naturally caused the European powers to have misgivings, and they asked for more information concerning Austria-Hungary's intentions before acting on the suggestions. In a second note of August 29, Berchtold explained that he had not intended to intervene in Turkish affairs but only to support the reform efforts of the existing Turkish cabinet. At the same time, he suggested that the Balkan states could probably be quieted through individual representations of the powers.[99]

In line with the Austrian note, Russian suggested to the powers on September 17 that they join in advising the Porte to satisfy the wishes of the Balkan Christians and to extend the promised Albanian reforms to all nationalities in European Turkey.[100] France expressed her willingness to cooperate, but pointed out that Russia's proposal was not acceptable to the other powers, especially Great Britain. As has been noted, Great Britain opposed any concerted pressure on Turkey largely because of commercial interests in the Near East and her position as a colonial power in Moslem areas. Poincaré, interested above all in Entente solidarity, suggested on September 22 that Britain, France, and Russia agree among themselves and then present their views to Germany and Austria-Hungary.[101] The four points that Poincaré suggested at this time served as a basis for the diplomatic action of the great powers three weeks later at Constantinople and the Balkan capitals.

Largely as a result of the efforts of Kiderlen and Poincaré, the formula was worked out that Russia and Austria-Hungary, as the two most interested powers, should inform the Balkan states that the powers would tolerate no territorial changes in the peninsula, while all five powers were to emphasize collectively at Constantinople their interest in Ottoman reforms. In associating himself in this way with Poincaré, Kiderlen did pretty much the same thing he had accused Berchtold of doing previously: he acted in a matter of common interest without consulting his ally beforehand. Moreover, he had confidentially told the French that Austria-Hungary would no doubt agree to act jointly with Russia before Vienna had publicly taken a stand on joint action.

Kiderlen's behavior naturally vexed Berchtold,[102] but he had done much to tie his own hands by having failed to elaborate a reasonable alternative proposal. Moreover, on September 21 he had cooperated with Russia at Constantinople by instructing the Austrian Ambassador to join his Russian colleague in encouraging the Porte to make a number of specific reforms. As was to be expected, the Turkish Foreign Minister interpreted this move as interference in Turkish internal affairs.[103] Kiderlen-Wächter strongly disapproved of Berchtold's assistance to Russian diplomatic maneuvers at Constantinople, especially when related to reforms that seemed to aim at the dissolution of the Ottoman Empire.[104] But Berchtold's cooperation with Russia made it difficult for Austria-Hungary to avoid acceding to the wishes of the other powers, and on October 2 Vienna assured St. Petersburg that Austria-Hungary would participate in common Russo-Austrian action in the Balkans based on the principle of maintaining the status quo.[105]

Sazonov, who was then in Paris following his visit with the British at Balmoral, welcomed the prospect of joint Russo-Austrian action. He had, in fact, favored an Austro-Russian understanding to deal with the Balkan crisis as early as mid-September.[106] Sazonov explained to Nicholas II several days before the outbreak of the First Balkan War that he had agreed to common action with Austria-Hungary because such action would limit the Habsburg monarchy's freedom of action in the Balkans.[107] Although Sazonov did not know that Vienna had no intention of resorting to military action, he and Poincaré must be given credit for keeping the initiative in the hands of the Entente and skillfully working to prevent Vienna from doing anything that would adversely affect the interests of the Balkan states, Russia, and the Entente in the peninsula. Austria-Hungary and Germany, on the other hand, coordinated their efforts badly and did little in October 1912 to defend vital Austrian interests in the western Balkans.

Once Austria-Hungary agreed to joint action with Russia in the Balkans, the powers moved fairly rapidly. Only British objections concerning the wording of Article III of the Balkan note delayed agreement on a final draft several additional days.[108] By October 7, however, Sazonov was able to communicate the final version to the Balkan capitals.[109] On October 8, the same day Montenegro declared war on Turkey, Russian and Austrian representatives officially delivered the powers' note in the four Balkan capitals. Most important was Article III which stated unequivocally that the powers would permit no change in the Balkan status quo at the end of a war between Turkey and the Balkan allies.[110] Two days later, on October 10, the powers collectively notified Turkey of their willingness to assist her in carrying out the reforms she had already publicly announced. Turkey understandably was not interested in such assistance, describing it as interference in Turkish internal affairs. The Turkish Government therefore rejected the powers' collective note.[111]

No one seriously believed that the status-quo declaration by Austria-Hungary and Russia in the name of the powers would prevent the Balkan states from attacking Turkey. The powers were really more interested in avoiding a war among themselves than a localized war in the Balkans. Indeed, they had very little right to moralize about the sanctity of the status quo, for they themselves had set a poor example with numerous seizures of territory in Europe and elsewhere during the preceding decades. Kaiser Wilhelm, who despite all his shortcomings was honest, even felt that it was wrong for the powers to stand in the way of the aspirations of the Balkan states. He compared them with Prussia of 1864, 1866, and 1870 and refused to approve taking from them what they might gain by right of conquest.[112] Prussia of course was not alone in practicing the dictum "might is right." After 1870 all the European great powers madly scrambled after African and Asian colonies and spheres of influence. With particular regard to the Near East, the annexation of Bosnia-Herzegovina and the Tripolitan War were especially instructive examples for the Balkan states to follow.

The absurdity of the powers' insistence on the inviolability of the status quo has been particularly well described by Gabriel Hanotaux, a French historian writing on the eve of World War I:

> The Tripolitan War having provoked the events, it was from this quarter that the cards were on the table. How could one say and believe that such a blow to the status quo—to that famous status quo that the diplomats do not grow weary of invoking with an irony a bit strong or a candor a bit naive— how could one say and believe that the status quo would be respected by everyone when two provinces were torn from the Ottoman Empire, when all the islands of the Aegean were occupied, when the enemy fleets operated near Arabia, at Smyrna, and even up to the Dardanelles? Really, the fiction was a bit strong. Because one of the powers of the European concert had declared war on Turkey the sick man was indeed sick.[113]

Chapter 7

CONCLUSION

After 1905 pressing internal problems made it difficult for tsarist diplomats to act resolutely abroad. Yet the Ilinden uprising, growing Austro-Hungarian influence, the Young-Turk Revolution, and continuing unrest among the subject Christians forced Russia to repair her deteriorating position in the Balkans. But St. Petersburg not only wanted to prevent, or at least delay and localize war, but even to avoid any suspicion of being associated with the war plans of the Balkan states. In late September, when the Russian army began a trial mobilization in Poland and western Russia, Neratov assured the Russian press and European governments that the trial mobilization had been planned since spring and had no connection with the mobilization of the Balkan armies.[1]

Nevertheless war came and complicated Russia's task of maintaining her influence and prestige in the Balkans. Irritated with the Balkan states, St. Petersburg terminated military and financial aid to Montenegro[2] but did not dare punish Sofia and Belgrade. Indeed, their importance quickly forced St. Petersburg to defend Balkan territorial changes which it had just condemned.[3]

Russia consistently avoided military and diplomatic adventures in the Balkans after 1908. This caution is at odds with the

131

common view that the tsarist government repeatedly and energetically tried to create a Balkan alliance directed against either Turkey or Austria-Hungary.[4] It is particularly doubtful that Russia intended to use the Balkan alliance against Turkey. Even in 1912 Sazonov did not pursue an anti-Turkish policy *à outrance*. He unquestionably favored the cause of the Slavic states, but this preference did not include support of their war plans. St. Petersburg feared dissolution of the Ottoman Empire in 1912; a Turkish debacle promised to open a Pandora's box of Black Sea and Balkan problems with which Russia was in no position to cope.

A particular bugbear was that if Turkey collapsed Bulgaria might gain possession of the Straits. Russian diplomats had persistently discouraged Bulgarian expansion toward Constantinople. Prior to the First Balkan War they repeatedly rejected Sofia's request that Adrianople be included in Bulgaria's sphere of influence.[5] After hostilities began, the rapid advance of Bulgarian troops toward Constantinople so frightened the Russian Foreign Ministry that in November it proposed sending 5,000 troops to Constantinople to defend Russia's interests should the Bulgarians take the Turkish capital. To protect Russian interests from what it called "Bulgarian imperialism," [6] the foreign ministry even discussed seizing a strip of land on the Bosphorus. The chief of the naval staff considered such action futile,[7] however, and it became unnecessary when the Turks stopped the Bulgarians at the Chatalja fortifications.

Austrophobia, on the other hand, is a fairly accurate description of the attitude of most Russian diplomats. The suspicion and hostility aroused by Austria-Hungary's annexation of Bosnia-Herzegovina had abated considerably by 1911. Yet Sazonov's first reaction upon learning of the Serbo-Bulgarian negotiations was to visualize 500,000 bayonets closing the Balkans forever to further Austro-German penetration. Vienna's efforts to curry Bulgarian and Montenegrin favor during 1911 and 1912 reawakened Russian apprehension. And despite Aehrenthal's victory over

Conclusion

Conrad von Hötzendorf in November 1911, tsarist diplomats could never be absolutely sure that Austria-Hungary would not launch a preventive war against Serbia or expand elsewhere to the south. They valued Serbo-Bulgarian unity above all as an obstacle to Vienna's apparent *Drang nach Saloniki.* For this reason, once war had started, St. Petersburg supported the principal Balkan territorial demands. Without such support, as Sukhomlinov warned in November 1912, the Balkan states would soon lose their warm feelings for Russia, in which case "we could hardly count on them in the event of armed conflict with Germany and Austria-Hungary." [8]

It is not, however, fair to argue that Russia systematically prepared the Balkan alliance for aggression against Austria and Germany. The Balkan alliance was originally conceived by the Balkan peoples themselves, not Russia. In 1908 and in 1911 the Serbs took the initiative in beginning alliance talks, and when serious negotiations began in the fall of 1911 Russia was relatively passive. Although confidence in Russian support no doubt encouraged the Serbs and Bulgarians to proceed with their talks, there is no convincing evidence that Russian diplomats tried to influence the Balkan states to direct the alliance against Austria-Hungary. Such encouragement was unnecessary, and St. Petersburg seems to have intended that the alliance should play a defensive, not aggressive role in regard to the dual monarchy.

Russian Balkan policy should not be too closely identified with the extremely anti-Austrian views of Izvol'skii and Hartwig. Even while still foreign minister Izvol'skii exerted less influence over Balkan policy than has generally been assumed. And his influence naturally diminished when in 1910 he moved to Paris. Hartwig, to be sure, being in Belgrade, was an essential source of ideas and information for Neratov and Sazonov. Hartwig's pronounced pro-Serbian and anti-Austrian views, driving ambition, and determination to shape Russian Balkan policy are well known. He was not, however, always successful. Neratov, who advised Serbia and Bulgaria to draft a defensive treaty and to leave open the possibility of Turkey's joining them, certainly did not take seriously Hartwig's talk about Russia's "secular task" and Serbia as Russia's vanguard in the Near East. Nor did Sazonov accept Hartwig's recommendations uncritically, deciding in the spring of 1912 on a pro-Bulgarian orientation of Russian policy. The need to weaken Austria's and strengthen Russia's influence in Bulgaria was the main argument for such a policy. At the same time, it was clear that too much support of Serbia might intensify agitation by her extremists against Austria-Hungary. Russia definitely did not want to encourage Serbian extremists. A *modus vivendi* with Austria-Hungary was necessary for both powers; if need be, they could act in concert to prevent a European war arising out of a Balkan conflict. Hartwig, of course, disapproved of such common diplomatic action with Vienna because of the bad impression it made in Serbia.[9]

Nor should the influence of the press in 1912 on Sazonov's Balkan policy be exaggerated. True, the press aided Stolypin late in 1908 when he forced Izvol'skii to abandon compensation for Russia in the Straits and to be more mindful of the interests of the Balkan Slavs. And contemporary foreign diplomats frequently commented on "unofficial Russia's" influence on Sazonov during the period of the Balkan wars. Even such a competent observer as Baron Boris E. Nol'de has referred to Sazonov as a "representative of Russian public opinion."[10] But comparison of Russian press opinion with policy decisions made by Neratov and Sazonov reveals that they were quite capable of ignoring the press and arriving at their own conclusions. They were especially independent between October 1911 and the late summer of 1912. The Charykov episode was the one matter about which the Russian public was relatively well informed during these months. But the Russian bureaucracy and the Balkan governments carefully kept the secret of the Balkan alliance from the press. Neratov and Sazonov were therefore able to deal with the Balkan states as they saw fit during this crucial period without having to worry much about Russian public opinion. Indeed, Sazonov strove to use rather than serve Russian public opinion. He even commented in October 1912 how convenient it was to have Russia's opponents believe that the foreign ministry was in a difficult position and constantly obliged "to struggle against the pressure of public opinion." [11]

Nevertheless, few significant differences separated Sazonov from Russian public opinion in regard to Balkan and European policy. Such a determined critic of official Russian policy after 1909 as Miliukov realized this even before the outbreak of World War I. In speeches before the Duma in 1913 and 1914 he praised Sazonov for having encouraged the formation of the Balkan alliance and for having worked closely with France to halt Austro-German expansion and make it possible for Russia to fulfill her "historic task in the Near East." [12]

Like Miliukov, many Russian diplomats hoped that at some future date Russia might gain control of the Straits and firmly establish her hegemony in the Balkans. They did not, however, expect that Russian military power and the international situation would permit such an ideal solution of the Eastern Question for many years. Meanwhile, Russia, weakened by internal problems, had to defend her national interests in the Black Sea and along the Caucasian frontier and maintain prestige and influence in the Balkans. Lacking the material means to support a vigorous and imaginative policy in these areas, Russian diplomacy had to adapt its policies to the vicissitudes of Balkan and Near Eastern politics. In more ways than one, St. Petersburg's position was similar to Vienna's. Like Russia, Austria-Hungary was hindered from acting aggressively in the Balkans by internal weakness. She was interested in Bulgarian friendship for much the same reason that Russia encouraged Serbo-Bulgarian unity: both countries wanted Balkan allies for a general European war that could break out at any time.

Russia's Balkan policy during 1911 and 1912 was highly realistic and her objectives limited. By encouraging the Balkan alliance, tsarist diplomats, as Langer has aptly remarked, "were merely trying to prevent the exploitation of their weaknesses by their rivals." [13] They realized that the alliance, though useful strategically and as a deterrent to an active Austrian policy, could easily lead to a Balkan-Turkish war, arouse suspicions in Europe, and cause misunderstandings with Great Britain and France. In 1912 Sazonov could not restrain the Balkan allies but nevertheless managed to maintain Russia's prestige and predominant influence in Belgrade, Cetinje, and Sofia. By outmaneuvering Berchtold he also effectively limited Austria-Hungary's freedom of action at the height of the Balkan crisis, simultaneously convincing not only Poincaré and Grey but also Kiderlen-Wächter of Russia's sincerity and desire to avoid a Balkan war. Moreover, his confidential discussions with Grey and Poincaré in September and October 1912 greatly helped to reinforce Franco-Russian and Anglo-Russian friendship. France at that time reinterpreted the Franco-Russian Alliance in an especially important fashion; for the first time St. Petersburg could be reasonably certain of French assistance should a Russo-Austrian war arise out of a purely Balkan issue.

After the fall of 1912 Russia was in a much stronger position than she had been previously—not so much from increased military appropriations or better army and naval organization, but from the skill of the Russian Foreign Ministry in dealing with the Balkan crisis. Not only was Balkan friendship for Russia at its height, but French and British understanding for Russian interests in the Balkans and the Straits augured well for the future. By 1917, had it not been for the October Revolution, Russia was much closer to fulfilling her "historic task in the Near East" than tsarist diplomats and Miliukov had dared hope in 1911–12 or even in 1914.

NOTES

Abbreviations for most frequently used sources—all references following abbreviated titles are to document number except where page number is specifically indicated.

APS—Die auswärtige Politik Serbiens, 1903–1914.
BD—British Documents on the Origins of the War 1898–1914.
Benckendorff—Graf Benckendorffs diplomatischer Schriftwechsel.
Doklad—Narodno sŭbranie, *Doklad na parlamentarnata izpitatelna komisiia.*
DDF—Ministère des Affaires étrangères, *Documents diplomatiques français.*
GP—Auswärtiges Amt, *Die grosse Politik der europäischen Kabinette 1871–1914.*
IB—Komissiia po izdaniiu dokumentov, *Die internationalen Beziehungen im Zeitalter des Imperialismus: Dokumente aus den Archiven der zarischen und der provisorischen Regierungen.*
MO—Komissiia po izdaniiu dokumentov, *Mezhdunarodynye otnosheniia v epokhu imperializma: Dokumenty iz arkhivov tsarskogo i vremennogo pravitel'stv 1878–1917.*
OUA—Österreich-Ungarns Aussenpolitik von der bosnischen Krise 1908 bis zum Kriegsausbruch 1914: Diplomatische Aktenstücke des öster-reich-ungarischen Ministeriums des Äussern.
Prilozhenie—Narodno sŭbranie, *Prilozhenie kŭm tom pŭrvi ot doklada na parlamentarnata izpitatelna komisiia.*
Schriftwechsel Iswolskis—Der diplomatische Schriftwechsel Iswolskis 1911–1914: Aus den Geheimakten der russischen Staatsarchive.

PREFACE

1. Otto Bickel, *Russland und die Entstehung des Balkanbundes 1912: Ein Beitrag zur Vorgeschichte des Weltkrieges* (Königsberg-Berlin: Osteuropa Verlag, 1933). W. L. Langer, "Russia, the Straits Question and the Origins of the Balkan League, 1908–1912," *Political Science Quarterly,* XLIII (September 1928), 321–63. Hans Kiendl, *Russische Balkanpolitik von der Ernennung Sasonows bis zum Ende des zweiten Balkankrieges* (Munich doctoral dissertation; Garmisch: Druck von A. Adam, 1925).

2. Bickel, pp. 95–96, 98–99, 116, 154–55.

3. Ibid., pp. 1–2, 8, 119, 159–60.

4. Documents published by A. L. Popov in the *Krasnyi Arkhiv* in 1925 and 1926 had been the main source of information concerning Russia's role in the Balkan alliance: "Diplomaticheskaia podgotovka Balkanskoi voiny 1912," ed. A. L. Popov, *Krasnyi Arkhiv,* VIII (1925), 3–48, and IX (1925), 3–23; Pervaia Balkanskaia voina," *ibid.,* XV (1926), 1–29, and XVI (1926), 3–23. Only a limited selection of the documents pertaining to the conduct of Russian Balkan policy during 1911 and 1912 was published by Popov. Almost all of these were reproduced fully or with deletions in footnotes by the editors of *Mezhdunarodnye otnosheniia.* Of approximately 750 pieces of diplomatic correspondence exchanged between St. Petersburg and Cetinje, Athens, Belgrade, Constantinople, and Sofia, reproduced fully in *Mezhdunarodnye otnosheniia,* only sixty had been published by Popov. *Mezhdunarodnye otnosheniia* included hundreds of other new documents pertaining to Russian Balkan policy in 1911–12: diplomatic correspondence of the foreign office with the European capitals, special memoranda drafted within the foreign office, reports to Nicholas II, notes on special meetings of the council of ministers, and letters exchanged between administrative heads of departments and ministries in the tsarist government.

5. "Russian Policy in 1911–12," *Journal of Modern History,* XII (March 1940), 71–78 and 86.

6. Especially important is I. V. Bestuzhev's *Bor'ba v Rossii po voprosam vneshnei politiki 1906–1910* (Moscow: Akademiia Nauk, 1961). See also I. S. Galkin, "Obrazovanie Balkanskogo soiuza 1912 g. i politika evropeiskikh derzhav," *Vestnik Moskovskogo Universiteta,* 1956, no. 4, pp. 9–40; Galkin, *Diplomatiia evropeiskikh derzhav v sviazi s osvoboditel'nym dvizheniem narodov evropeiskoi Turtsii nakanune Balkanskikh voin 1912–1913 gg.* (Moscow: Izdatel'stvo Moskovskogo Universiteta, 1960.)

INTRODUCTION

1. B. A. Dranov, *Chernomorskie prolivy: Mezhdunarodno-pravovoi rezhim* (Moscow: Iuridicheskoe Izdatel'stvo Ministerstva Iustitsii SSSR, 1948), pp. 63–67. P. E. Mosely, *Russian Diplomacy and the Opening of the Eastern Question in 1838–39* (Cambridge: Harvard University Press, 1934), pp. 7–30. Theodor von Sosnosky, *Die Balkanpolitik Österreich-Ungarns seit 1866* (Stuttgart: Deutsche Verlags-Anstalt, 1913), I, 16–42, 53–63, II, 66–68 and 129–139. Hans Uebersberger, *Russlands Orientpolitik in den letzten zwei Jahrhunderten* (Stuttgart: Deutsche Verlags-Anstalt, 1913), Vol. I.

2. Charles Jelavich, *Tsarist Russia and Balkan Nationalism: Russian Influence in the Internal Affairs of Bulgaria and Serbia 1879–1886* (Berkeley: University of California Press, 1958), pp. 237, 274. A. V. Bogdanovich, *Journal de la Générale A. V. Bogdanovitch,* tr. M. Lefebvre (Paris: Payot, 1926), p. 42.

3. William L. Langer, *The Diplomacy of Imperialism 1890–1902* (New York: Alfred A. Knopf, 1935), I, 303–83. Wayne S. Vucinich, *Serbia between East and West: The Events of 1903–1908* (Stanford: Stanford University Press, 1954), pp. 125–127. Andrew Malozemoff, *Russian Far Eastern Policy 1881–1904* (Berkeley: University of California Press, 1958), pp. 37–39.

4. Between 1901 and 1910, 87.2% of Russian wheat exports passed through the Straits. In 1910, 92.9% of manganese ore, 61.5% of the iron ore, 70% of the cement, and 100% of the iron rails exported from Russia were shipped via the same route. See Dranov, p. 140; A. F. Miller, *Turtsiia i problema prolivov* (Moscow: Izdatel'stvo "Pravda," 1947), p. 4.

5. "Tsarskoe pravitel'stvo o probleme prolivov v 1896–1911 gg.," ed. V. M. Khvostov and E. M. Gliazer, *Krasnyi Arkhiv,* LXI (1933), 138–40. W. M. Carlgren, *Iswolsky und Aehrenthal vor der bosnischen Annexionskrise: Russische und österreichisch-ungarische Balkanpolitik 1906–1908* (Uppsala: Almqvist & Wiksells Boktryckeri AB, 1955), pp. 54–56.

6. M. N. Pokrovskii, *Drei Konferenzen: Zur Vorgeschichte des Krieges* (Berlin: Arbeiter Buchhandlung, 1920), pp. 23–25, 29–30.

7. A. S. Suvorin, *Dnevnik A. S. Suvorina,* ed. M. Krichevskii (Moscow-Petrograd: Izdatel'stvo L. D. Frenkel', 1923), p. 376. M. A. Taube, *La politique russe d'avant-guerre et la fin de l'empire des tsars* (1904–1917) (Paris: Librairie Ernest Leroux, 1928), p. 100. Carlgren, pp. 87, 179. E. M. Rozental', *Diplomaticheskaia istoriia russko-frantsuzskogo soiuza v nachale XX veka* (Moscow: Izdatel'stvo Sotsial'no-Ekonomicheskoi Literatury, 1960), pp. 228–61. Harold Nicolson, *Portrait of a Diplomatist* (Cambridge, Mass.: The Riverside Press, 1930), pp. 149–88. Pierre Renouvin, *Les questions méditerranéennes de 1904 à 1914* (Paris: Centre de Documentation Universitaire, 1954), pp. 18–19.

8. Gosudarstvennaia duma, Third Duma, first session, *Stenografi-cheskiia otchety*, Part II, Meeting 49 (April 4/17, 1908), col. 1763 ff. Bestuzhev, p. 191.

9. A. J. May, "The Novibazar Railway Project," *Journal of Modern History*, X (December 1938), 507–8, 514. Carlgren, pp. 218–25, 263.

10. A. J. May, "Trans-Balkan Railway Schemes," *Journal of Modern History*, XXIV (December 1952), 353–56. Vucinich, pp. 210–17. Carlgren, pp. 264–65.

11. Carlgren, pp. 281–283, 310–313. Bernadotte E. Schmitt, *The Annexation of Bosnia 1908–1909* (Cambridge: Cambridge University Press, 1937), pp. 9–10.

12. Speeches of P. N. Miliukov (Kadet), M. Ia. Kapustin (Octobrist), V. M. Purishkevich (extreme right), I. I. Balakleev (extreme right), and I. P. Pokrovskii (Social Democrat), *Stenografcheskiia otchety*, Meeting 49, cols. 1786–1824.

13. V. N. Kokovtsov, *Out of my Past: The Memoirs of Count Ko-kovtsov*, ed. H. H. Fisher. (Stanford: Stanford Uniersity Press, 1935.)

14. Bestuzhev, pp. 186, 222–25.

15. *Novoe Vremia*, 1908, September 26/October 9.

16. Bestuzhev, pp. 200–207, 212–16. Schmitt, *Annexation of Bosnia*, pp. 9–10, 35–36.

17. Bestuzhev, pp. 204–5.

18. *Ibid.*, pp. 213–21. A. M. Zaionchkovskii, *Podgotovka Rossii k mirovoi voine v mezhdunarodnom otnoshenii* (Leningrad: Voennaia Tipo-grafiia Upravleniia Delami Narkomvoenmor i RVS SSSR, 1926), pp. 166–68, 357–58. N. V. Charykov, *Glimpses of High Politics: Through War and Peace 1855–1929* (George Allen & Unwin, 1931), pp. 269–70, 276.

19. M. P. Bok, *Vospominaniia o moem ottse P. A. Stolypine* (New York: Izdatel'stvo imeni Chekhova, 1935), pp. 257–258; *Novoe Vremia*, 1908, October 23/November 5, November 2/15 and 4/17.

20. Bestuzhev, p. 239. *Golos Moskvy*, 1908, October 1/14, October 22/November 4, October 24/November 6.

21. *Rech'*, 1908, October 15/28, November 30/December 13; December 5/18, 13/26. P. N. Miliukov, *Balkanskii krizis i politika A. P. Izvol'skago* (St. Petersburg: Tipografiia Tovarishchestva "Obshchestvennaia Pol'za," 1910), pp. 51–55. Miliukov, *Vospominaniia (1859–1917)*, ed. M. N. Karpo-vich and B. I. El'kin (New York: Izdatel'stvo imeni Chekhova, 1955), II, 40–41.

22. *Novoe Vremia*, 1908, September 29/October 11, October 21/November 3, October 29/November 11, November 1/14 and 5/18. *Golos Moskvy*, 1909, February 14/27. Guchkov speech (December 12/25, 1908), Gosudarstvennaia duma, Third Duma, second session, *Stenografcheskiia otchety*, Part I, Meeting 31, col. 2675. Even some people associated with the extreme right, which was more interested in Balkan peace than Slavic solidarity, then favored an anti-Austrian Balkan bloc including Turkey. Thus the journalist S. F. Sharapov of the rightest newspaper *Svet* urged

Notes to Chapter 1

the creation of a "mighty Balkan alliance" to tear the Slavic states and Turkey away from the "spider's web" of Austria-Hungary and Germany. (S. F. Sharapov, *Blizhaishiia zadachi Rossii na Balkanakh*—Moscow: "Svidetel'" [1909]—p. 3.)

23. Pokrovskii, *Drei Konferenzen*, pp. 29–30. Bestuzhev, pp. 219–20. Carlgren, p. 232.

24. Bestuzhev, pp. 258–64. Gustav Lambsdorff, *Die Militärbevollmächtigten Kaiser Wilhelms II am Zarenhofe, 1904–1914* (Berlin: Schlieffen Verlag, 1937), p. 318. *Die grosse Politik der europäischen Kabinette 1871–1914* (Berlin: Deutsche Verlagsgesellschaft für Politik und Geschichte, 1922–27—hereinafter cited as *GP*), XXVI-1, 9146, Pourtalès to Bulow, December 9, 1908.

25. Third Duma, second session, *Stenograficheskiia otchety*, Part I, Meeting 31, cols. 2616–30. Taube, pp. 194–98.

26. *Stenograficheskiia otchety*, cols. 2648–52, 2673–77.

27. *Ibid.*, cols. 2677–2704.

28. *Ibid.*, cols. 2632–33, 2636–42, 2653–58, 2661–66. Iu. Ia. Solov'ev, *Vospominaniia diplomata 1893–1922* (Moscow: Izdatel'stvo Sotsial'no-Ekonomicheskoi Literatury, 1959), p. 209.

29. The most complete accounts of the diplomatic crisis of 1909 are given by Mončilo Ninčić (Montchilo Nintchitch), *La crise bosniaque (1908–1909) et les puissances européennes* (Paris: Alfred Costes, Editeur, 1937), II, 96–188; and Schmitt, *The Annexation of Bosnia*, pp. 186–207.

30. V. I. Bovykin, *Ocherki istorii vneshnei politiki Rossii: Konets XIX veka-1917 god* (Moscow: Gosudarstvennoe Uchebno-Pedogogicheskoe Izdatel'stvo Ministerstva Prosvescheniia RSFSR, 1960), p. 89. *Rech'*, 1909, March 17/30, March 20/April 2, and March 25/April 7. *Novoe Vremia*, 1909, March 15/28, 16/29, and 17/30. *Golos Moskvy*, 1909, March 17/30.

31. Bestuzhev, pp. 339–42. *Rech'*, 1909, November 18/December 1.

32. "Soglashenie mezhdu Rossiei i Italiei, Rakkonidzhi, 11/24 oktiabria 1909 g.," *Sbornik dogovorov Rossii s drugimi gosudarstvami 1856–1917*, ed. E. A. Adamov and I. V. Koz'menko (Moscow: Gosudarstvennoe Izdatel'stvo Politicheskoi Literatury, 1952), pp. 402–4.

33. Third Duma, third session, *Stenograficheskiia otchety*, Part II, Meeting 60 (March 2/15, 1910), cols. 2753–61.

CHAPTER 1

1. Jagoš Jovanović, *Stvaranje Crnogorske države i razvoj crnogorske nacionalnosti* (Cetinje: Izdanie Štamparsko-Izdavačkog Preduzeća "Obod," 1947), p. 96.

2. L. S. Stavrianos, *Balkan Federation: A History of the Movement Toward Balkan Unity in Modern Times* (Northampton, Mass.: Smith College Studies in History, XXVII, nos. 1–4, 1944), pp. 9–10. Stavrianos, *The Balkans since 1453* (New York: Holt, Rinehart and Winston, 1961), 180–81, 187–97, 204–11. George Vernadsky, "Alexandre ler et le problème slave pendant la première moitié de son règne," *Revue des Etudes Slaves*, VII (1927), 94–111.

3. I. S. Aksakov, *Ivan Sergeevich Aksakov v ego pis'makh* (Moscow: M. G. Volchaninov, 1888–92), II, 154–55.

4. S. A. Nikitin, "Russkaia politika na Balkanakh i nachalo vostochnoi voiny," *Voprosy Istorii*, 1946, No. 4, pp. 3–29. Standard discussions in English of Nicholas I's foreign policy are G. H. Bolsover, "Nicholas I and the Partition of Turkey," *Slavonic and East European Review*, XXVII (1948), 115–45; and N. V. Riasanovsky, *Nicholas I and Official Nationality in Russia 1825–1855* (Berkeley: University of California Press, 1959), pp. 235–65.

5. S. A. Nikitin, *Slavianskie komitety v Rossii v 1858–1876 godakh* (Moscow: Izdatel'stvo Moskovskogo Universiteta, 1960), pp. 24–44. Stavrianos, *The Balkans since 1453*, pp. 394–95.

6. Nikitin, *Slavianskie komitety*, pp. 260–342. B. H. Sumner, *Russia and the Balkans 1870–1880* (Oxford: At the Clarendon Press, 1937), pp. 56–80. E. C. Thaden, *Conservative Nationalism in Nineteenth-Century Russia* (Seattle: University of Washington Press, 1964), chapters 6 and 10.

7. Nikitin, *Slavianskie komitety*, pp. 328–29, 340–42, 349–51. Sumner, pp. 334–35 and 554–55. V. I. Ado, "Berlinskii kongress 1878 g. i pomeshchich'e-burzhuaznoe obshchestvennoe mnenie Rossii," *Istoricheskie Zapiski*, LXIX (1961), 101–41. Charles Jelavich, *Tsarist Russia and Balkan Nationalism* (Berkeley: University of California Press, 1958). "Perepiska I. S. Aksakova s kn. V. A. Cherkasskim (1875–1878)," ed. I. V. Koz'menko, in *Slavianskii sbornik: Slavianskii vopros i russkoe obshchestvo v 1867–1878*, ed. N. M. Druzhinin (Moscow: Publichnaia Biblioteka imeni Lenina, 1948), pp. 136–38, 176–78.

8. Wadham Peacock, "Nicholas of Montenegro and the Czardom of the Serbs," *Nineteenth Century and After*, LXXII (1912), 881–82. M. E. Durham, "King Nikola of Montenegro," *Contemporary Review*, CXIX (April 1921), 473. Spiridion Gopčević, *Geschichte von Montenegro und Albanien* (Gotha: F. A. Perthes, 1914), p. 455. Jagoš Jovanović, pp. 391–94.

9. Durham, p. 473.

10. Peacock, p. 886. Cf. Jagoš Jovanović, pp. 327–99.

11. Joseph Swire, *Albania, the Rise of a Kingdom* (London: Williams & Norgate, Ltd., 1929), pp. 91–100. E. C. Helmreich, *The Diplomacy of the Balkan Wars, 1912–1913* (Cambridge: Harvard University Press, 1938), pp. 91–92. I. G. Senkevich, *Osvoboditel'noe dvizhenie albanskogo naroda v 1905–1912 gg.* (Moscow: Izdatel'stvo Akademii Nauk SSSR, 1959), p. 180. Stavro Skendi, "Beginnings of Albanian Nationalist Trends

in Culture and Education (1878–1912)," *Journal of Central European Affairs*, XII (1953), 356–67.

12. M. E. Durham, *Struggle for Scutari (Turk, Slav, and Albanian)* (London: E. Arnold, 1914), pp. 18–19. Wladimir Giesl von Gieslingen, *Zwei Jahrzehnte im Nahen Osten: Aufzeichnungen des Generals der Kavallerie Baron Wladimir Giesl*, ed. Eduard Ritter von Steinitz (Berlin: Verlag der Kulturpolitik, 1927), p. 223.

13. *Mezhdunarodnye otnosheniia* . . . (hereinafter cited as *MO*), 2nd series, XVIII-1, 13, Arsen'ev to Neratov, May 17, 1911.

14. *Ibid.*, p. 10 note 3, Arsen'ev to Neratov, May 20, 1911.

15. Bogdanovich, p. 39.

16. *MO*, 3d series, I, 165, Report on the question of renewing the military convention with Montenegro, February 3, 1914.

17. *MO*, 2nd series, XVIII-2, 518, Report of Sukhomlinov and Zhilinskii, October 2, 1911.

18. *MO*, XVIII-1, 24, Arsen'ev to Neratov, May 22, 1911.

19. *Ibid.*, 13, p. 10 note 3, p. 117 note 1, Arsen'ev to Neratov, May 17, 20, and June 16, 1911; 108, Potapov to Zhilinskii, June 16, 1911. Giesl, p. 223, E. C. Thaden, "Charykov and Russian Foreign Policy at Constantinople in 1911," *Journal of Central European Affairs*, XVI-1 (1956), 28.

20. *MO*, XVIII-1, p. 118 note 1, Arsen'ev to Neratov, June 19, 1911; 142, Neratov to Nicholas II, June 30, 1911.

21. *British Documents on the Origins of the War 1898–1914*, eds. G. P. Gooch and Harold Temperley (London: HM Stationery Office, 1926–38—hereinafter cited as *BD*), Akers-Douglas to Grey, June 24, 1911.

22. *MO*, XVIII-1, 27, Neratov to Charykov, May 23, 1911.

23. *Novoe Vremia*, 1911, June 14/27.

24. *MO*, XVIII-1, 142.

25. *Ibid.*, 108, Potapov to Zhilinskii, June 16, 1911.

26. *Ibid.*, p. 117 note 1, Arsen'ev to Neratov, June 16, 1911.

27. *Ibid.*, 131, Arsen'ev to Neratov, June 26, 1911; p. 143 note 1, pp. 156–57 note 1, Neratov to Arsen'ev, June 29, 1911.

28. *Ibid.*, 150, Potapov to Zhilinskii, July 2, 1911.

29. *Ibid.*

30. *Ibid.*, p. 179 note 2, Arsen'ev to Neratov, July 4, 1911.

31. *Ibid.*, 25, 26, 27, Neratov to Arsen'ev, Charykov, and the ambassadors in London, Paris, Rome, Berlin, and Vienna, May 23, 1911.

32. *Ibid.*, 43, 67, Charykov to Neratov, May 24, 30, 1911. *Novoe Vremia*, 1911, May 11/24. *Rech'*, 1911, May 11/24 and May 12/25.

33. *MO*, XVIII-1, 99, Shcheglov to Eberhard, June 11, 1911.

34. *Ibid.*, 67, 198, 234, 284, Charykov to Neratov, May 30, July 14 and 21, and August 2, 1911.

35. *Ibid.*, 144, Benckendorff to Neratov, July 1, 1911. Cf. London *Times*, June and July 1911.

36. *BD*, IX-1, 489, Grey to Russell, June 21, 1911.

37. *Ibid.*, 497–99, Grey to Russell, June 24; Grey to Count de Salis, June 26; O'Beirne to Grey, June 26, 1911. *MO*, XVIII-1, 139, Neratov to Benckendorff, June 29, 1911.

38. *BD*, IX-1, 504, Lowther to Grey, July 2, 1911.

39. *Ibid.*, 501, Salis to Grey, June 28, 1911.

40. *MO*, XVIII-1, 139, Neratov to Benckendorff, June 29, 1911.

41. *Ibid.*, 135, Giers to Neratov, June 27, 1911.

42. *Documents diplomatiques français 1871–1914* (Paris: Alfred Costes, 1929–59—hereinafter cited as *DDF*), 2nd series, XIII, 336, Crozier to Cruppi, June 4, 1911. *Österreich-Ungarns Aussenpolitik* . . . , eds. Ludwig Bittner and Hans Uebersberger (Vienna: Bundesverlag, 1930—hereinafter cited as *OUA*), III, 2479, Vienna to Constantinople, March 10, 1911; 2539, private note of Conrad von Hötzendorf to Constantinople, May 11, 1911. *BD*, IX-1, 475–79, Cartwright to Nicolson and Grey, June 7, 8, 12, 14, 1911; 510, Bax-Ironside to Grey, July 24, 1911. Giesl, p. 223. Senkevich, pp. 46–56, 183–84.

43. *MO*, XVIII-1, p. 224 note 4, memo Thurn to Neratov, July 12, 1911; p. 225 note 2, memo Neratov to Thurn, July 18, 1912; 206, 254, Neratov to Nicholas II, July 18, 28, 1911; 212, Korf to Neratov, July 18, 1911; 223, 288, Giers to Neratov, July 19 and August 3, 1911, *ibid.*, 234, 270, 284, Charykov to Neratov, July 21, 30, August 2, 1911; 224, 226, 238, 252, 263, 345, Neratov to Giers, Korf, Charykov, July 20, 23, 27, 29, August 19, 1911; 241, Thurn to Neratov, July 24, 1911; 262, Neratov to Thurn, July 29, 1911. *OUA*, III, 2568, Aehrenthal to Conrad, July 21, 1911. *DDF*, 2nd series, XIII, 358, 372 and XIV, 133, Bompard to Cruppi, June 17, 30, August 1, 1911. *BD*, IX-1, 512, Buchanan to Grey, July 27, 1911.

44. *BD*, IX-1, 480, 495, Lowther and Douglas to Grey, June 14, 24, 1911. *MO*, XVIII-1, 104, p. 225 note 1, Arsen'ev to Neratov, June 15 and July 12, 1911; 132, 139, Neratov to Benckendorff, June 27 and 29, 1911; 188, Charykov to Neratov, July 10, 1911. Durham, *Struggle for Scutari*, pp. 58–71. London *Times*, July 3, 1911.

45. *MO*, XVIII-1, 234, Charykov to Neratov, July 21, 1911. *OUA*, III, 2581, Thurn to Vienna, August 4, 1911.

46. *MO*, XVIII-1, 234, 284, Charykov to Neratov, July 21 and August 2, 1911.

47. Durham, *Struggle for Scutari*, p. 73. London *Times*, July 14, 1911.

48. *MO*, XVIII-1, 198, p. 213 note 4, Charykov and Arsen'ev to Neratov, July 14, 1911.

49. *Ibid.*, 251, Arsen'ev to Neratov, July 26, 1911.

50. Swire, pp. 109–10. Durham, pp. 76–83. *Novoe Vremia*, 1911, July 22/August 4, and August 2/15.

51. *MO*, XVIII-1, 318, Polivanov to Neratov, August 14, 1911.

52. E. C. Thaden, "Montenegro: Russia's Troublesome Ally, 1911–1912," *Journal of Central European Affairs*, XVIII (1958), 123–24. *MO*,

XIX-2, 583, Miller to Sazonov, March 4, 1912; 651, p. 229 note 3, Nicholas I (Montenegro) to Nicholas II, March 17, 1912; p. 293 note 2, Potapov to Zhilinskii, May 3, 1912; XX-1, 19, Potapov to Danilov, May 17, 1912.

CHAPTER 2

1. *MO*, xviii-1, 119, 364, 425, Korf to Neratov, June 20, August 29, September 12, 1911; 360, Neratov to Korf, August 26, 1911; 435, Svechin to Neratov, September 13, 1911. William C. Askew, *Europe and Italy's Acquisition of Libya 1911–1912* (Durham, North Carolina: Duke University Press, 1942), pp. 19–22, 42–76.

2. *MO*, xviii-1, 372, Protocol of the conference of the French and Russian general staffs, August 31, 1911.

3. A. K. Martynenko, "Pozitsiia Rossii v sviazi s provozglasheniem nezavisimosti Bolgarii v 1908 godu.," *Iz istorii russko-bolgarskikh otnoshenii: Sbornik statei*, ed. L. B. Valev, V. N. Kondrat'eva, and S. A. Nikitin (Moscow: Izdatel'stvo Akademii Nauk sssr, 1958), pp. 62–67, 81–104. Bickel, *Russland und die Entstehung des Balkanbundes 1912*, pp. 20–29.

4. Martynenko, pp. 54, 90–96. *BD*, v, 443, Whitehead to Grey, November 13, 1908; 447, Grey to Whitehead, November 14, 1908; 452, Grey to Nicolson, November 17, 1908; 470, Nicolson to Grey, December 1, 1908.

5. Martynenko, pp. 104–12. Bestuzhev, pp. 276–78. *BD*, v, 542, Nicolson to Grey, January 30, 1909; 556, 857, Buchanan to Grey, February 3 and April 28, 1909.

6. Charykov, *Glimpses of High Politics*, p. 239. Bestuzhev, pp. 339–40.

7. *Die auswärtige Politik Serbiens, 1903–1914* (Berlin: Brücken-verlag, 1928–31—hereinafter cited as *APS*), i, 22, Milovanović to Belgrade, October 29, 1908; 115, Gruić to Belgrade, May 25, 1909; 100, 103, Milovanović to Gruić, April 14, 16, 1909. *BD*, v, 427, Buchanan to Grey, November 4, 1908; 432, Lowther to Grey, November 6, 1908; 447, Grey to Whitehead, November 14, 1908; 515, Grey to Cartwright, January 16, 1909. Bickel, pp. 30–32.

8. Bestuzhev, pp. 339–41. Charykov, *Glimpses of High Politics*, pp. 273–76. Erich Lindow, *Freiherr Marschall von Bieberstein als Botschafter in Konstantinopel 1897–1912* (Danzig: A. W. Kafemann, 1934), pp. 97–98, 133–34.

9. *Graf Benckendorffs diplomatischer Schriftwechsel* (Berlin and Leipzig: Verlag Gruyter, 1928—hereinafter cited as *Benckendorff*), ii, 372,

Charykov to Sazonov, February 28, 1911; 392, Charykov to Neratov, April 15, 1911. *MO*, xviii–1, 35, 67, Charykov to Neratov, May 23 and 30, 1911.

10. *MO*, xviii–1, 2, 34, 35, and p. 50 note 2, Charykov to Neratov, May 14, 23 and July 11, 1911; 44, Polivanov to Stolypin, May 24, 1911; also p. 1 note 2. *DDF*, 2nd. series, xiii, 209, Bompard to Cruppi, April 1, 1911. John A. DeNovo, "A Railroad for Turkey," *Business History Review*, xxxiii (Autumn 1959), 304.

11. *MO*, xviii–1, p. 227 note 2, memo of A. Giers, May 11, 1911.

12. *Ibid.*, 231, "Opinion of the general staff of marine affairs on the question of the Straits," July 20, 1911.

13. *Ibid.*, 233, memo of A. Giers, July 21, 1911; 310, Sukhomlinov to Neratov, August 11, 1911.

14. *Ibid.*, 274, Sukhomlinov to Neratov, July 31, 1911.

15. *Ibid.*, enclosure ii in 319, Neratov to Nicholas ii, August 15, 1911.

16. DeNovo, 310–21.

17. In 1900 Russia had persuaded Turkey to grant Russian entrepreneurs the exclusive right to construct railways in northeastern Anatolia. German negotiations with the Porte concerning the projected Berlin-to-Bagdad railway had then raised the general question of railway construction in the Ottoman Empire. Russia lacked the requisite capital to finance Turkish railway construction and, indeed, opposed such construction for military reasons. At this moment the Turks respected Russian power and agreed not to construct railways in this area without first consulting St. Petersburg. (G. L. Bondarevskii, *Bagdadskaia doroga i proniknovenie germanskogo imperializma na Blizhnii Vostok 1888–1903*—Tashkent: Gosudarstvennoe Izdatel'stvo Uzbekskoi ssr, 1955—pp. 209–26.)

18. *MO*, xviii–1, 202 with enclosure, Neratov to Sukhomlinov, Kokovtsov, and Timashev, July 17, 1911. *DDF*, 2nd series, xiv, 150, Bompard to de Selves, August 6, 1911.

19. *MO*, xviii–1, 293, Charykov to Neratov, August 4, 1911.

20. *Ibid.*, 301, Neratov to Kokovtsov, August 7, 1911.

21. *Ibid.*, pp. 360–7 note 2, Kokovtsov to Neratov, August 10, 1911.

22. *MO*, xviii–2, 509, Neratov to Charykov, October 2, 1911. Cf. P. E. Mosely, "Russian Policy in 1911–12," p. 72.

23. *MO*, xviii–2, 466, Izvol'skii to Neratov, September 26, 1911.

24. Langer, "Russia, the Straits Question and the Origins of the Balkan League, 1908–1912," *Political Science Quarterly*, xliii, 360.

25. This date is given in Stieve's collection of Izvol'skii's correspondence: Izvol'skii to Neratov, September 26, 1911, *Der diplomatische Schriftwechsel Iswolskis 1911–1914* (Berlin: Deutsche Verlagsgesellschaft für Politik und Geschichte, 1925—hereinafter cited as *Schriftwechsel Iswolskis*), i, 125.

26. *MO*, xviii–2, 483, Neratov to Charykov, September 29, 1911.

27. *Ibid.*, 496, 497, 498, Charykov to Neratov, September 30, 1911.

146

Notes to Chapter 2

28. *Ibid.*, 498.

29. *Ibid.*, 496; cf. 470, Charykov to Neratov, September 26, 1911.

30. *Ibid.*, 496.

31. *Ibid.*, 509 with enclosure, 690, Neratov to Charykov, October 2 and 22, 1911; xviii–1, pp. 306–7 note 2, Kokovtsov to Neratov, August 10, 1911.

32. Charykov acknowledged receipt of these instructions in a letter of October 7: *MO*, xviii–2, 556.

33. *Ibid.*, 538, 548, 550, Neratov to Charykov, October 6 and 7, 1911.

34. *Ibid.*, 570, Charykov to Neratov, October 9, 1911.

35. N. V. Charykov, "Sazonoff," *Contemporary Review*, cxxxiii (1928), 287.

36. During nine months (March–December 1911) while Sazonov convalesced from a serious illness in Switzerland, his assistant Neratov administered the foreign office. Although Neratov had been a classmate of Sazonov at the exclusive St. Petersburg Alexander Lyceum, he was essentially a routine bureaucrat and a man with little authority. He had spent his entire diplomatic career in the St. Petersburg foreign office. As his colleagues put it, he was sort of a Jules Verne who had traveled around the world many times in his official reports without leaving his desk in St. Petersburg. A Russian journalist, Eugene Schelking, described him in the following words:

> His mental capacity was hardly mediocre. His entire success he owed to his zeal and to his very thorough knowledge of the contents of our diplomatic archives. He had been at college with Sazonoff, who later appointed him Assistant Minister, and since then he always had the sense to make himself indispensable to all foreign ministers, despite their widely divergent mentalities and ideas . . . he was ever the same as on the first day he entered the service, always very eager to execute the orders of his superiors, a hard worker, but painfully narrow minded, and wholly devoid of the attributes of the great statesman he fondly imagined he resembled.

(Eugene de Schelking, *Suicide of Monarchy: Recollections of a Diplomat—* Toronto: The Macmillan Company of Canada, Ltd., 1918—pp. 229–30. *Istoricheskii ocherk Imperatorskago Aleksandrovskago [b. Tsarskosel'skago] Litseia*, ed. A. N. Iakhontov—Paris: Izdanie Ob"edineniia b. Vospitannikov Imperatorskago Litseia, 1936—pp. 203–4. Solov'ev, p. 29.

37. *MO*, xviii–2, 564, Charykov to Neratov, October 8, 1911.

38. *Ibid.*, 570, Charykov to Neratov, October 9, 1911.

39. *Ibid.*, 590, Charykov to Neratov, October 11, 1911.

40. *Ibid.*, 595, Neratov to Charykov, October 12, 1911.

41. *Ibid.*, 601, Charykov to Neratov, October 12, 1911; 602, Charykov to Said Pasha, October 12, 1911.

42. N. V. Charykov, *Glimpses of High Politics.*

43. *MO*, xvIII-2, 596, Izvol'skii to Neratov, October 12, 1911.

44. Taube, p. 209.

45. *MO*, xvIII-2, 629, Charykov to Neratov, October 14, 1911; also p. 114 note 5.

46. *Ibid.*, 690, Neratov to Charykov, October 22, 1911; also p. 206 note 2.

47. *Ibid.*, 690, Neratov to Charykov, October 22, 1911.

48. *Ibid.*, 628, Charykov to Neratov, October 14, 1911.

49. *Ibid.*, 704, Charykov to Neratov, October 23, 1911; also p. 203 note 3. *OUA*, III, 2800, Pallavicini to Aehrenthal, October 21, 1911.

50. *Novoe Vremia*, 1911, October 11/24.

51. *Rech'*, 1911, October 14/27 and October 23/November 5.

52. *Rech'*, 1911, October 14/27, 18/31, October 23/November 5, and October 26/November 8.

53. *MO*, xvIII-2, 796, Neratov to Hartwig and Nekliudov, November 4, 1911.

54. *Ibid.*, 780, Neratov to Osten-Sacken, November 2, 1911; 820, Neratov to Charykov, November 7, 1911.

55. *Ibid.*, 498, Charykov to Neratov, September 30, 1911. I. S. Galkin, "Demarsh Charykova v 1911 g. i pozitsiia evropeiskikh derzhav," in *Iz istorii obshchestvennykh dvizhenii i mezhdunarodnykh otnoshenii: Sbornik statei v pamiat' Akademika Evgeniia Viktorovicha Tarle*, ed. A. M. Pankratova *et al.* (Moscow: Izdatel'stvo Akademii Nauk SSSR, 1957), p. 640.

56. *MO*, xvIII-2, 610, Dolgorukii to Neratov, October 13, 1911.

57. *GP*, xxx-1, 10976, Bethmann-Hollweg to William II, November 24, 1911; 10971, 10973, Kiderlen-Wächter to William II and Tschirschky, November 19, 1911. *MO*, xIX-1, 76, Osten-Sacken to Neratov, November 23, 1911. Galkin, "Demarsh Charykova," p. 651. Oswald Hauser, "Die englisch-russische Konvention von 1907 und die Meerengenfrage," *Geschichtliche Kräfte und Entscheidungen: Festschrift zum fünfundsechzigsten Geburtstage von Otto Becker*, ed. Martin Göhring and Alexander Scharff (Wiesbaden: Franz Steiner Verlag, 1954), p. 253. Askew, *Acquisition of Libya*, pp. 137–38.

58. Askew, *Acquisition of Libya*, pp. 137–39. *OUA*, III, 2968, A. Hoyos to Berlin, November 22, 1911; 3023, Aehrenthal to Berlin, November 30, 1911.

59. Galkin, "Demarsh Charykova," pp. 652–53. *OUA*, III, 2998, Vienna to St. Petersburg, November 26, 1911; 3008, 3103, Constantinople to Vienna, November 28, December 14, 1911; 3047, Vienna to Constantinople, December 5, 1911. *GP*, xxx-1, 10947, Tschirschky to Berlin, November 20, 1911. German policy changed in December, especially because of the insistence of German Ambassador Marschall von Bieberstein that Germany risked losing Turkish friendship unless she defended the Porte against

Russian diplomatic pressure. However, this happened after the Russian Government had lost interest in Charykov's ideas.

60. *MO*, xviii-2, 623, Izvol'skii to Neratov, October 14, 1911. *DDF*, 2nd series, xiv, 441, de Selves to Bompard, October 15, 1911.

61. *MO*, xviii-2, 723, Benckendorff to Neratov, October 25, 1911.

62. *Ibid.*, 778, Neratov to Izvol'skii, November 2, 1911.

63. Raymond Poincaré, *Au service de la France* (Paris: Librairie Plon: 1926–33), i, 297–303. *DDF*, 3d series, i, 465, Bompard to de Selves, January 13, 1912. Ima Christina Barlow, *The Agadir Crisis* (Chapel Hill, N. C.: University of North Carolina Press, 1940), pp. 357–62.

64. *DDF*, 3d series, i, 106, de Selves to Daeschner, November 13, 1911; 114, Daeschner to de Selves, November 14, 1911.

65. Askew, *Europe and Italy's Acquisition of Libya*, p. 132.

66. *BD*, ix-1, 221, Grey to Rodd, July 28, 1911; 231, Grey to Nicolson, September 19, 1911.

67. *Ibid.*, Appendix iv, pp. 779–80, Tewfik Pasha to Grey, October 31, 1911; p. 780, Grey's memorandum, October 31, 1911.

68. *MO*, xviii-2, 789, 824, Benckendorff to Neratov, November 3, 7, 1911. *DDF*, 3d series, i, 53, Bompard to de Selves, November 8, 1911.

69. *BD*, ix-1, p. 521, minute to no. 530.

70. *MO*, xviii-2, 700, 723, 824, Benckendorff to Neratov, October 23 and 25, November 7, 1911; see also pp. 214–15 note 1.

71. *Ibid.*, 723, 824; 779, Neratov to Benckendorff, November 2, 1911; 836, Benckendorff to Neratov, November 8, 1911.

72. *BD*, ix-1, 346, Grey to Lowther, December 12, 1911.

73. See *BD*, ix-1, 335, 340 with minutes, 346, 348.

74. *DDF*, 3d series, i, 433, de Selves to Izvol'skii, January 4, 1912.

75. Askew, *Europe and Italy's Acquisition of Libya*, pp. 106–8, 135–36, 160–62.

76. See especially *GP*, xxx-1, 10978, Marschall to Berlin, December 1, 1911; also 10982, 10983, 10987.

77. *DDF*, 3d series, i, 28, Bompard to de Selves, November 6, 1911.

78. *Ibid.*, 53, Bompard to de Selves, November 8, 1911.

79. *Ibid.*, 94, Daeschner to de Selves, November 11, 1911.

80. *MO*, xviii-2, 806, Hartwig to Neratov, November 5, 1911; xix-1, 66, Nekliudov to Neratov, November 22, 1911.

81. *MO*, xix-1, 7, Charykov to Neratov, November 14, 1911.

82. *Ibid.*, 24, Neratov to Fredericks, November 17, 1911.

83. *Ibid.*, 124, Charykov to Neratov, November 30, 1911.

84. *Ibid.*, 6, Charykov to Neratov, November 14, 1911.

85. See the telegrams sent by Charykov and Dolgorukii to Neratov and by Neratov to the Russian ambassadors in Berlin, Constantinople, London, Paris, Rome, and Vienna, November 20 and 25, 1911, *ibid.*, 44, 93, and 95.

86. *BD*, ix–1, 319, Lowther to Grey, November 25, 1911.

87. Charykov, *Glimpses of High Politics*, p. 277.

88. *MO*, xix–1, 48, Neratov to Dolgorukii and Charykov, November 21, 1911; 93, Neratov to Izvol'skii, Benckendorff, Dolgorukii, N. Giers, and Charykov, November 25, 1911.

89. *Ibid.*, 27, Neratov to Charykov, November 17, 1911.

90. *Ibid.*, 124, "Prilozhenie" to dispatch of Charykov to Neratov, November 30, 1911.

91. *Ibid.*, 164, Neratov to Charykov, December 6, 1911.

92. *Ibid.*, p. 173 note 2; 186, Sazonov to Neratov, December 9, 1911.

93. N. V. Charykov, "Sazonoff," p. 287.

CHAPTER 3

1. Stavrianos, *Balkan Federation*, pp. 111–13, 128–29, 133–36. Vucinich, pp. 132–33. Edouard Driault and Michel Lhéritier, *Histoire diplomatique de la Grèce de 1821 à nos jours* (Paris: Presses Universitaires de France, 1925–26), iv, 290–91.

2. Dino G. K'osev, *Istoriia na makedonskoto natsionalno revoliutsionno dvizhenie* (Sofia: Izdatelstvo na Natsionalniia Otechestveniia Front, 1954), pp. 37–39, 189, 402–7. Slobodan Jovanović, *Vlada Aleksandra Obrenovića* (Belgrade: Izdavačko i Knjižarsko Preduzeće Geca Kon A. D., 1934–36), i, 147–70. Langer, *Diplomacy of Imperialism*, i, 306–12, 355. Stavrianos, *The Balkans since 1453*, pp. 374, 519–21. Bŭlgarska Akademiia na Naukite, *Istoriia na Bŭlgariia*, ed. Dimitŭr Kosev, Khristo Khristov, *et al.* (Sofia: Dŭrzhavno Izdatelstvo "Nauka i izkustvo," 1954–55), i, 352–54.

3. K'osev, pp. 66–68.

4. Sumner, *Russia and the Balkans*, pp. 662–63.

5. K'osev, p. 154.

6. *Ibid.*, pp. 108–33, 316–20.

7. *Ibid.*, pp. 182–212, 341–72.

8. *Ibid.*, pp. 139–40, 372, 395. Léon Lamouche, *Quinze ans d'histoire balkanique (1904–1918)* (Paris: Payot, 1928), pp. 52–66. Vucinich, pp. 154–60.

9. *MO*, xviii–1, 50, Nekliudov to Neratov, May 25, 1911.

10. *MO*, xix–1, 145, Hartwig to Neratov, December 3, 1911.

11. K'osev, pp. 139–40. Lamouche, *Quinze ans d'histoire balkanique*, pp. 115–16. A. Toshev, *Balkanskite voini* (Sofia: Knigoizdatelstvo "Fakel," 1929), i, 308–9, 361. *Istoriia na Bŭlgariia*, ii, 149, 222–23. I. E. Geshov,

Notes to Chapter 3

The Balkan League, tr. Constantin Mincoff (London: John Murray, 1915), pp. 16–17, 38–40. Basil Laourdas, *La lotta per la Macedonia dal 1903 al 1908* (Thesalonike: Hetaireia Makedonikon Spoudon Hidryma Meleton Chersonesou tou Haimou, 1962), pp. 1–14.

12. Vucinich, pp. 132–57.

13. Stavrianos, *The Balkans since 1453*, pp. 374–75, 437, 519. *Istoriia na Bŭlgariia*, ii, 121–23.

14. Langer, *Diplomacy of Imperialism*, ii, 310–11. Driault and Lhéritier, *Histoire diplomatique de la Grèce*, iv, 178, 182–86. S. Jovanović, *Vlada Aleksandra Obrenovića*, ii, 364–68. Vucinich, pp. 156–57. Bickel, pp. 20–28. Geshov, *Balkan League*, pp. 2–10.

15. E. C. Helmreich and C. E. Black, "The Russo-Bulgarian Military Convention of 1902," *Journal of Modern History*, ix (December 1937), 471–82. S. Danev, *Ocherki na diplomaticheskata istoriia na balkanskite dŭrzhavi* (Sofia: Pechatnitsa "Nov Zhivot," 1931), p. 106. *Istoriia na Bŭlgariia*, ii, 192–93. A. F. Pribram, *The Secret Treaties of Austria-Hungary, 1879–1914*, ed. A. C. Coolidge (Cambridge: Harvard University Press, 1920), i, 203–7.

16. For a recent Bulgarian account of the views and motivations of Russophobes in Bulgaria, see Tushe Vlakhov, "Vŭnshnata politika na Ferdinand i Balkanskiia Sŭiuz," *Istoricheski Pregled*, nos. 4–5 (1950), pp. 422–44.

17. S. Jovanović, *Vlada Aleksandra Obrenovića*, i, 125–43; ii, 219–20, 352–57, 441–42; iii, 62, 97–101. Vucinich, pp. 5–7. Dimitrije Popović, "Nikola Pašić i Rusija: Iz mojih ličnih sečanje," *Godišnjica Nikole Čupnica*, xlvi (1937), 137.

18. Vucinich, pp. 67–68.

19. Vucinich, pp. 125–32, 158–69. E. C. Helmreich, *The Diplomacy of the Balkan Wars 1912–1913* (Cambridge: Harvard University Press, 1938), pp. 40–41. S. B. Fay, *The Origins of the World War*, 2nd ed. (New York: Macmillan, 1935), ii, 80–92. B. E. Schmitt, *The Coming of the War, 1914* (New York: Charles Scribner's Sons, 1930), i, 179–84. Dimitrije Djordjević, *Carinski rat Austro-Ugarske i Srbije 1906–1911* (Belgrade: Izdanje Istorijski Institut, 1962).

20. Stavrianos, *The Balkans since 1453*, pp. 526–28. Assen I. Krainikowsky, *La question de Macédoine et la diplomatie européenne* (Paris: Librairie Marcel Rivière et Co., 1938), pp. 208–17. A. F. Miller, "Mladoturetskaia revoliutsiia," *Pervaia russkaia revoliutsiia 1905–1907 gg. i mezhdunarodnoe revoliutsionnoe dvizhenie* (Moscow: Gospolitizdat, 1956), ii, 342–47.

21. *Benckendorff*, ii, 405, Hartwig to Neratov, May 27, 1911.

22. *MO*, xviii–1, 65, Neratov to Hartwig and notation by Nicholas ii, May 30, 1911.

23. *Ibid.*, enclosure in Appendix iii, Romanovskii to quarter-master division of the general staff, August 2, 1911; Appendix i, Nekliudov to

Neratov, August 5, 1911; Appendix II, Neratov to Nicholas II, August 12, 1911; Appendix III, Polivanov to Neratov, August 24, 1911; Appendix IV, Neratov to Polivanov, August 26, 1911.

24. *Ibid.*, 6, Urusov to Neratov, May 15, 1911; *MO*, XVIII-2, 526, Neratov to Nekliudov, October 4, 1911; XVIII-2, 598, Nekliudov to Neratov, October 12, 1911.

25. *MO*, XVIII-1, 6.

26. *BD*. IX-1, 737 with minute, Barclay to Grey, September 23, 1912. Cf. Helmreich, *Diplomacy of the Balkan Wars*, pp. 154–55.

27. *MO*, XVIII-2, 512, Nekliudov to Neratov, October 2, 1911.

28. *Ibid.*, 526, Neratov to Nekliudov, October 4, 1911.

29. *Ibid.*, 752, Neratov to Nekliudov, October 30, 1911.

30. *Ibid.*, 850, Neratov to Hartwig, November 10, 1911.

31. Nicolson, *Portrait of a Diplomatist*, pp. 256–57. A. V. Nekliudov, *Diplomatic Reminiscences before and during the World War, 1911–1917*, tr. Alexandra Paget (London: J. Murray, 1920), p. 49.

32. Marco [Božin Simić], "Nikola Hartvig: Spoljna politika Srbije pred Svetski Rat," *Nova Evropa*, knjiga XVII, broj 8 (April 26, 1928), pp. 271–72. B. E. Schmitt, *The Coming of the War*, I, 200–201. Hans Uebersberger, *Österreich zwischen Russland und Serbien* (Köln-Graz: Verlag Hermann Böhlaus Nachf., 1958), p. 251.

33. Schelking, *Suicide of Monarchy*, pp. 241–42.

34. Marco, "Nikola Hartvig," p. 259. Cf. Uebersberger, *Österreich zwischen Russland und Serbien*, pp. 52, 298.

35. Nekliudov, *Diplomatic Reminiscences*, pp. 49–50.

36. Marco, "Nikola Hartvig," p. 257.

37. *MO*, XVIII-2, 806, Hartwig to Neratov, November 11, 1911.

38. *MO*, XIX-1, 277, Hartwig to Sazonov, December 28, 1911.

39. *MO*, XIX-2, 448, Hartwig to Sazonov, February 11, 1912.

40. *MO*, XVIII-2, 697; and XIX-1, 39, p. 73 note 2, Hartwig to Neratov, October 22, November 19, December 3, 1911.

41. Giesl, *Zweijahrzehnte im Nahen Orient*, p. 260.

42. *MO*, XIX-2, 643, Giers to Sazonov, March 16, 1912.

43. Sazonov, *Fateful Years 1909–1916* (New York: F. A. Stockes, 1928), p. 80. *Die internationalen Beziehungen im Zeitalter des Imperialismus*, ed. Otto Hoetzsch (Berlin: Steiniger Verlag, 1942—hereinafter cited as *IB*), 3d series, IV-1, 354, Sazonov to Hartwig, November 27, 1912.

44. Marco, "Nikola Hartwig," p. 258.

45. Nekliudov, *Diplomatic Reminiscences*, pp. 66, 90–91, 201, 218–19. Schelking, *Suicide of Monarchy*, pp. 244–45.

46. *MO*, XVIII-2, 512, Nekliudov to Neratov, October 2, 1911; 526, Neratov to Nekliudov, October 4, 1911.

47. *Ibid.*, 512, 598, 758, Nekliudov to Neratov, October 2, 12, 30, 1911. The Sanjak of Novibazar was a narrow strip separating Serbia from Montenegro. From the Congress of Berlin until 1908 it was garrisoned by

Austria-Hungary but remained under Turkish civil administration; Austrian troops were evacuated in 1908. Old Serbia is the present Autonomous Kosovo-Metohija Region that contains most of Yugoslavia's sizeable Albanian minority. It remained in Turkish hands until 1913. Both the Sanjak and Old Serbia had long been coveted by Serbian nationalists.

48. Nekliudov, *Diplomatic Reminiscences,* p. 45.

49. *MO,* xviii–2, 758, 769, Nekliudov to Neratov, October 30 and 31, 1911.

50. *Ibid.,* 769.

51. *Ibid.;* also *MO,* xix–1, 66, Nekliudov to Neratov, November 22, 1911.

52. Nekliudov, *Diplomatic Reminiscences,* p. 50.

53. *MO,* xviii–2, 758.

54. *MO,* xviii–1, Appendix i, Nekliudov to Neratov, August 5, 1911.

55. *MO,* xix–1, p. 258 note 1, Nekliudov to Sazonov, December 29, 1911.

56. Toshev, *Balkanskite voini,* i, 287–90, 294–95, 301–2.

57. *Ibid.,* pp. 298–300 and 307–10. *MO,* xviii–1, pp. 3–4 note 7, and no. 6, Urusov to Neratov, April 26, May 11 and 15, 1911; pp. 3–4 note 7, Hartwig to Neratov, April 29, 1911; no. 31, Hartwig to Neratov, May 23, 1912; no. 50, Nekliudov to Neratov, May 25, 1911.

58. *MO,* xviii–1, 50 and 298, Nekliudov to Neratov, May 25 and August 5, 1911. Geshov, pp. 2–7; Lamouche, pp. 115–16. M., "The Balkan League, History of its Formation," *Fortnightly Review,* new series, xcii (March 1913), 430–39. J. D. Bourchier, "Articles on the Origin of the Balkan League," London *Times,* June 5, 1913.

59. Geshov, p. 8. London *Times,* October 3, 1911.

60. *MO,* xviii–1, p. 29 note 1, and nos. 77 and 298, Nekliudov to Neratov, May 25, June 2, August 5, 1911. Geshov, p. 9. London *Times,* November 22, 1911.

61. Geshov, pp. 9–10.

62. Askew, *Acquisition of Libya,* pp. 47–51. *MO,* xviii–1, 119, 364, 425, Korf to Neratov, June 20, August 29, September 12, 1911; 410, 435, Svechin to Neratov, September 7 and 13, 1911; 360, Neratov to Korf, August 26, 1911.

63. Geshov, pp. 10–12. Nadejda Muir, *Dimitri Stancioff: Patriot and Cosmopolitan 1864–1940* (London: J. Murray, 1957), pp. 140–41.

64. *MO,* xviii–2, 545, Hartwig to Neratov, October 6, 1911. Geshov, pp. 10–13.

65. Geshov, pp. 13–14.

66. *Ibid.,* pp. 12–15.

67. The Serbo-Bulgarian alliance negotiations were conducted in utmost secrecy. Only the Russian and British governments learned of these negotiations in the course of October 1911; other European governments were not informed. The general public in Europe and Russia heard about

Balkan confederation including Turkey in the fall of 1911 but knew nothing about the Serbo-Bulgarian negotiations until some time after they had been concluded in the spring of 1912.

When Hartwig requested permission to go to Sofia in May 1911, Neratov answered in the following words: "As desirable as is our assistance to mutual discussions of the Serbs and Bulgarians, under the present circumstances your trip to Sofia for this purpose is likely to attract attention and excite suppositions about the existence of negotiations, for which utmost secrecy serves as the best assurance of success." (*MO*, xviii–1, 65, Neratov to Hartwig, May 30, 1911.)

68. *Ibid.*, pp. 15–17; *MO*, xviii–2, 625, Hartwig to Neratov, October 14, 1911.

69. Geshov, p. 16.

70. *Ibid.*, p. 17.

71. *Ibid.*, pp. 17–36.

72. *MO*, xviii–2, 526, Neratov to Nekliudov, October 4, 1911.

73. *Ibid.*, 598, 758, Nekliudov to Neratov, October 12, 30, 1911.

74. *Ibid.*, 563, 696, Hartwig to Neratov, October 8, 22, 1911.

75. *Ibid.*, 506, 697; and *MO*, xix–1, 39, Hartwig to Neratov, October 1, 22, November 19, 1911.

76. Nekliudov, p. 45.

77. *OUA*, iii, 2809, Denkschrift Hietzing, October 22, 1911.

78. *Ibid.*, 2823, Aehrenthal to Giesl, October 25, 1911.

79. *MO*, xviii–2, 845, Giers to Neratov, November 9, 1911.

80. *Ibid.*, 526, Neratov to Nekliudov, October 4, 1911; 634, Neratov to Urusov, October 15, 1911; 781, Neratov to Giers, November 2, 1911; xix–1, 49, Neratov to Kokovtsov and Sukhomlinov, November 21, 1911.

81. *MO*, xix–1, 171, Giers to Neratov, December 7, 1911.

82. Conrad von Hötzendorf, *Aus meiner Dienstzeit* (Vienna: Rikola Verlag, 1921–25), i, 57–63, 153–75, 640–55; ii, 11, 281–83, 436–52. Uebersberger, *Österreich zwischen Russland und Serbien*, pp. 65–66. *OUA*, iii, 2809, Denkschrift Hietzing, October 22, 1911.

83. *MO*, xviii–2, 696, Hartwig to Neratov, October 22, 1911.

84. *Ibid.*, 757, Nekliudov to Neratov, October 30, 1911.

85. *Ibid.*

86. During the second half of November and the early part of December 1911, Neratov made no changes in the policies of the previous months. Thus the possibility of a Balkan confederation including Turkey was left open and no new commitments to Serbia and Bulgaria were undertaken.

87. *MO*, xviii–2, 801, Hartwig to Neratov, November 4, 1911. Geshov, pp. 19–21.

88. *MO*, xviii–2, 813, Nekliudov to Neratov, November 6, 1911.

89. Geshov, pp. 19–21.

90. *MO*, xix–1, 4, Nekliudov to Neratov, November 14, 1911.

91. Geshov, pp. 23–25. *MO*, xviii–2, 829, Hartwig to Neratov, November 7, 1911.

92. Geshov, pp. 24–33. *MO*, xix–1, 145, Hartwig to Neratov, December 3, 1911.

93. *MO*, xviii–2, 850, Neratov to Hartwig, November 10, 1911; xix–1, 163, Neratov to Hartwig and Nekliudov, December 6, 1911.

94. *MO*, xix–1, 163.

95. *Ibid.*, p. 151 note 3, Nekliudov to Neratov, December 11, 1911.

96. *MO*, xviii–2, 850, Neratov to Hartwig, November 10, 1911; *MO*, xix–1, 162, Neratov to Nekliudov, December 6, 1911; xix, 163, Neratov to Hartwig and Nekliudov, December 6, 1911.

CHAPTER 4

1. Luigi Albertini, *The Origins of the War of 1914*, tr. and ed. Isabella M. Massey (London: Oxford University Press, 1952–57), i, 366.

2. Taube, p. 249.

3. Albertini, i, 367.

4. Kiendl, pp. 7–8. P. N. Miliukov, *Vospominaniia*, eds. M. N. Karpovich and B. I. El'kin (New York: Izdatel'stvo imeni Chekhova, 1955), ii, 110. Taube, p. 249.

5. Bickel, pp. 99–100.

6. Langer, "Straits Question," 335.

7. Bestuzhev, pp. 219–20, 339–44.

8. *Benckendorff*, i, 290, Sazonov to Sementovskii-Kurilo, September 28, 1910.

9. *MO*, xix–1, 171, Giers to Neratov, December 7, 1911.

10. *Ibid.*, 244, 361, Giers to Sazonov, December 21, 1911, January 17, 1912. Uebersberger, *Österreich zwischen Russland und Serbien*, pp. 65–66.

11. *MO*, xviii–1, 93, Giers to Neratov, June 7, 1911. Herbert Feis, *Europe the World's Banker 1870–1914* (New Haven: Yale University Press, 1930), p. 279.

12. *MO*, xviii–1, 93. *OUA*, iii, 2501, Giskra to Vienna, April 14, 1911. Cemal Tukim, *Die politischen Beziehungen zwischen Österreich-Ungarn und Bulgarien von 1908 bis zum Bukarester Frieden* (Hamburg: H. Christian, 1936), p. 80. Hans R. Madol, *Ferdinand von Bulgarien: Der Traum von Byzanz* (Berlin: Universitas, 1931), pp. 126–28.

13. *MO*, xviii–1, 93. Tukim, p. 80. *OUA*, iii, 2547, Aehrenthal to Sofia, June 23, 1911.

14. *MO*, xix-2, 710, Urusov to Sazonov, March 30, 1912. *OUA*, iv, 3539, Tarnowski to Vienna, May 23, 1912.

15. *MO*, xix-1, 203, Sazonov to Giers, December 14, 1911.

16. *OUA*, iii, 2774, Giesl to Vienna, October 17, 1911.

17, *Ibid.*, 2857, Giesl to Vienna, November 1, 1911.

18. *Ibid.*, 2580, 3247, Giesl to Vienna, August 4, 1911, January 25, 1912; 2903, Aehrenthal to Giesl, November 11, 1911. Giesl, pp. 224–25.

19. *OUA*, iii, 2903. *MO*, xix-1, p. 220 note 2, Arsen'ev to Sazonov, December 18, 1911; 425, Sazonov to Nicholas ii, February 6, 1912.

20. *MO*, xix-2, 477, 521, Miller to Sazonov, February 15 and 23, 1912; p. 175 note 3, Arsen'ev to Sazonov, April 22, 1912. Giesl, p. 224.

21. *MO*, xix-1, p. 180 note 1, Arsen'ev to Sazonov, December 12, 1911.

22. *MO*, xix-2, 425, Sazonov to Nicholas ii, February 6, 1912; 500, Sazonov to Miller, February 20, 1912.

23. *Ibid.*, 425.

24. *Ibid.*, 500.

25. Giesl, p. 224. Cf. *MO*, xix-2, p. 138 note 4, Miller to Sazonov, February 14, 1912.

26. Sazonov, p. 55.

27. *Ibid.*

28. *MO*, xix-2, 878, Sazonov's memorandum, May 10, 1912.

29. *MO*, xix-1, 145, Hartwig to Neratov, December 3, 1911.

30. *Ibid.*, 228, Hartwig to Neratov, December 19, 1911.

31. *Ibid.*, p. 229 note 2, Nekliudov to Hartwig, December 20, 1911.

32. *Ibid.*, 245, Hartwig to Nekliudov, December 21, 1911.

33. *Ibid.*, 277, Hartwig to Sazonov, December 28, 1911.

34. Geshov, p. 33.

35. *MO*, xix-1, 291, Nekliudov to Hartwig, December 31, 1911 (Hartwig's letter to Nekliudov of December 28 is contained within the text of Nekliudov's letter of December 31)

36. *Ibid.*, 277, Hartwig to Sazonov, December 28, 1911.

37. *Ibid.*, 293, Sazonov to Nekliudov, January 1, 1912.

38. *Ibid.*, p. 258 note 1, Nekliudov to Sazonov, December 29, 1911.

39. *Ibid.*, 313, Nekliudov to Sazonov, January 4, 1912.

40. *Ibid.*, 327, Nekliudov to Sazonov, January 6, 1912.

41. *Ibid.*, 338, Nekliudov to Sazonov, January 11, 1912.

42. *Ibid.*, 354, Nekliudov to Sazonov, January 16, 1912.

43. *Ibid*

44. *MO*, xix-2, 371, Sazonov to Hartwig, January 19, 1912.

45. *Ibid.*, 374, Hartwig to Sazonov, January 20, 1912.

46. *Ibid.*

47. *Ibid.*, 448, Hartwig to Sazonov, February 11, 1912.

48. *Ibid.*, 388, Sazonov to Hartwig, January 25, 1912; p. 40 note 3, Sazonov to Nekliudov, January 25, 1912.

49. On the Serbian cabinet crisis, *ibid.*, 439, 449, Hartwig to Sazonov, February 8 and 11, 1912; 443, Artamonov to quartermaster division of general staff, February 10, 1912.

50. *Ibid.*, p. 147 note 1, Nekliudov to Sazonov, February 16, 1912.

51. *Ibid.*, p. 161 note 3, Nekliudov to Sazonov, February 15, 1912; p. 161 note 4, Romanovskii to quartermaster division of the general staff, February 14, 1912; 501, Romanovskii to Sazonov, February 20, 1912; p. 162 note 2, Nekliudov to Sazonov, February 23, 1912.

52. *Ibid.*, 489, Sazonov to Hartwig, February 17, 1912.

53. *Ibid.*, 520, Nekliudov to Sazonov, February 23, 1912.

54. *Ibid.*, 512, Hartwig to Sazonov, February 21, 1912.

55. *Ibid.*, 527, Sazonov to Hartwig, February 24, 1912.

56. *Ibid.*, 528, Sazonov to Nekliudov, February 24, 1912; p. 180 note 8.

57. *Ibid.*, p. 186 note 1.

58. *MO*, xix–1, 291, Nekliudov to Hartwig, December 31, 1911.

59. *MO*, xix–2, 535, Hartwig to Nekliudov, February 24, 1912.

60. *Ibid.*, pp. 187–88 note 2, Nekliudov to Hartwig, February 28, 1911.

61. *Ibid.*, 546, Nekliudov to Sazonov, February 27, 1912.

62. *Ibid.*, p. 199 note 1, Sazonov to Hartwig and Nekliudov, March 1, 1912.

63. *Ibid.*, 774, Sazonov to Hartwig, April 18, 1912; 775, Sazonov to Polivanov, April 18, 1912. Later Sazonov seems to have changed his mind, for a special Serbian delegation, headed by Pašić, was sent to Russia with a copy of the treaty of alliance in June 1912. See the letter of King Peter to Nicholas ii, June 8, 1912, *MO*, xx–1, 159.

64. *MO*, xix–2, 731, Urusov to Sazonov, April 4, 1912; p. 376 note 3, Sazonov to Izvol'skii and Urusov, April 6, 1912; 878, Sazonov's memorandum, May 10, 1912.

65. *Ibid.*, 536, p. 188 note 4, Nekliudov to Sazonov, February 25, April 30, 1912; p. 188 note 4, Sazonov to Nekliudov, July 5, 1912; 678, Urusov to Sazonov, March 24, 1912; p. 317 note 8, Sazonov to Urusov, March 27, 1912. Nekliudov, pp. 59–61.

66. *MO*, xix–2, 599, Hartwig to Sazonov, March 7, 1912.

67. *Ibid.*, 613, Hartwig to Sazonov, March 11, 1912.

68. *Ibid.*, 625, Nekliudov's memorandum on conversation with King Ferdinand, March 13, 1912; 626, Romanovskii to quartermaster division of general staff, March 13, 1912.

69. Geshov, Appendix i, pp. 112–14. The treaty and secret annex have also been published as enclosures in *MO*, xix–2, 625, and in the *Krasnyi Arkhiv*, ix, no. 79, pp. 23–26.

70. Geshov, Appendix ii, pp. 114–15.

71. *MO*, xix–2, 613, Hartwig to Sazonov, March 11, 1912.

72. *MO*, xx–1, 283, Nekliudov to Sazonov, July 10, 1912.

RUSSIA AND THE BALKAN ALLIANCE

73. *Ibid.*, p. 87 note 4, and no. 100, Nekliudov to Sazonov, May 21, 29, 1912.

74. *Ibid.*, 278, Sazonov to Nekliudov, July 8, 1912; p. 271 notes 4 and 7.

75. *Ibid.*, 64, Sazonov to Nekliudov, May 23, 1912. Cf. *MO*, xix–2, 878, Sazonov's memorandum, May 10, 1912.

76. *MO*, xix–2, 708, Sazonov to Izvol'skii, March 30, 1912.

77. *Ibid.*, 625, Nekliudov's memorandum, March 13, 1912.

78. *Ibid.*, 878; xx–1, 64.

79. Geshov, pp. 115–16.

80. *MO*, xix–2, 626, Romanovskii to quartermaster division of the general staff, March 13, 1912.

81. Cf. P. E. Mosely, "Russian Policy in 1911–12," p. 76.

82. Geshov, pp. 116–17.

83. *MO*, xix–2, 772, Romanovskii to quartermaster division of the general staff, April 17, 1912.

84. Geshov, Appendix iii, pp. 117–22.

85. *Ibid.*, Appendices iii and iv, pp. 117–24.

86. *MO*, xx–2, 660, 762, Artamonov to Danilov, September 10 and 24, 1912; 950, Hartwig to Neratov, October 8, 1912.

87. Ivan I. Fichev, *Balkanskata voina 1912–1913* (Sofia: Dŭrzhavna Pechatnitsa, 1940), pp. 62–63.

88. *MO*, xx–1, 308, Hartwig to Neratov, July 16, 1912; xx–2, 555, Strandtman to Sazonov, August 25, 1912; xx–2, 660, Artamonov to Danilov, September 10, 1912.

89. *MO*, xx–2, 678 and p. 206 note 1, Hartwig to Sazonov, September 13, 1912. London *Times*, September 13, 1912.

90. Toshev, i, 381–82. Bulgaria, Narodno sŭbranie, *Doklad na parlamentarnata izpitatelna komisiia* (Sofia: Dŭrzhavna Pechatnitsa, 1918–19—hereinafter cited as *Doklad*), i, pp. 139–40, Toshev to Bulgarian foreign office, September 25 and 26, 1912.

91. Toshev, i, 383. *MO*, xx–2, 795, Hartwig to Neratov, September 27, 1912; 776, Nekliudov to Neratov, September 25, 1912. *GP*, xxxiii, 12159, 12164, 12165, Wangenheim to German foreign office, September 23, 24, and 25, 1912.

92. Toshev, i, 384–85; *Doklad*, i, p. 138, Geshov to the legations at Belgrade and Athens, September 25, 1912; p. 139, Toshev to Bulgarian foreign office, September 25 and 26, 1912. I. V. Holmsen, *Na voennoi sluzhbe v Rossii: Vospominaniia ofitsera general'nago shtaba* (New York: Izd. Russkago-Istoriko-Rodoslovnago Obshchestva v Amerike, 1953), p. 60.

93. Geshov, pp. 126–27.

94. The Bulgarians were aware that Pašić intended to claim additional territory in Macedonia not specified in the alliance of March 13, 1912, for they intercepted a copy of a letter sent by Pašić on September 28 which outlined Serbian territorial demands in Macedonia (see *Doklad*, i, pp. 123, 142–45).

3

CHAPTER 5

1. J. D. Bourchier, London *Times,* June 5 and 6, 1913. Ellinor Flora Bosworth (Smith), Lady Grogan, *The Life of J. D. Bourchier* (London: Hurst & Blackett, Ltd., 1926), p. 136. Helmreich, *Diplomacy of the Balkan Wars,* p. 73.

2. Geshov, p. 37.

3. *Ibid.*

4. Bourchier, London *Times,* June 6, 1913.

5. *MO,* xix–2, 712, Urusov to Sazonov, March 30, 1912; 844, Nekliudov to Sazonov, May 1, 1912.

6. Geshov, pp. 37–38. Helmreich, p. 75. Grogan, p. 137.

7. Geshov, pp. 38–39. *MO,* xix–2, 712.

8. *MO,* xviii–2, 667, Urusov to Neratov, October 19, 1911.

9. I. S. Galkin, *Diplomatiia,* pp. 89–95, 99–100.

10. *MO,* xviii–2, 717, Nekliudov to Neratov, October 24, 1911.

11. *Ibid.,* 769, Nekliudov to Neratov, October 31, 1911.

12. *Ibid.,* 768, Nekliudov to Neratov, October 31, 1911.

13. *Ibid.,* p. 280 note 4, Neratov to Nekliudov, November 4, 1911; The full text of this telegram is to be found in *Krasnyi Arkhiv,* viii, no. 43, p. 43.

14. *MO,* xix–2, 534, Nekliudov to Sazonov, February 24, 1912

15. Bourchier, London *Times,* June 6, 1913. Grogan, pp. 137–38.

16. *MO,* xix–2, 534, Nekliudov to Sazonov, February 24, 1912.

17. *Ibid.,* p. 357 note 2, Roshchakovskii to Sazonov, March 5, 1912.

18. *Ibid.,* 712, Urusov to Sazonov, March 30, 1912.

19. *Ibid.,* 844, Nekliudov to Sazonov, May 1, 1912.

20. *MO,* xx–1, 1, Nekliudov to Sazonov, May 14, 1912.

21. See Geshov, Appendix vii, pp. 127–30, for the text of the Greco-Bulgarian treaty.

22. *MO,* xx–1, 1; p. 1 note 2. Sazonov to Nekliudov, May 17, 1912.

23. *Ibid.,* p. 1 note 2

24. *Ibid.,* p. 87 note 3, and no. 100, Nekliudov to Sazonov, May 21 and 29, 1912.

25. *Ibid.,* 214, Nekliudov to Sazonov, June 20, 1912.

26. *Ibid.,* p. 87 note 4, Nekliudov to Sazonov, May 21, 1912.

27. Toshev, i, 344. Geshov, p. 41. Helmreich, *Diplomacy of the Balkan Wars,* p. 86. *MO,* xx–1, p. 205 note 4. A week earlier, between June 1 and June 3, King Ferdinand of Bulgaria had also made an official visit in Vienna (see London *Times,* June 3, 1912, and *MO,* xx–1, 148, N. Giers to Sazonov, June 6, 1912).

28. Geshov, Appendix viii, pp. 130–33.

29. *MO,* xx–1, 3, and p. 3 note 1, Potapov to Zhilinskii, May 14 and June 28, 1912.

30. *Ibid.,* 272, A. Giers to Sazonov, July 6, 1912.

31. *Ibid.*, p. 265 note 1, Potapov to quartermaster branch of general staff, July 12, 1912.

32. *Ibid.*, 291, 328, 406, Obnorskii to Neratov, July 13, 18, August 3, 1912; 405, Neratov to Obnorskii, August 3, 1912; p. 408 note 1, Potapov to quartermaster branch of general staff, August 3, 1912.

33. *Ibid.*, 446, M. Giers to Neratov, August 10, 1912; p. 437 note 1, A. Giers to Neratov, August 10, 1912.

34. *MO*, xx-2, 508, Potapov to quartermaster branch of general staff, August 19, 1912; p. 49 note 2, A. Giers to Neratov, August 19, 1912.

35. *Ibid.*, 513, Neratov to the chargés d'affaires in Paris and London, August 20, 1912; 565, Sazonov to the chargés d'affaires in Paris, London, Berlin, and Vienna, August 27, 1912; p. 65 note 2, Neratov to A. Giers, August 23, 1912.

36. Zhebokritskii, *Bolgariia na nakanune balkanskikh voin*, p. 198. Bŭlgarska Akademiia na Naukite, *Istoriia na Bŭlgariia*, ii, 256. Helmreich, *Diplomacy of the Balkan Wars*, pp. 37, 39, 104; *MO*, xx-1, p. 425 note 2, and no. 429, Giers to Neratov, August 2, 7, 1912.

37. *MO*, xx-1, 364, Nekliudov to Sazonov, July 26, 1912; xx-2, p. 56 note 5, Romanovskii to Danilov, August 8, 1912.

38. Geshov, p. 19. K'osev, p. 474. Zhebokritskii, *Bolgariia na nakanune balkanskikh voin*, pp. 197–202. *MO*, xx-1, 364, Nekliudov to Sazonov, July 26, 1912.

39. *MO*, xx-2, p. 56 note 5.

40. *MO*, xx-1, 434, Nekliudov to Neratov, August 8, 1912.

41. *Ibid.*, 455, and xx-2, 499, Nekliudov to Neratov, August 12, 18, 1912; xx-2, 517, Romanovskii to Danilov, August 20, 1912. Zhebokritskii, *Bolgariia na nakanune balkanskikh voin*, pp. 198–200.

42. Geshov, pp. 49–50.

43. *OUA*, iv, 3687, Berchtold to St. Petersburg, Berlin, London, Paris, Rome, Constantinople, and Bucharest, August 13, 1912.

44. *MO*, xx-2, 517, Romanovskii to Danilov, August 20, 1912. *Doklad*, i, p. 104, Rizov to Bulgarian foreign office, August 16, 1912; pp. 104–5, Toshev to Bulgarian foreign office, August 20, 1912; p. 108, Rizov to foreign office, August 21, 1912. Toshev, i, 358.

45. Senkevich, pp. 230–34. *MO*, xx-1, 456, Nekliudov to Neratov, August 12, 1912; 457, M. Giers to Neratov, August 12, 1912; xx-2, 502, Holmsen to quartermaster division of the general staff, August 18, 1912.

46. *MO*, xx-1, 380, Obnorskii to Neratov, July 28, 1912; p. 386 note 1; 395, 411, 464, Strandtman to Neratov, July 30, August 4, 13, 1912.

47. *Ibid.*, 411, 464; 394, Strandtman to Neratov, July 30, 1912.

48. *Doklad*, i, p. 110, Mishev to Bulgarian foreign office, August 23, 1912; p. 200, Kolushev to foreign office, September 3, 1912. *MO*, xx-2, 529, A. Giers to Neratov, August 21, 1912; 542, Strandtman to Neratov, August 23, 1912; 558, Nekliudov to Sazonov, August 26, 1912.

49. *Doklad,* ɪ, p. 193; p. 197, Kolushev to Bulgarian foreign office, July 18, 1912; p. 197, Geshov to Cetinje legation, July 27, 1912; p. 198, Kolushev to foreign office, July 30, 1912; pp. 198–99, Geshov to Cetinje legation, August 14, 20, 1912. Geshov, p. 42. Zhebokritskii, *Bolgariia na nakanune,* p. 182.

50. *MO,* –2, 546, Nekliudov to Neratov, August 24, 1912.

51. Toshev, ɪ, 360–61. Zhebokritskii, *Bolgariia nakanune,* pp. 182, 230. Helmreich, *Diplomacy of the Balkan Wars,* p. 87. Bulgaria, Narodno sŭbranie, *Prilozhenie kŭm tom pŭrvi ot doklada na parlamentarnata izpitatelna komisiia* (Sofia: Dŭrzhavna Pechatnitsa, 1918), p. 118.

52. *MO,* xx–2, 668, 669, Potapov to quartermaster branch of general staff, September 11, 1912; 699, Sazonov to Obnorskii, September 18, 1912. *Krasnyi Arkhiv,* xv (1926), p. 22, Potapov to general staff, September 16, 1912.

53. Geshov, p. 41.

54. *Doklad,* ɪ, p. 202, Geshov to Cetinje legation, September 28, 1912. *Prilozhenie,* p. 118.

55. *MO,* xx–2, 669, Potapov to quartermaster branch of general staff, September 11, 1912.

56. *Doklad,* ɪ, p. 141, Kolushev to Bulgarian foreign office, September 25, 1912.

57. J. Jovanović, *Stvaranje crnogorske države,* p. 400.

58. *MO,* xx–2, p. 297 note 2, Potapov to quartermaster branch of general staff, September 26, 1912.

59. *Ibid.,* 802, p. 297 note 3, Potapov to quartermaster branch of general staff, September 28 and October 3, 1912.

60. E. C. Helmreich, "The Serbian-Montenegrin Alliance of September 23/October 6, 1912," *Journal of Central European Affairs,* xɪx (January 1960), 411–15.

61. *Doklad,* ɪ, p. 200, Kolushev to Sofia, September 13, and Geshov to Cetinje, September 17, 1912.

62. *MO,* xx–2, 736, A. Giers to Neratov, September 22, 1912.

63. *Ibid.,* 763, A. Giers to Neratov, September 24, 1912.

64. *Ibid.,* 735, Nekliudov to Neratov, September 22, 1912.

65. *Ibid.,* 829, 830, 831, Nekliudov, Urusov, Hartwig to Neratov, September 30, 1912; 849, 850, Giers to Neratov, October 1, 1912.

66. *Ibid.,* 954, Holmsen to general staff, October 8, 1912; 961, 962, Demidov to Neratov, October 9, 1912; 947, Hartwig to Neratov, October 8, 1912. Helmreich, *Diplomacy of the Balkan Wars,* pp. 138–45.

67. *Doklad,* ɪ, p. 202, Geshov to Cetinje, September 28, 1912.

68. *MO,* xx–2, 1012, notes of the Bulgarian, Greek, and Serbian Governments to the Turkish Government, October 13, 1912; 1043, Giers to Sazonov, October 15, 1912; also 1047, 1075, 1089. *OUA,* ɪv, 4098, Pallavicini to Vienna, October 15, 1912.

CHAPTER 6

1. *DDF,* 3d series, III, 466, Doulcet to Poincaré, September 27, 1912.

2. *MO,* xx–1, 100, Nekliudov to Sazonov, May 29, 1912.

3. See *MO,* xx–1, 267 and 359, xx–2, 591 and 621, Nekliudov to Sazonov, July 4 and 25, August 29, and September 4, 1912; *MO,* xx–2, p. 56 note 5, and nos. 517, 610, and 623, Romanovskii to Danilov, August 8 and 20, and September 2 and 4, 1912.

4. *MO,* xx–1, 267, 359. *Schriftwechsel Iswolskis,* II, 366, Sazonov to Benckendorff, July 8, 1912. *DDF,* 3d series, III, 174, Louis to Poincaré, July 8, 1912; 180, 198, Panafieu to Poincaré, July 9 and 12, 1912. *BD,* IX–1, 585, Obeirne to Grey, July 8, 1912; 590, Obeirne to Nicolson, July 11, 1912; 589, Barclay to Grey, July 11, 1912.

5. *MO,* xx–1, 359. *BD,* IX–1, 589. *DDF,* III, 198.

6. Nekliudov, pp. 96–97.

7. *MO,* xx–1, 146, Izvol'skii to Sazonov, June 6, 1912.

8. *Ibid.,* 256, Krupenskii to Sazonov, July 2, 1912.

9. *Ibid.,* 278, Sazonov to Nekliudov, July 8, 1912.

10. *Ibid.,* 256.

11. *Ibid.,* 352, Neratov to Hartwig, Nekliudov, and Urusov, July 22, 1912.

12. *Ibid.,* 413, Neratov to Nekliudov, Strandtman, and Urusov, August 5, 1912.

13. Geshov, p. 2.

14. *MO,* xvIII–2, 487, p. 43 notes 1, 2, Nekliudov to Neratov and Sazonov, September 29, October 1 and 2, 1911; xx–1, 283, July 10, 1912.

15. *MO,* xx–1, 283.

16. *Ibid.,* 298, Giers to Neratov, July 15, 1912; xx–2, 590, 591, 618, 629, Nekliudov to Sazonov, August 29, September 3, 5, 1912; xx–2, 623, Romanovskii to Danilov, September 4, 1912.

17. *MO,* xx–1, 298; 343, M. Giers to Neratov, July 20, 1912.

18. *Ibid.,* 381, Artamonov to Danilov, July 29, 1912; xx–2, 480, Zankevich to Danilov, August 15, 1912. Spalajković and Panafieu, the Serbian and French ministers in Sofia, reported an alleged Russian request that the Balkan states maintain peace until September. According to Spalajković, Danev had been told in Russia that trouble was to be avoided in the Balkans until after the Duma elections in September. Geshov and King Ferdinand supposedly had been similarly informed, and Guchkov made the same point while in Sofia. Guchkov may have asked the Bulgarians to postpone trouble until after the Duma elections in Russia. It is, however, doubtful whether the Russian Government or Russian diplomats ever made such a request officially. Hartwig and Nekliudov, to be sure, suggested that Russia gain time by persuading the Balkan states to delay

war until 1913. But Neratov rejected this suggestion on the ground that such action would not prevent war but would implicitly commit Russia to support the Balkan states once war started. (*APS*, ɪ, 180, Spalajković to Serbian foreign office, August 12, 1912—Bogićević erroneously dates this communication July 30; Helmreich, *Diplomacy of the Balkan Wars*, p. 104, correctly points out that it must have been sent thirteen days later. *DDF*, 3d series, ɪv, 39, Panafieu to Poincaré, October 3, 1912. *MO*, xx–2, 637, Nekliudov to Sazonov, September 6, 1912; 740, Hartwig to Neratov, September 23, 1912; 822, Neratov to Hartwig, September 30, 1912).

19. *MO*, xx–2, 629, 637, Nekliudov to Sazonov, September 5 and 6, 1912; 686, Sazonov to Izvol'skii, A. Krupenskii, Etter, Bronevskii, and Kudashev, September 17, 1912.

20. *Ibid.*, 591, Nekliudov to Sazonov, August 29, 1912.

21. *Ibid.*, 541, 683, Nekliudov to Neratov and Sazonov, August 23, 29, September 15, 1912.

22. *Ibid.*, 698, Sazonov to Nekliudov, September 18, 1912.

23. *Ibid.*, 683, 719, Nekliudov to Sazonov, September 15 and 20, 1912.

24. Toshev, ɪ, 342–43. S. Danev, *balkanskite derzhavi*, pp. 117–18. *MO*, xx–1, 64, Sazonov to Nekliudov, May 23, 1912.

25. Danev, *balkanskite derzhavi*, pp. 118–20.

26. *MO*, xx–2, 657, Hartwig to Sazonov, September 10, 1912.

27. Askew, *Acquisition of Libya*, pp. 176–78.

28. *DDF*, 3d series, ɪ, 539, Poincaré to Louis, January 27, 1912; 625, Louis to Poincaré, February 7, 1912; ɪɪ, 10, Poincaré to Louis, February 9, 1912.

29. Ibid., ɪɪ, 43, Louis to Poincaré, February 15, 1912.

30. *Ibid.*, 48, Poincaré to Louis, February 17, 1912; 202, Poincaré to Vieugué, March 14, 1912.

31. Poincaré, ɪɪ, 32. *DDF*, 3d series, ɪɪ, 298, Poincaré to the French ambassadors at Constantinople and London, April 4, 1912. Soviet historians insist that Poincaré must have known about the Serbo-Bulgarian negotiations earlier and assume that French historians chose not to publish documents illustrating Poincaré's knowledge in order to hide aspects of French imperialistic policy during 1911–12. See Iu. O. Boiev, *Polityka Frantsii na Balkanakh naperedodni pershoi svitovoi imperialistychnoi viiny, 1911–1913 rr.* (Kiev: Vid.-vo Akademii, Nauk URSR, 1958), pp. 9–10 and 47–53; V. I. Bovykin, "Russko-frantsuzskie protivorechiia na Balkanakh i Blizhnem Vostoke nakanune pervoi mirovoi voiny," *Istoricheskie Zapiski*, ʟɪx (1957), 91; I. S. Galkin, "Obrazovanie balkanskogo soiuza 1912 g. i politika evropeiskikh derzhav," *Vestnik Moskovskogo Universiteta*, 1956, no. 4 (April), pp. 25–26.

32. *DDF*, 3d series, ɪɪ, 297, Panafieu to Poincaré, April 3, 1912.

33. Poincaré, ɪɪ, 31–66, 99–132.

34. *Ibid.*

35. Poincaré, ii, 83–85, 112. *DDF*, 3d series, iii, 56, Fleriau to Poincaré, May 30, 1912; 189, 207, Captain Le Gouz de Saint-Seine to Delcassé, July 10 and 18, 1912; 206, draft Franco-Russian Naval convention, July 16, 1912. *MO*, xx–1, 299, 300, 301, draft naval convention and agreement for a Franco-Russian exchange of naval information, July 16, 1912. G. M. Derenkovskii, "Franko-russkaia morskaia konventsiia 1912 g. i anglo-russkie morskie peregovory nakanune pervoi mirovoi voiny," *Istoricheskie Zapiski,* xxix (1949), 95–101.

36. *MO*, xx–2, 474, Sazonov to Poincaré, August 15, 1912; 484, Poincaré to Sazonov, August 16, 1912; 489, Sazonov to Nicholas ii, August 17, 1912.

37. *MO*, xx–1, 288, Protocol of conference of French and Russian chiefs of staff, July 13, 1912.

38. *MO*, xx–2, 489.

39. *Ibid.*, 672, Izvol'skii to Sazonov, September 12, 1912. *DDF,* 3d series, iii, 359, memorandum of the French general staff, September 2, 1912.

40. *MO*, xx–2, 672. *IB,* 46, Izvol'skii to Sazonov, October 24, 1912.

41. Poincaré, ii, 339.

42. Cf. Albertini, i, 406–9. Poincaré, in effect, confirmed the general accuracy of Izvol'skii's interpretation of French policy in the letter he sent to Georges Louis on November 19, 1912, *DDF*, 3d series, iv, 494.

43. Albertini, i, 373.

44. *MO*, xix–2, 748, Izvol'skii to Sazonov, April 10, 1912.

45. *DDF*, 3d series, iii, 45, Paléologue to Poincaré, February 16, 1912. A month later the Russian chargé d'affaires at Sofia wrote that France had told Bulgaria that a French loan was contingent upon Bulgaria's entry into the orbit of the powers of the Triple Entente (*Benckendorff*, ii, 584, Urusov to Sazonov, April 4, 1912).

46. *MO*, xix–2, 752, Izvol'skii to Poincaré, April 11, 1912; cf. p. 397 note 2.

47. *DDF*, 3d series, ii, 324, Poincaré to Panafieu, April 11, 1912.

48. *MO*, xx–1, 211, Izvol'skii to Sazonov, June 20, 1912. Cf. Poincaré, ii, 49.

49. *MO*, xx–1, 489.

50. *DDF*, 3d series, iv, 39, Panafieu to Poincaré, October 3, 1912.

51. They also conflicted with France's relations with Russia. As late as May 1912, at a meeting of the council of ministers, Sazonov regretted that Russia was not in a position to oppose Franco-Turkish negotiations concerning the construction of railways in eastern Anatolia. (*MO*, xx–1, 63, Special journal of the council of ministers, May 23, 1912. Holmsen, p. 59.)

52. Herbert Feis, pp. 276–77. *MO*, xx–2, 587, Sevastopulo to Sazonov, August 29, 1912. *DDF*, 3d series, iii, 339, 393, Poincaré to Panafieu, August 29 and September 12, 1912; 434, Panafieu to Poincaré, September 19, 1912.

53. Feis, p. 277. *IB*, 228, p. 236 note 1, Izvol'skii to Sazonov, November 12 and 13, 1912. *GP*, xxxiv, 12963, Jagow to Lichnowsky, March 14, 1913. German and Russian banks made similar advances to the Bulgarian government at the time.

54. Albertini, ɪ, 412–13; Pierre Renouvin, *La politique extérieure de la IIIe République de 1904 à 1919* (Paris: Centre de Documentation Universitaire, 1949), pp. 112–13. Bovykin, "Russko-frantsuzskie protivorechiia," 102–4; John C. Cairns, "International Politics and the Military Mind: The Case of the French Republic, 1911–1914," *Journal of Modern History*, xxv (September 1953), 276–81. Millerand and General Edouard de Curières de Castelnau, the deputy chief of staff of the French army, are quoted at length by Bovykin from reports now located in the Soviet Foreign Ministry and military archives.

55. Werner Schröder, *England, Europa und der Orient: Untersuchung zur englischen Vorkriegspolitik in Vorgeschichte der Balkankrise 1912* (Stuttgart: Kohlhammer, 1938), pp. 1–12, 67–68. Nicolson, pp. 222–23. G. M. Trevelyan, *Grey of Fallodan* (Boston: Houghton Mifflin Co., 1937), pp. 251–52. Oswald Hauser, *Deutschland und der englisch-russische Gegensatz 1910–1914* (Göttingen: Musterschmidt Verlag, 1958), pp. 266–69. John E. Tyler, *The British Army and the Continent 1904–1914* (London: E. Arnold & Co., [1938]), pp. 166–70.

56. Mosa Anderson, *Noel Buxton: A Life* (London: Allen & Unwin, [1952]), pp. 36–39, 54–55. T. P. Conwell-Evans, *Foreign Policy from a Back Bench: A Study Based on the Papers of Lord Noel Buxton* (London: Oxford University Press, 1932), pp. 3–13, 26–32. Grogan, pp. 84–87, 134–40.

57. *BD*, ɪx–1, 525, 544, 555, 558, 559 with enclosure, 560, 566, 572, Bax-Ironside to Grey, October 23, 1911, January 31, February 26, March 14, 18, and 28, and June 1, 1912.

58. *Ibid.*, p. 501, note to no. 517.

59. *BD*, v, 427, Buchanan to Grey, November 4, 1908; 447, 468, ɪx–1, 2, Grey to Whitehead, November 14, December 1, 1908, April 15, 1909; v. 858, ɪx–1, 81, Whitehead to Grey, April 28, November 24, 1909; ɪx–1, 59, Findlay to Grey, September 27, 1909.

60. Schröder, pp. 77–78. Cf. *BD*, ɪx–1, 352, 537, 552; and Alfred F. Pribram, *Austria-Hungary and Great Britain, 1908–1914*, tr. Ian F. D. Morrow (London: Oxford University Press, 1951), pp. 152–53, 160–61.

61. *MO*, xx–1, 419, 453, xx–2, 553, 708, 732, 768, Neratov to M. Giers, August 6, 12, 25, September 19, 22, 25, 1912; xx–2, 495, Neratov to Sevastopulo and Etter, August 18, 1912; xx–2, 686, Sazonov to Izvol'skii, A. Krupenskii, Etter, Bronevskii, and Kudashev, September 17, 1912; xx–2, 597, 687, Sazonov to M. Giers, August 31, September 17, 1912.

62. *MO*, xx–2, 769, Neratov to Nekliudov, Hartwig, A. Giers, and Urusov, September 25, 1912; 781, Neratov to Sazonov, September 26, 1912; 930, Sazonov to Neratov, October 7, 1912; 1006, Sazonov to Demidov, October 13, 1912.

63. *Ibid.*, 597, Sazonov to M. Giers, August 31, 1912; 613, Sazonov to Sevastopulo, September 3, 1912.

64. *Ibid.*, 608, 663, Etter to Sazonov, September 2 and 11, 1912; 726, 771, Sazonov to Neratov, September 21 and 25, 1912; 914, Benckendorff to Neratov, October 6, 1912; 1034, Sazonov to Nicholas II, October 15, 1912.

65. *Ibid.*, 915, Sazonov to Neratov, October 6, 1912; 979, Izvol'skii to Sazonov, October 11, 1912. *BD*, IX–2, 85, Buchanan to Grey, November 1, 1912; p. 71 note 3 to no. 85; Appendix II, pp. 1010–11. Cf. Schröder, pp. 88–89.

66. *MO*, xx–2, 1034, Sazonov to Nicholas II, October 15, 1912.

67. Derenkovskii, 111–20.

68. Hauser, pp. 117–81, 243–53. Schröder, pp. 20–43.

69. *BD*, IX–2, Appendix II, p. 1008. Soviet historian I. S. Galkin has recently argued that Anglo-Russian differences in the Balkans were deepseated enough to make the weakening of Russian influence in the peninsula a major objective of British policy in 1912. According to Galkin, Britain maintained "secret contact" with Austria-Hungary and worked closely with the dual monarchy to maintain the status quo. A second tactic was to bring Greece, where Britain's influence was particularly strong, into the Balkan alliance. Bourchier, according to Galkin, was an "active agent and scout [*razvedchik*] of the foreign office" and acted directly under the orders of Grey.

Galkin's interpretation lacks adequate documentation and is based on questionable conjecture. Great Britain undeniably wanted to maintain good relations with Austria-Hungary, but did not necessarily seek to weaken Russian influence in the Balkans. And Bourchier's articles in the *Times* then nettled the Foreign Office; he vigorously asserted his right as a correspondent to tell the truth as he knew it rather than to conform "with a preconceived policy in London." Greece was exceedingly angry at England because of the latter's opposition to the union of Crete with the Greek motherland. At such a time of strained relations could the Foreign Office really have counted on Greece as a dependable and effective counterweight to Russian influence on the Balkan alliance? The final proof of the value Great Britain attached to Russian goodwill was her promise in November 1914 of Constantinople and the Straits. Such a promise would scarcely have been made if, as Galkin suggests, Britain considered checking Russia in the Near East one of her major tasks prior to the Revolution of 1917. (Galkin, "Obrazovanie balkanskogo soiuza," pp. 33–36, 38–39. Galkin, *Politika evropeiskikh derzhav v sviazi s osvoboditel'nym dvizheniem narodov evropeiskoi Turtsii v 1908–1912 gg.: Avtoreferat dissertatsii na soiskanie stepeni doktora istoricheskikh nauk* [Moscow: Izdatel'stvo Moskovskogo Universiteta, 1956], pp. 34–35. Galkin, *Diplomatiia*, pp. 95–104. Pribram, pp. 152–62. Grogan, p. 140. *MO*, XIX–2, 664, Sverbeev to Sazonov, March 21, 1912; xx–2, 866, 1045, memorandum of Buchanan to Neratov,

October 3, 16, 1912; 1076, Demidov to Sazonov, October 17, 1912. Galkin refers to Grey's letter of January 31, 1913, to Sir W. E. Goschem, British Ambassador at Vienna—*BD*, ix–2, 581—as corroboration of his characterization of Bourchier as an agent of the Foreign Office. The cited document is, however, no proof of Galkin's assumption.)

70. *BD*, ix–1, enclosure in no. 190, Napier to Findlay, October 11, 1910.

71. M. I. Madzharov. *Diplomaticheska podgotovka na nashite voini: Spomeni, chastni pisma, shifrovani telegrami i poveritelni dokladi* (Sofia: "Mir," 1932), pp. 9–11 and 35–38.

72. *Ibid.*, pp. 37–38. *MO*, xviii–2, p. 43 note 2, Nekliudov to Neratov, October 2, 1911. *DDF*, 3d series, iii, 36, 45, Paléologue to Poincaré, February 15 and 16, 1912. *MO*, xx–2, 623, Romanovskii to Danilov, September 4, 1912; 762, Artamonov to Danilov, September 24, 1912. Muir, *Dimitri Stancioff: Patriot and Cosmopolitan 1864–1940*, pp. 140–43. *APS*, i, 193, 194, 195, Spalajković to Belgrade, October 1, 2, 3, 1912.

73. Theobald von Bethmann-Hollweg, *Reflections on the World War*, tr. George Young, i (London: T. Butterworth, Ltd., [1920]), 73.

74. *GP*, xxxiii, 12252, Berchtold to Kiderlen-Wächter, October 8, 1912.

75. *Kiderlen-Wächter: Der Staatsmann und Mensch, Briefwechsel und Nachlass*, ed. Ernst Jäckh (Stuttgart: Deutsche Verlags-Anstalt, 1924), ii, 186. Helmreich, *Diplomacy of the Balkan Wars*, p. 63.

76. Bethmann-Hollweg, i, 72. *OUA*, iv, 3771, Berchtold memorandum concerning his Buchlau conversations with Bethmann-Hollweg, September 7–8, 1912.

77. *OUA*, iv, 3540, Berchtold memorandum concerning his conversations with German political leaders and diplomats at Berlin between May 24 and May 26, 1912.

78. *OUA*, iv, 3612, protocol of the Ministerrat für gemeinsame Angelegenheiten, July 8 and 9, 1912.

79. *Ibid.*, 3607, 3703, 3764, Tarnowski to Berchtold, July 6, August 16, September 4, 1912.

80. *Ibid.*, 3549, Berchtold memorandum concerning King Ferdinand's visit to Vienna of June 1–5, 1912.

81. *Ibid.*, 3678, Berchtold to Tarnowski, August 10, 1912.

82. *Ibid.*, 3734, Tarnowski to Berchtold, August 26, 1912.

83. Danev, *balkanskite dŭrzhavi*, p. 118.

84. Oswald W. Wedel, *Austro-German Diplomatic Relations 1908–1914* (Stanford: Stanford University Press, 1932), pp. 132–35, 138–45. Helmreich, *Diplomacy of the Balkan Wars*, pp. 179–83. *OUA*, iv, 3991, memorandum of section chief Count Friedrich Szápáry, October 7, 1912. *GP*, xxxiii, 12162, Kiderlen-Wächter to Stolberg, September 25, 1912.

85. Askew, *Acquisition of Libya 1911–1912*, pp. 252–63. Albertini, i, 388–89. Danev, *balkanskite dŭrzhavi*, p. 118. Bethmann-Hollweg, i, 70–71.

86. *MO*, xx–2, 660, 762, Artamonov to Danilov, September 10, 24, 1912.

87. Helmreich, *Diplomacy of the Balkan Wars*, p. 182.

88. *OUA*, iv, 4022, Szögyény to Vienna, October 10, 1912. Albertini, i, 380.

89. Wedel, p. 154. *Kiderlen-Wächter*, ii, 188 ff.

90. On German-Bulgarian trade relations, see M. L. Flaningam, "German Economic Controls in Bulgaria: 1894–1914," *American Slavic and East European Review*, xx (February 1961), 99–108.

91. *GP*, xxxiii, 12202, Jenisch to Bethmann-Hollweg, October 2, 1912; p. 148 note 3.

92. *Ibid.*, 12225, note by William ii, October 4, 1912.

93. *OUA*, iv, 3869, Schemua to Franz Josef, September 28, 1912. Helmreich, *Diplomacy of the Balkan Wars*, pp. 186–87. Albertini, i, 387–88.

94. *OUA*, iv, 4118, 4128, 4140, 4170, protocols of conferences in the Austro-Hungarian foreign ministry, October 16–19, 25–30, 1912; 4171, memorandum on the Sanjak question, October 25, 1912; 4205, Berchtold to Szögyény, October 30, 1912.

95. *GP*, xxxiii, 12087, note by Kiderlen-Wächter, August 15, 1912; 12135, Kiderlen-Wächter to Bethmann-Hollweg, September 2, 1912. *OUA*, iv, 3714, Szögyény to Berchtold, August 19, 1912.

96. *OUA*, iv, 3714.

97. *MO*, xx–2, 543, M. Giers to Neratov, August 23, 1912.

98. *OUA*, vi, note to 3678, Berchtold to Franz Josef, August 13, 1912.

99. *Ibid.*, 3744, Berchtold to St. Petersburg, Berlin, London, Rome, and Paris, August 29, 1912. Helmreich, *Diplomacy of the Balkan Wars*, pp. 117–19.

100. *MO*, xx–2, 686, Sazonov to Izvol'skii, A. Krupenskii, Etter, Bronevskii, and Kudashev, September 17, 1912; 687, Sazonov to Giers, September 17, 1912; 729, M. Giers to Sazonov, September 21, 1912.

101. *Ibid.*, 732, Izvol'skii to Neratov, September 22, 1912; 733. *DDF*, 3d series, iii, 451, 453, Poincaré to P. Cambon, September 22, 1912.

102. *OUA*, iv, 3991, memorandum by Szápáry, October 7, 1912; 3996, Berchtold to Kiderlen-Wächter, October 8, 1912. *DDF*, 3d series, iv, 9, 18, Jules Cambon to Poincaré, October 1 and 2, 1912. *GP*, xxxiii, 12213, Kiderlen-Wächter to Tschirschky, October 3, 1912.

103. *OUA*, iv, 3821, Berchtold to Pallavicini, September 21, 1912; 3832, Pallavicini to Berchtold, September 23, 1912.

104. *GP*, xxxiii, 12151, 12162, Kiderlen-Wächter to Stolberg, September 19, 25, 1912; 12163, Kiderlen to Wangenheim, September 25, 1912. *OUA*, iv, 3943, report by Berchtold concerning visit of German ambassador, October 4, 1912.

105. *MO*, xx–2, p. 326 note 5, Neratov to Sazonov, October 2, 1912.

106. *Ibid.*, 688, Sazonov to Kudashev, September 17, 1912; 858, Sazonov to Neratov, October 2, 1912.

107. *Ibid.*, 1034, Sazonov to Nicholas II, October 15, 1912.

108. *Ibid.*, 912, Benckendorff to Neratov, October 6, 1912; 915, Sazonov to Neratov, October 6, 1912.

109. *Ibid.*, 927, Sazonov to St. Petersburg, Athens, Belgrade, Cetinje, and Sofia, October 7, 1912.

110. *Ibid.*, 945, 946, 948, 951, Nekliudov, Demidov, Hartwig, and A. Giers to Neratov, October 8, 1912. *OUA*, IV, 3992, 3993, 3997, 4009, Braun, Ugron, Giesl, and Tarnowski to Vienna, October 8, 1912.

111. *MO*, XX–2, 975, M. Giers to Neratov, October 10, 1912. *GP*, XXXIII, 12273, Wangenheim to German foreign office, October 14, 1912.

112. *GP*, XXXIII, 12225, note by Wilhelm II, October 4, 1912.

113. Gabriel Hanotaux, *La guerre des Balkans et l'Europe*, 2nd ed. (Paris: Plon-Nourrit et Cie., 1914), p. 112.

CONCLUSION

1. *MO*, XX–2, 823, Neratov to Sazonov, September 30, 1912; p. 313 notes 4, 5, and 6; p. 335 note 3. Neratov seems to have made this assurance in good faith. He desired better coordination between the army and navy and the foreign ministry. As he wrote in October 1912, the trial mobilization "coinciding with the news of the mobilization in the Balkan states . . . caused distrust in Austria and Germany and awakened unfounded hopes in the Balkan states, which undoubtedly complicated our task of pacifying the existing situation." Although Sazonov approved a Germany request that, to avoid unnecessary rumors, Russia inform Germany of future trial mobilizations near her frontier, Sukhomlinov, the war minister, brushed it aside, saying it would facilitate espionage. (*MO*, XX–2, 870, Neratov to Sukhomlinov, October 3, 1912. *IB*, 335, Sazonov to Sukhomlinov and Kokovtsov, November 25, 1912; p. 331 note 1, Sukhomlinov to Sazonov, November 30, 1912. Cf. Helmreich, *Diplomacy of the Balkan Wars*, pp. 161–62.)

2. Thaden, "Montenegro," p. 130.

3. *IB*, 100, Sazonov to the Russian representatives in Paris, London, Berlin, Vienna, Rome, Constantinople, and the Balkan capitals, October 31, 1912.

4. See Sidney B. Fay, I, 429; Langer, "Russia, the Straits Question and the Origins of the Balkan League, 1908–1912," *Political Science*

Quarterly, XLIII, 359–360; Bickel, pp. 159–160; Hauser, *Der englisch-russische Gegensatz*, pp. 265–66; Uebersberger, *Österreich zwischen Russland und Serbien*, pp. 70–73.

5. *IB*, 204, Nekliudov to Sazonov, November 9, 1912; p. 214 note 1.

6. *Ibid.*, 227, memorandum drafted in the Russian Foreign Ministry, November 12, 1912.

7. *Ibid.*, 246, Sazonov to M. Giers, November 14, 1912; 374, Lieven to Grigorovich, November 28, 1912.

8. *Ibid.*, 351, Sukhomlinov to Sazonov, November 26, 1912.

9. See *MO*, xx-2, 958, 974, Hartwig to Neratov, October 9, 10, 1912.

10. B. E. Nol'de, *Dalekoe i blizkoe: Istoricheskie ocherki* (Paris: Izdatel'stvo "Sovremennyia Zapiski," 1930), p. 225.

11. *IB*, 100.

12. Fourth Duma, *Stenograficheskiia otchety*, First Session, Part III, Meeting 66, June 19, 1913, cols. 1019–21; Second Session, Part IV, Meeting 80, May 23, 1914, cols. 348–49.

13. Langer, "Russia, the Straits Question, and Balkan League," p. 361.

BIBLIOGRAPHY

DOCUMENTS AND OFFICIAL PUBLICATIONS

AUSTRIA-HUNGARY

Hötzendorf, Franz Conrad von. *Aus meiner Dienstzeit 1906–1918.* Vienna: Rikola Verlag, 1921–25. 5 vols.
Österreich-Ungarns Aussenpolitik von der bosnischen Krise 1908 bis zum Kriegsausbruch 1914: Diplomatische Aktenstücke des österreich-ungarischen Ministeriums des Äussern, eds. Ludwig Bittner and Hans Uebersberger. Vienna: Österreichischer Bundesverlag für Unterricht, Wissenschaft und Kunst, 1930. 9 vols.
Pribram, A. F. *The Secret Treaties of Austria-Hungary 1879–1914,* trans. A. C. Coolidge. Cambridge: Harvard University Press, 1920. 2 vols.

BULGARIA

Kesiakov, B. D. *Prinos kŭm diplomaticheskata istoriia na Bŭlgariia, 1878–1925.* Sofia: T. L. Klisarov, 1925–26. 4 vols.
Narodno sŭbranie. *Doklad na parlamentarnata izpitatelna komisiia.* Sofia: Dŭrzhavna Pechatnitsa, 1918–19. 4 vols.
———. *Prilozhenie kŭm tom pŭrvi ot doklada na parlamentarnata izpitatelna komisiia.* Sofia: Dŭrzhavna Pechatnitsa, 1918.

FRANCE

Ministère des Affaires étrangères. *Documents diplomatiques français 1871–1914.* Paris: Alfred Costes, 1929–59. 41 vols.

BIBLIOGRAPHY

GERMANY

Auswärtiges Amt. *Die grosse Politik der europäischen Kabinette 1871–1914,* eds. Johannes Lepsius, Albrecht Mendelsohn-Bartholdy, and Friedrich Thimme. Berlin: Deutsche Verlagsgesellschaft für Politik und Geschichte, 1922–27. 40 vols. in 54.

GREAT BRITAIN

British Documents on the Origins of the War 1898–1914, eds. G. P. Gooch and Harold Temperley. London: His Majesty's Stationery Office, 1926–38. 11 vols.

RUSSIA

Gosudarstvennaia duma, *Stenograficheskiia otchety.* St. Petersburg: Gosudarstvennaia Tipografiia, 1906–17.

Hoetzsch, Otto (ed.). *Die internationalen Beziehungen im Zeitalter des Imperialismus*—see under Komissiia po izdaniiu dokumentov.

Izvol'skii, A. P. *Au service de la Russie: Correspondance diplomatique 1906–1911,* eds. Hélène Isvolsky and G. Chklaver. Paris: Les Editions Internationales, 1937–39. 2 vols.

Khvostov, V. M., and Gliazer, E. M. (eds.). "Tsarskoe pravitel'stvo o probleme prolivov v 1896–1911 gg.," *Krasnyi Arkhiv,* LXI (1933), 135–140.

Komissiia po izdaniiu dokumentov epokhi imperializma, *Mezhdunarodnye otnosheniia v epokhu imperializma: Dokumenty iz arkhivov tsarskogo i vremennogo pravitel'stv 1878–1917,* eds. A. P. Bol'shemennikov, A. S. Erusalimskii, A. A. Mogilevich, and F. A. Rotshtein.

Series I, 1878–99—no volumes published.

Series II, 1900–1913, Volumes XVIII–XX published. Moscow: Gospolizdat, 1938–40.

Series III, 1914–17, Volumes I–X published. Moscow: Gosudarstvennoe Sotsial'no-Ekonomicheskoe Izdatel'stvo, 1931–38.

Most of the volumes published in Series II and III have been translated, in an authorized edition, into German. However, what would have been Volume XXI, part 1, of Series II, covering the period from October 18 to December 4, 1912, does not seem to be available in the Russian original. The manuscript of the Russian original was apparently routinely sent to Germany at some time before June 22, 1941, and the German translation of this volume was published at Berlin in 1942: *Die internationalen Beziehungen im Zeitalter des Imperialismus: Dokumente aus den Archiven der zarischen und der provisorischen Regierungen,* 3d series. Volume IV, part 1, ed. Otto Hoetzsch. Berlin: Steiniger-Verlage, 1942.

Bibliography

Pokrovskii, M. N. (ed.). *Drei Konferenzen: Zur Vorgeschichte des Krieges.* [Berlin: Arbeiterbuchhandlung,] 1920.

Popov, A. L. (ed.). "Diplomaticheskaia podgotovka balkanskoi voiny 1912 g.," *Krasnyi Arkhiv*, VIII (1925), 3–48, and IX (1925), 3–31.

——. "Pervaia Balkanskaia voina," *Krasnyi Arkhiv*, XV (1926), 1–29, and XVI (1926), 3–23.

Siebert, Benno von (ed.). *Graf Benckendorffs diplomatischer Schriftwechsel.* Berlin and Leipzig: Verlag von Walter de Gruyter & Co., 1928. 3 vols.

——, and Schreiner, George A. (eds.). *Entente Diplomacy and the World: Matrix of the History of Europe, 1909–1914.* New York and London: G. P. Putnam's Sons, 1921.

Sbornik dogovorov Rossii s drugimi gosudarstvami 1856–1917, ed. E. A. Adamov and I. V. Koz'menko. Moscow: Gospolizdat, 1952.

Stieve, Friedrich (ed.). *Der diplomatische Schriftwechsel Iswolskis 1911–1914: Aus den Geheimakten der russischen Staatsarchive.* Berlin: Deutsche Verlagsgesellschaft für Politik und Geschichte, 1925. 4 vols.

Svod zakonov rossiiskoi imperii [vol. I, part 1:], *Svod osnovnykh gosudarstvennykh zakonov: Izdanie 1906 goda.* St. Petersburg: Gosudarstvennaia Tipografiia, 1906.

SERBIA

Bogićević, Miloš [Boghitschewitsch, Milosch] (ed.). *Die auswärtige Politik Serbiens, 1903–1914.* Berlin: Brückenverlag, 1928–31. 3 vols.

NEWSPAPERS

London *Times.*

Moscow *Golos Moskvy.*

St. Petersburg *Novoe Vremia* and *Rech'.*

MEMOIRS AND BIOGRAPHIES

Aksakov, I. S. *Ivan Sergeevich Aksakov v ego pis'makh.* Moscow: N. G. Volchaninov, 1888–92. 4 vols.

Anderson, Mosa. *Noel Buxton: A Life.* London: Allen & Unwin [1952].

Bethmann-Hollweg, Theobald von. *Reflections on the World War* [vol. 1], trans. George Young. London: T. Butterworth, Ltd. [1920].

Bobchev, S. S. *Stranitsi iz moiata diplomaticheska misiia v Petrograd (1912–1913).* Sofia: Slavianskoto Druzhestvo v Bŭlgariia, 1940.

BIBLIOGRAPHY

Bogdanovich, A. V. *Journal de la Générale* A. V. *Bogdanovitch,* tr. M. Lefebvre. Paris: Payot, 1926.

Bok, M. F. *Vospominaniia o moem ottse P. A. Stolypine.* New York: Izdatel'stvo imeni Chekhova, 1953.

Bosdari, Alessandro de. *Delle Guerre Balcaniche della Grande Guerra e alcuni fatti precedenti ad esse.* Milan: A Mondadori, 1928.

Charykov, N. V., *Glimpses of High Politics: Through War and Peace 1855–1929.* London: George Allen & Unwin, 1931.

Chastenet, J. *Raymond Poincaré.* Paris: R. Julliard [1948].

Conwell-Evans, T. P. *Foreign Policy from a Back Bench: A Study Based on the Papers of Lord Noel Buxton.* London: Oxford University Press, 1932.

Geshov, Ivan E. *The Balkan League,* tr. Constanin C. Nincoff. London: J. Murray, 1915.

Giesl, Wladimir. *Zwei Jahrzehnte im nahen Osten: Aufzeichnungen des Generals der Kavallerie Baron Wladimir Giesl,* ed. Ritter von Steinitz. Berlin: Verlag der Kulturpolitik, 1927.

Giolitti, Giovanni. *Memoirs of My Life,* tr. Edward Storer. London and Sydney: Chapman & Dodd, Ltd., 1923.

Grey, Edward, Viscount of Fallodon. *Twenty-Five Years 1892–1916.* New York: Frederick A. Stockes, Co., 1925. 2 vols.

Grogan, Ellinor Flora Bosworth (Smith), Lady. *The Life of J. D. Bourchier.* London: Hurst & Blackett, Ltd., 1926.

Gurko, V. I. *Features and Figures of the Past: Government and Opinion in the Reign of Nicholas II.* Stanford: Stanford University Press, 1939.

Holmsen, I. A. *Na voennoi sluzhbe v Rossii: Vospominaniia ofitsera general'nago shtaba.* New York: Izdanie Russkago Istoriko-Rodoslovnago Obshchestva v Amerike, 1953.

Ignat'ev, A. A. *Piat'desiat let v stroiu.* Moskva: Goslitizdat, 1959. 2 vols.

Izvol'skii, A. P., *The Memoirs of Alexander Isvolsky,* ed. and trans. C. L. Seeger. London: Hutchinson and Co., 1920.

Kiderlen-Wächter: Der Staatsmann und Mensch: Briefwechsel und Nachlass, ed. Ernst Jäckh. Stuttgart: Deutsche Verlags-Anstalt, 1924. 2 vols.

Kokovtsov, V. N. *Out of my Past: The Memoirs of Count Kokovtsov,* ed. H. H. Fisher. Stanford: Stanford University Press, 1935.

Lambsdorff, Gustav. *Die Militärbevollmächtigten Kaiser Wilhelms II am Zarenhofe 1904–1914.* Berlin: Schlieffen Verlag, 1937.

Lamouche, Léon. *Quinze ans d'histoire balkanique (1904–1918).* Paris: Payot, 1928.

Lindow, Erich. *Freiherr Marschall von Bieberstein als Botschafter in Konstantinopel 1897–1912.* Danzig: A. W. Kafemann, 1934.

Louis, Georges. *Les carnets de Georges Louis.* Paris: F. Rieder et Cie., 1926. 2 vols.

Madol, Hans R. *Ferdinand von Bulgarien, der Traum von Byzanz.* Berlin: Universitas, 1931.

Bibliography

Madzharov, Mikhail. *Diplomaticheska podgotovka na nashite voini: Spomeni, chastni pisma, shifrovani telegrami i poveritelni dokladi.* Sofia: "Mir," 1932.

Miliukov, P. N. *Vospominaniia,* eds. M. N. Karpovich and B. I. El'kin. New York: Izdatel'stvo imeni Chekhova, 1955. 2 vols.

Muhdar Pasha, M. *La Turquie, l'Allemagne et l'Europe depuis le traité de Berlin jusqu'à la guerre mondiale.* Paris: Berger-Levrault, 1924.

Muir, Nadejda. *Dimitri Stancioff: Patriot and Cosmopolitan 1864–1940.* London: J. Murray, 1957.

Nekliudov, A. V. *Diplomatic Reminiscences before and during the World War,* trans. Alexandra Paget. London: J. Murray, 1920.

Nicolson, Harold. *Portrait of a Diplomatist.* Cambridge, Mass.: The Riverside Press, 1930.

Poincaré, Raymond. *Au service de la France: Neuf année de souvenirs.* Paris: Librairie Plon, 1926–33. 10 vols.

Pomiankowski, Joseph. *Der Zusammenbruch des Ottomanischen Reiches: Erinnerungen an die Türkei aus der Zeit des Weltkrieges.* Zurich, Vienna, and Leipzig: Amalthea-Verlag [1928].

Rerlich, Josef, *Schicksalsjahre Österreichs 1908–1919: Das politische Tagebuch Josef Redlichs,* ed. Fritz Fellner. Graz: Hermann Bölau, 1953–54. 2 vols.

Rosen, R. R. *Forty Years of Diplomacy.* New York: Alfred A. Knopf, 1922. 2 vols.

Savinsky, Alexander A. *Recollections of a Russian Diplomat.* London: Hutchinson & Co. [1927].

Sazonov, S. D., *Fateful Years 1909–1916: The Reminiscences of Serge Sazonov.* New York: Frederick A. Stockes Co., 1928.

Schelking, Eugene de. *Suicide of Monarchy: Recollections of a Diplomat.* Toronto: The Macmillan Company of Canada, Ltd., 1918.

Solov'ev, Iu. Ia. *Vospominaniia diplomata 1893–1922.* Moscow: Izdatel'stvo Sotsial'no-Ekonomicheskoi Literatury, 1959.

Steed, H. W. *Through Thirty Years 1892–1922.* Garden City, N. Y.: Doubleday, Page & Co., 1924. 2 vols.

Sukhomlinov, V. A. *Erinnerungen.* Berlin: Verlag von Reimar Hobbing, 1925.

Suvorin, A. S. *Dnevnik A. S. Suvorina,* ed. M. Krichevskii. Moscow-Petrograd: Izdatel'stvo L. D. Frenkel', 1923.

Szilassy, Gyula. *Der Untergang der Donau-Monarchie: Diplomatische Erinnerungen.* Berlin: Verlag Neues Vaterland, E. Berger & Co., 1921.

Tommasini, Francesco. *L'Italia alla vigilia della guerra: La politica estera di Tommaso Tittoni.* Bologna: Nicola Zanichelli, editore, 1934–41. 5 vols.

Toshev, A. *Balkanskite voini.* Sofia: Knigoizdatelstvo "Fakel," 1929–31. 2 vols.

Trevelyan, G. M. *Grey of Fallodon.* Boston: Houghton Mifflin Co., 1937.

Venizelos, Eleutherios. *The Vindication of Greek National Policy 1912–1917.* London: G. Allen & Unwin, Ltd., 1918.

MONOGRAPHS AND
GENERAL HISTORICAL WORKS

Albertini, Luigi. *The Origins of the War of 1914,* trans. and ed. Isabella M. Massey. London: Oxford University Press, 1952–57. 3 vols.

Askew, William C. *Europe and Italy's Acquisition of Lybia, 1911–1912.* Durham, N. C.: Duke University Press, 1942.

Barlow, Ima C. *The Agadir Crisis.* Chapel Hill, N. C.: University of North Carolina Press, 1940.

Bestuzhev, I. V. *Bor'ba v Rossii po voprosam vneshnei politiki 1906–1910.* Moscow: Akademiia Nauk, 1961.

Bickel, Otto. *Russland und die Entstehung des Balkanbundes 1912: Ein Beitrag zur Vorgeschichte des Weltkrieges.* Königsberg-Berlin: Osteuropa Verlag, 1933.

Boiev, Iu. O. *Polityka Frantsii na Balkanakh naperedodni pershoi svitovoi imperialistychnoi vijny (1912–1913 vv.).* Kiev: Akademiia Nauk URSR, 1958.

Bondarevskii, G. L. *Bagdadskaia doroga i proniknovenie germanskogo imperializma na Blizhnii Vostok 1888–1903.* Tashkent: Gosudarstvennoe Izdatel'stvo Uzbekskoi SSR, 1955.

Bovykin, V. I. *Iz istorii vozniknoveniia pervoi mirovoi voiny: Otnosheniia Rossii i Frantsii v 1912–1914 gg.* Moscow: Izdatel'stvo Moskovskogo Unversiteta, 1961.

——. *Ocherki istorii vneshnei politiki Rossii: Konets XIX veka-1917 god.* Moscow: Gosudarstvennoe Uchebno-Pedagogicheskoe Izdatel'stvo Ministerstva Prosveshcheniia RSFSR, 1960.

Brandt, Johanna (van der Veen). *De voorgeschiedenis van de Balkanoorloog.* Utrecht: Kemink en Zoon n.v., 1935.

Bŭlgarska Akademiia na Naukite. *Istoriia na Bŭlgariia,* eds. Dimitŭr Kosev, Khristo Khrisov, *et al.* Sofia: Dŭrzhavno Izdatelstvo "Nauka i izkustva," 1954–55. 2 vols.

Carlgren, W. M. *Iswolsky und Aehrenthal vor der bosnischen Annexionskrise: Russische und österreich-ungarische Balkanpolitik 1906–1908.* Uppsala: Almqvist & Wiksells, Boktr., 1955.

Carnegie Endowment for International Peace. *Report of the International Commission to Inquire into the Causes and Conduct of the Balkan Wars.* Washington, D. C.: The Endowment, 1914.

176

Bibliography

Danev, Stoian. *Ocherk na diplomaticheskata istoriia na balkanskite dŭrzhavi.* Sofia: Pechatnitsa "Nov Zhivot," 1931.

Derzhavin, N. S. *Bolgarsko-serbskiia vzaimootnosheniia i makedonskii vopros.* St. Petersburg: A. Smolinskii, 1914.

Djordjević, Dmitrije. *Carinski rat Austro-Ugarske i Srbije 1906–1911.* Belgrade: Izdanie Istorijski Institut, 1962.

Dobronravov, F. *Dostoevskii kak vyrazitel' narodnoi psikhologii i etiki.* St. Petersburg: V. S. Balashev i Ko., 1904.

Dranov, B. A. *Chernomorskie prolivy: Mezhdunarodno-pravovoi rezhim.* Moscow: Iuridicheskoe Izdatel'stvo Ministerstva Iustitsii sssr, 1948.

Driault, Edouard, and Lhéritier, Michel. *Histoire diplomatique de la Grèce de 1821 à nos jours.* Paris: Les Presses Universitaires de France, 1925–26. 5 vols.

Drossos, Demetrios I. D. *La fondation de l'alliance balkanique: Etude d'histoire.* Athens: Imprimerie J. Vartsos, 1929.

Durham, Mary Edith. *The Struggle for Scutari (Turk, Slav, and Albanian).* London: E. Arnold, 1914.

———. *Twenty Years of Balkan Tangle.* London: G. P. Putnam's Sons, 1920.

Efremov, P. N. *Vneshniaia politika Rossii (1907–1914 gg.).* Moscow: Institut Mezhdunarodnykh Otnoshenii, 1961.

Fadner, Frank. *Seventy Years of Pan-Slavism in Russia: Karazin to Danilevskii 1800–1870.* Washington, D. C.: Georgetown University Press, 1962.

Fay, Sidney B. *The Origins of the World War,* 2nd revised ed. New York: The Macmillan Company, 1935. 2 vols.

Feis, Herbert. *Europe the World's Banker 1870–1914.* New Haven: Yale University Press, 1930.

Fellner, Fritz. *Der Dreibund: Europäische Diplomatie vor dem Ersten Weltkrieg.* Munich: Verlag R. Oldenbourg, 1960.

Fichev, Ivan I. *Balkanskata voina 1912–1913.* Sofia: Dŭrzhavna Pechatnitsa, 1940.

Fischel, Alfred. *Der Panslavismus bis zum Weltkriege.* Berlin: Cotta, 1919.

Galkin, I. S. *Diplomatiia evropeiskikh derzhav v sviazi s osvoboditel'nym dvizheniem narodov evropeiskoi Turtsii 1905–1912 gg.* Moscow: Izdatel'stvo Moskovskogo Universiteta, 1960.

———. *Politika evropeiskikh derzhav v sviazi s osvoboditel'nym dvizheniem narodov evropeiskoi Turtsii v 1908–1912 gg.: Avtoreferat dissertatsii na soiskanie stepeni doktora istoricheskikh nauk.* Moscow: Izdatel'stvo Moskovskogo Universiteta, 1956.

Geisman, P. A. *Slavianskii krestovyi pokhod: Po sluchaiu 25-letiia so vremeni nachala voiny 1877–1878 gg.* St. Petersburg: S.-Peterburgskoe Slavianskoe Blagotvoritel'noe Obshchestvo, 1902.

Gooch, G. P. *Before the War: Studies in Diplomacy.* London: Longmans, Green & Co., 1936–38. 2 vols.

177

BIBLIOGRAPHY

————. *History of Modern Europe, 1878–1919.* New York: H. Holt and Company, 1923.

Gopčević, Spiridion. *Geschichte von Montenegro und Albanien.* Gotha: F. A. Perthes, 1914.

Gurko-Kriazhin, V. A. *Blizhnii Vostok i derzhavy.* Moscow: Nauchnaia Assotsiatsiia Vostokovedeniia pri Ts.I.K. sssr, 1925.

Hanotaux, G. *La guerre des Balkans et l'Europe 1912–1913: Etudes diplomatiques,* 2nd ed. Paris: Plon-Nourrit et Cie, 1914.

Hauser, Oswald, *Deutschland und der englisch-russische Gegensatz 1910–1914.* Göttingen: Musterschmidt Verlag, 1958.

Helmreich, E. C. *The Diplomacy of the Balkan Wars 1912–1913.* Cambridge: Harvard University Press, 1938.

Holdegel, K. *Frankreichs Politik im Nahen Orient und im Mittelmeer in der Zeit vom Ausbruch des italienisch-türkischen Krieges bis zum Zusammentritt der Londoner Botschafterkonferenz Oktober 1911–Dezember 1912.* Dresden: Risse Verlag, 1934.

Iakhontov, A. N. (ed.). *Istoricheskii ocherk Imperatorskago Aleksandrovskago (b. Tsarskosel'skago) Litseia* . . . Paris: Izdanie Ob"edineniia b. Vospitannikov Imperatorskago Litseia, 1936.

Ignat'ev, A. V. *Russko-angliiskie otnosheniia nakanune pervoi mirovoi voiny (1908–1914 gg.).* Moscow: Izdatel'stvo Sotsial'no-Ekonomicheskoi Literatury, 1962.

Jelavich, Barbara. *A Century of Russian Foreign Policy 1814–1914.* Philadelphia and New York: J. B. Lippincott Company, 1964.

Jelavich, Charles. *Tsarist Russia and Balkan Nationalism: Russian Influence in the Internal Affairs of Bulgaria and Serbia 1879–1886.* Berkeley: University of California Press, 1958.

Jovanović, Jagoš. *Stvaranje crnogorske države i razvoj crnogorske nacionalnosti.* Cetinje: Izdanje Štamparsko-izdavačkog Preduzeća "Obod," 1947.

Jovanović, Slobodan. *Vlada Aleksandra Obrenovića,* 2nd. ed. Belgrade: Izdavačko i Knjižarsko Preduseće Geca Kon A. D., 1934–1936. 3 vols.

Khvostov, V. M. *Istoriia diplomatii* [vol. II:], *Diplomatiia v novoe vremia 1871–1914.* Moscow: Gospolitizdat, 1963.

Kiendl, Hans. *Russische Balkanpolitik von der Ernennung Sasonows bis zum Ende des zweiten Balkankrieges,* Munich University doctoral dissertation. Garmisch: Druck von A. Adam, 1925.

Kohn, Hans. *Pan-Slavism: Its History and Ideology,* 2nd ed. New York: Vintage Books, 1960.

K'osev, Dino G. *Istoriia na makedonskoto natsionalno revoliutsionno dvizhenie.* Sofia: Izdatelstvo na Natsionalniia Sŭvet na Otechestveniia Front, 1954.

Krainikovsky, Assen I. *La question de Macédoine et la diplomatie européenne.* Paris: Librairie Marcel Rivière et Co., 1938.

Langer, W. L. *European Alliances and Alignments 1871–1890.* New York:

Bibliography

Alfred A. Knopf, 1935.

————. *The Diplomacy of Imperialism 1890–1902.* New York: Alfred A. Knopf, 1935. 2 vols.

Laourdas, Basil. *La lotta per la Macedonia dal 1903 al 1908.* Thesalonike: Hetaireia Makedonikon Spoudon Hidryma Meleton Chersonesou tou Haimou, 1962.

Lederer, Ivo (ed.). *Russian Foreign Policy: Essays in Historical Perspective.* New Haven: Yale University Press, 1962.

Lutz, Hermann. *Lord Grey and the World War,* trans. E. W. Dickes. New York: Alfred A. Knopf, 1928.

Malozemoff, Andrew. *Russian Far Eastern Policy 1881–1904.* Berkeley: University of California Press, 1958.

Miliukov, P. N. *Balkanskii krizis i politika A. P. Izvol'skago.* St. Petersburg: Tipografia Tovarishchestva "Obshchestvennaia Pol'za," 1910.

Miller, A. F. *Turtsiia i problema prolivov.* Moscow: Izdatel'stvo "Pravda," 1947.

Mogilevich, A. A., and Airapetian, M. E. *Na putiakh k mirovoi voine 1914–1918 gg.* Moscow: Gospolitizdat, 1940.

Mosely, P. E. *Russian Diplomacy and the Opening of the Eastern Question in 1838–39.* Cambridge: Harvard University Press, 1934.

Nikitin, S. A. *Slavianskie komitety v Rossii.* Moscow: Izdatel'stvo Moskovskogo Universiteta, 1960.

Ninčić, Mončilo [Nintchitch, Montchilo]. *La crise bosniaque (1900–1908) et les puissances européennes.* Paris: Alfred Costes, 1937. 2 vols.

Nol'de, B. E. *Dalekoe i blizkoe: Istoricheskie ocherki.* Paris: Izdatel'stvo "Sovremennyia Zapiski," 1930.

Petrovich, Michael B. *The Emergence of Russian Panslavism, 1856–1870.* New York: Columbia University Press, 1956.

Preobrazhenskii, I. V. *Za brat'ev-slavian: Po povodu 25-letiia sviashchennoi voiny 1877–1878 gg.* St. Petersburg: P. Soikin, 1903.

Pribram, A. F. *Austria-Hungary and Great Britain 1908–1914,* trans. Ian F. D. Morrow. London: Oxford University Press, 1951.

Renouvin, Pierre. *La politique extérieure de la IIIe République de 1904 à 1919,* roneotyped "Cours de la Sorbonne." Paris: Centre de Documentation Universitaire, 1949. 4 fascicles.

————. *Le XIXe siècle* [*Histoire des relations internationales,* t. 5–6]. Paris: Hachette, 1954–55. 2 vols.

————. *Les question méditerranéennes de 1904 à 1914,* roneotyped "Cours de la Sorbonne." Paris: Centre de Documentation Universitaire, 1954.

Riasanovsky, N. V. *Nicholas I and Official Nationality in Russia 1825–1855.* Berkeley: University of California Press, 1959.

Rozental', E. M. *Diplomaticheskaia istoriia russko-frantsuzskogo soiuza v nachale XX veka.* Moscow: Izdatel'stvo Sotsial'no-Ekonomicheskoi Literatury, 1960.

Schmitt, Bernadotte E. *The Annexation of Bosnia 1908–1909.* Cambridge:

BIBLIOGRAPHY

Cambridge University Press, 1937.

————. *The Coming of the War: 1914.* New York: Charles Scribner's Sons, 1930. 2 vols.

Schröder, Werner. *England, Europa und der Orient: Untersuchung zur englischen Vorkriegspolitik in Vorgeschichte der Balkankrise 1912.* Stuttgart: Kohlhammer, 1938.

Sharapov, S. F. *Blizhaishiia zadachi Rossii na Balkanakh.* Moscow: "Svidetel'" [1909].

Senkevich, I. G. *Osvoboditel'noe dvizhenie albanskogo naroda v 1905–1912 gg.* Moscow: Akademiia Nauk, 1959.

Smith, C. Jay, Jr. *The Russian Struggle for Power.* New York: Philosophical Library, 1956.

Sosnosky, Theodor von. *Die Balkanpolitik Österreich-Ungarns seit 1866.* Stuttgart: Deutsche Verlag-Anstalt, 1913. 2 vols.

Stavrianos, L. S. *Balkan Federation: A History of the Movement Toward Balkan Unity in Modern Times* [Smith College Studies in History, xxvii, nos. 1–4]. Northampton, Mass., 1944.

————. *The Balkans since 1453.* New York: Holt, Rinehart and Winston, 1961.

Steinitz, Eduard Ritter von (ed.). *Rings um Sasonow: Neue dokumentarische Darlegungen zum Ausbruch des grossen Krieges durch Kronzeugen.* Berlin: Verlag für Kulturpolitik, 1928.

Sumner, B. H. *Russia and the Balkans 1870–1880.* Oxford: At the Clarendon Press, 1937.

Swire, Joseph. *Albania, the Rise of a Kingdom.* London: Williams & Norgate, Ltd., 1929.

Taube, M. A. *La politique russe d'avant-guerre et la fin de l'empire des tsars (1904–1917).* Paris: Librairie Ernest Leroux, 1928.

Thaden, E. C. *Conservative Nationalism in Nineteenth-Century Russia.* Seattle: University of Washington Press, 1964.

Törngren, Adolf. *Den Tredje Duman.* Stockholm: Albert Bonniers Förlag, 1912.

Tukim, Cemal. *Die politischen Beziehungen zwischen Österreich-Ungarn und Bulgarien von 1908 bis zum Bukarester Frieden.* Hamburg: H. Christian, 1936.

Tyler, John E. *The British Army and the Continent, 1904–1914.* London: E. Arnold & Co. [1938].

Uebersberger, Hans. *Österreich zwischen Russland und Serbien: Zur südslawischen Frage und der Entstehung des Ersten Weltkrieges.* Köln-Graz: Verlag Hermann Böhlaus Nachf., 1958.

————. *Russlands Orient Politik in den letzten zwei Jahrhunderten* [vol. i], *Bis zum Frieden von Jassy (1789).* Stuttgart: Deutsche Verlags-Anstalt, 1913.

Vucinich, Wayne S. *Serbia between East and West: The Events of 1903–1908.* Stanford: Stanford University Press, 1954.

Bibliography

Wedel, Oswald H. *Austro-German Diplomatic Relations, 1908–1914.* Stanford: Stanford University Press, 1932.

Zaionchkovskii, A. M. *Podgotovka Rossii k mirovoi voine v mezhdunarodnom otnoshenii.* Leningrad: Voennaia Tipografiia Upravleniia Delami Narkomvoenmor i RVS SSSR, 1926.

Zhebokritskii, V. A. *Bolgariia nakanune balkanskikh voin 1912–1913 gg.* Kiev: Izdatel'stvo Kievskogo Universiteta, 1960.

———. *Bolgariia v period balkanskikh voin 1912–1913 gg.* Kiev: Izdatel'stvo Kievskogo Universiteta, 1961.

ARTICLES

Ado, V. I. "Berlinskii kongress 1878 g. i pomeshchich'e-burzhuaznoe obshchestvennoe mnenie Rossii," *Istoricheskie Zapiski,* LXIX (1961), 101–41.

Artamonov, Victor V. "Erinnerungen an meine Militärattachézeit in Belgrad," *Berliner Monatshefte,* XVI (July–August 1938), 583–602.

Askew, William C. "The Austro-Italian Antagonism, 1896–1914," in *Power, Public Opinion, and Diplomacy: Essays in Honor of Eber Malcolm Carroll by his Former Students.* Durham, N. C.: Duke University Press, 1959.

Bolsover, G. H. "Nicholas I and the Partition of Turkey," *Slavonic and East European Review,* XXVII (1948), 115–45.

Bourchier, J. D. "Articles on the Origins of the Balkan League," London *Times,* June 4, 5, 6, 11, and 13, 1913.

Bovykin, V. I. "Russko-frantsuzskie protivorechiia na balkanakh i Blizhnem Vostoke nakanune pervoi mirovoi voiny," *Istoricheskie Zapiski,* LIX (1957), 84–124.

Cairns, John C. "International Politics and the Military Mind: The Case of the French Republic, 1911–1914," *Journal of Modern History,* XXV (September 1953), 273–86.

Charykov, N. V. "Sazonoff," *Contemporary Review,* CXXXIII (March 1928), 284–88.

Danev, Stoian. "Balkánsky svaz a valka s Tureckem, 1912–1913," *Slovanský ustav* [Prague], *Přednásky,* Svazek 7 (1937), pp. 1–27.

DeNovo, John A. "A Railroad for Turkey," *Business History Review,* XXXIII (Autumn 1959), 299–329.

Derenkovskii, G. M. "Franko-russkaia morskaia konventsiia 1912 g. i anglo-russkie morskie peregovory nakanune pervoi mirovoi voiny," *Istoricheskie Zapiski,* XXIX (1949), 80–122.

Durham, M. E. "King Nikola of Montenegro," *Contemporary Review,* CXIX (April 1921), 471–77.

181

BIBLIOGRAPHY

Flaningam, M. L. "German Eastward Expansion, Fact and Fiction: A Study in German-Ottoman Trade Relations 1890–1914," *Journal of Central European Affairs*, XIV (January 1955), 319–33.

——. "German Economic Controls in Bulgaria: 1894–1914," *American Slavic and East European Review*, XX (February 1961), 99–108.

Florinsky, M. T. "Russia and Constantinople: Count Kokovtsov's Evidence," *Foreign Affairs*, VIII (October 1929), 135–41.

Galkin, I. S. "Demarsh Charykova v 1911 g. i pozitsiia evropeiskikh derzhav," *Iz istorii obshchestvennykh dvizhenii i mezhdunarodnykh otnoshenii: Sbornik statei v pamiat' Akademika Evgeniia Viktorovicha Tarle*, eds. A. M. Pankratova *et al.* Moscow: Izdatel'stvo Akademii Nauk SSSR, 1957.

——. "Evropeiskie derzhavy i kritskii vopros v 1908–1912 godakh," *Voprosy Istorii*, 1956, no. 5, pp. 126–40.

——. "Iz istorii natsional'nogo osvoboditel'nogo dvizheniia v Albanii v 1910–1912 godakh," *Voprosy Istorii*, 1954, no. 11, pp. 35–46.

——. "Obrazovanie balkanskogo soiuza 1912 g. i politika evropeiskikh derzhav," *Vestnik Moskovskogo Universiteta*, 1956, no. 4, pp. 9–40.

Grinberg, S. Sh. "Vneshnepoliticheskaia orientatsiia Bolgarii nakanune pervoi mirovoi voiny (1912–1914)," *Slavianskii sbornik*, ed. V. Picheta. Moscow: Politizdat, 1947.

Hauser, Oswald. "Die Englisch-russische Konvention von 1907 und die Meerengenfrage," *Geschichtliche Kräfte und Entscheidungen: Festschrift zum fünfundsechzigsten Geburtstage von Otto Becker*, eds. Martin Göhring and Alexander Scharff. Wiesbaden: Franz Steiner Verlag, 1954.

Helmreich, E. C. "The Serbian-Montenegrin Alliance of September 23/October 6, 1912," *Journal of Central European Affairs*, XIX (January 1960), 411–15.

——, and Black, C. E. "The Russo-Bulgarian Military Convention of 1902," *Journal of Modern History*, IX (December 1937), 471–82.

Henderson, W. O. "German Economic Penetration in the Middle East, 1870–1914," *Economic History Review*, XVIII (1948), 54–64.

Jablonowski, Horst. "Die Stellungnahme der russischen Parteien zur Aussenpolitik der Regierung von der russisch-englischen Verständigung bis zum ersten Weltkriege," *Forschungen zur osteuropäischen Geschichte*, V (1957), 60–92.

Jelavich, Charles. "Nikola Pasic: Greater Serbia or Yugoslavia?," *Journal of Central European Affairs*, XI (July 1951), 133–52.

Jovanovic, S. "Nicholas Pasic: After Ten Years," *Slavonic and East European Review*, XV (January 1937), 368–76.

Kiktev, A. Ia. "Iz istorii obrazovaniia balkanskogo soiuza 1912 goda," Kiev University, *Trudy Istoricheskogo Fakulteta*, I (1939), 29–40.

Langer, W. L. "Russia, the Straits Question and the European Powers, 1904–1908," *English Historical Review*, XLIV (January 1929), 59–85.

Bibliography

————. "Russia, the Straits Question and the Origins of the Balkan League, 1908–1912," *Political Science Quarterly*, XLIII (September 1928), 321–63.

Levin, Alfred. "The Russian Voter in the Elections to the Third Duma," *Slavic Review*, XXII (December 1962), 660–77.

M. "The Balkan League, History of its Formation," *Fortnightly Review*, new series, XCII (March 1913), 430–39.

Mandelstam, A. N. "La politique russe d'accès à la Méditerranée au XXe siècle," *Académie de droit international: Recueil des cours*, XLVII (1934), 603–801.

Marco [Simić, Božin]. "Nikola Hartvig: Spoljna politika Serbije pred Svetski Rat," *Nova Evropa*, knjiga XVII,, broj 8 (April 26, 1928), pp. 256–78.

————. "Nikolaus Hartwig: Serbiens Aussenpolitik vor dem Weltkrieg," *Die Kriegsschuldfrage*, VI (August 1928), 745–69 [German translation of preceding article].

Martynenko, A. K. "Pozitsiia Rossii v sviazi s provozglasheniem nezavisimosti Bolgarii v 1908 godu," *Iz istorii russko-bolgarskikh otnoshenii: Sbornik statei*, ed. V. N. Kondrat'eva, S. A. Nikitin, and L. B. Valev, Moscow: Akademiia Nauk, 1958.

May, A. J. "The Novibazar Railway Project," *Journal of Modern History*, X (December 1938), 496–527.

————. "Trans-Balkan Railway Schemes," *Journal of Modern History* (December 1952), 352–67.

Miller, A. F. "Mladoturetskaia revoliutsiia," *Pervaia russkaia revoliutsiia 1905–1907 gg. i mezhdunarodnoe revoliutsionnoe dvizhenie*, ed. A. M. Pankratova. Moscow: Gospolitizdat, 1956. Vol. II, pp. 313–48.

Mosely, P. E. "Russian Policy in 1911–12," *Journal of Modern History*, XII (March 1940), 69–86.

Nikitin, S. A. "Russkaia politika na Balkanakh i nachalo vostochnoi voiny," *Voprosy Istorii*, 1946, no. 4, pp. 3–29.

Peacock, Wadham. "Nicholas of Montenegro and the Czardom of the Serbs," *Nineteenth Century and After*, LXXII, 879–88.

"Perepiska I. S. Aksakov s Kn. V. A. Cherkasskim (1875–1878)," *Slavianskii sbornik: Slavianskii vopros i russkoe obshchestvo v 1867–1878 gg*, eds. N. M. Druzhinin, I. V. Koz'menko, *et al.* Moscow: Publichnaia Biblioteka imeni Lenina, 1948.

Popović, Dimitrije. "Nikola Pašić i Rusija: Iz mojih ličnih sečanja," *Godišnjica Nikole Čupnica*, XLVI (1937), 137–56.

Renouvin, Pierre. "Les relations franco-russes à la fin du XIX et au début du XX siècle: Bilan des recherches," *Cahiers du monde russe et soviétique*, I (May 1959), 128–47.

Schmidt, H. T. "Österreich-Ungarn und Bulgarien, 1908–1913," *Jahrbücher für Kultur und Geschichte der Slawen*, neue Folge, XI (1935), 503–609.

BIBLIOGRAPHY

Skendi, Stavro. "Albanian Political Thought and Revolutionary Activity, 1881–1912," *Südostforschungen,* XIII (1954), 159–99.

———. "Beginnings of Albanian Nationalist Trends in Culture and Education (1878–1912)," *Journal of Central European Affairs,* XII (January 1953), 356–67.

Thaden, E. C. "Charykov and Russian Foreign Policy at Constantinople in 1911," *Journal of Central European Affairs,* XVI (April 1956), 25–44.

———. "Montenegro: Russia's Troublesome Ally, 1910–1912," *Journal of Central European Affairs,* XVIII (July 1958), 111–33.

Vernadsky, George. "Alexandre Ier et le problème slave pendant la première moitié de son règne," *Revue des Etudes Slaves,* VII (1927), 94–110.

Vlakhov, Tushe. "Bulgariia i tsentralnite sily v nadvecherieto na pŭrvata svetovna voina," *Bŭlgarska Akademiia na Naukite, Izvestiia,* I/II (1951), 39–80.

———. "Vŭnshnata politika na Ferdinand i balkanskiia sŭiuz," *Istoricheski Pregled,* 1950, nos. 4–5, pp. 422–44.

UNPUBLISHED DISSERTATIONS

Katsainos, Charles T. "The Theory and Practice of Russian Panslavism (in the Light of Russia's Expansion in the Balkans)." Ph.D. dissertation, Georgetown University, Washington, D. C., 1951.

Martynenko, A. K. "Russko-bolgarskie otnosheniia, 1908–1912." Kiev University Candidate's dissertation, Kiev, 1954.

Swanson, Jack R. "The Duma Debates on Russia's Balkan Policy, 1912–1914." Columbia University Russian Institute Certificate essay, New York, 1957.

INDEX